THE WIDENING SCOPE OF SELF PSYCHOLOGY

Progress in Self Psychology
Volume 9

Progress in Self Psychology

Editor, Arnold Goldberg, M.D.

THE WIDENING SCOPE OF SELF PSYCHOLOGY

Progress in Self Psychology
Volume 9

Arnold Goldberg

editor

THE ANALYTIC PRESS

1993   Hillsdale, NJ   London

Copyright © 1993 by The Analytic Press
365 Broadway
Hillsdale, NJ 07642

ISBN 0-88163-163-9
ISSN 0893-5483

Printed in the United States of America
10 9 8 7 6 5 4 3 2 1

Acknowledgment

We would like to thank Ms. Chris Susman, who provided secretarial and editorial assistance.

Contents

III AGGRESSION AND RAGE

IV CLINICAL

V APPLIED

Contributors

Lindsey Stroben Alper, Ph.D., Member, San Diego Self Psychology Group; Psychologist in private practice, San Diego and La Mesa, CA.

Howard A. Bacal, M.D., F.R.C.P.(C), Training and Supervising Analyst, Toronto Institute of Psychoanalysis; Associate Professor, Department of Psychiatry, University of Toronto.

Beatrice Beebe, Ph.D., Core Faculty, Institute for the Psychoanalytic Study of Subjectivity; Clinical Associate Professor, New York University Postdoctoral Program in Psychotherapy and Psychoanalysis.

Bernard Brandchaft, M.D., Training and Supervising Analyst, Los Angeles Psychoanalytic Institute.

Doris Brothers, Ph.D., Cofounder and Training and Supervising Analyst, The Training and Research Institute for Self Psychology; Founding Member, Society for the Advancement of Self Psychology, New York City.

Mark J. Gehrie, Ph.D., Training and Supervising Analyst, Chicago Institute for Psychoanalysis; private practice, Chicago.

Frank M. Lachmann, Ph.D., Senior Supervisor and Training Analyst, Postgraduate Center for Mental Health, New York City; Core Faculty, Institute for the Psychoanalytic Study of Subjectivity, New York City.

Robert J. Leider, M.D., Training and Supervising Analyst, Institute for Psychoanalysis, Chicago; Assistant Professor, Department of Psychiatry, Northwestern University Medical School.

Richard C. Marohn, M.D., Professor of Clinical Psychiatry, Northwestern University Medical School, Chicago; Faculty, Institute for Psychoanalysis, Chicago.

Diane Martinez, M.D., Teaching Analyst, Houston-Galveston Psychoanalytic Institute; Clinical Associate Professor of Psychiatry, The University of Texas Health Science Center at San Antonio.

Russell Meares, M.D., Professor of Psychiatry, University of Sydney; Director of Psychiatry, Westmead Hospital, Westmead, Australia.

Donna M. Orange, Ph.D., Psy.D., Institute for the Psychoanalytic Study of Subjectivity, New York City.

Paul H. Ornstein, M.D., Professor of Psychiatry and Codirector, International Center for the Study of Psychoanalytic Self Psychology, University of Cincinnati Department of Psychiatry; Training and Supervising Analyst, Cincinnati Psychoanalytic Institute.

Estelle Shane, Ph.D., Training and Supervising Analyst, Los Angeles Psychoanalytic Society/Institute; Founding Member, Training and Supervising Analyst, Institute of Contemporary Psychoanalysis, Los Angeles.

Morton Shane, M.D., Training and Supervising Analyst in Adult and Child, Los Angeles Psychoanalytic Society/Institute; Founding Member, Training and Supervising Analyst, Institute of Contemporary Psychoanalysis, Los Angeles.

R. Dennis Shelby, Ph.D., Faculty, Institute for Clinical Social Work; private practice, Chicago.

Robert D. Stolorow, Ph.D., Faculty, Training and Supervising Analyst, Institute of Contemporary Psychoanalysis, Los Angeles; Core Faculty, Institute for the Psychoanalytic Study of Subjectivity, New York City.

Paul H. Tolpin, M.D., Training and Supervising Analyst, Chicago Institute for Psychoanalysis; private practice, Chicago.

Ernest S. Wolf, M.D., Assistant Professor of Psychiatry, Northwestern University Medical School; Training and Supervising Analyst, Institute for Psychoanalysis, Chicago.

Chapter 1

Introduction: Is Self Psychology on a Promising Trajectory?

Paul H. Ornstein

How do we determine whether our discipline, our field of endeavor, the clinical–empirical science in which we are all active participants, is or is not on a promising developmental path? I do not know a satisfactory answer—perhaps one can only find that out retrospectively—but I do sense that the question is vital and that our periodic critical reflections on it may serve as a compass to keep us on the right course.

Our first task, then, is to find a few appropriate criteria around which an assessment of where we are and where we are heading might be possible. In the search for such criteria, we soon realize that they form two clusters: one relating to external successes, the other to intrinsic potentialities of self psychology. The first cluster includes those issues that lend themselves to historical-descriptive statements of self psychology or to the quantitative measurements of a statistical study (e.g., reflecting the evidence of changes in the level of interest in self psychology in this country and worldwide). The second cluster includes those issues that require a conceptual analysis of the foundational principles of self psychology and an estimate of its contemporary relevance and future prospects. These two clusters are not unrelated to each other. Measurable popularity and clinical–theoretical relevance may well be linked in some way (we hope), but it would require a sophisticated social psychological and historical research approach combined to pinpoint their precise relationship in the case of self psychology and its evident successes.

While I have chosen to focus mainly on some elements of the second cluster—which I view as the more significant one for the long run—I want to say a few words in passing about the first because the data, even without a formal statistical study, are reassuring (and uplifting) for those who have labored under the banner of self psychology during the last two decades.

Both interest in and knowledge about self psychology have been gaining ground in all mental health fields and simultaneously in, though at a slower pace, the humanities. Relevant articles in various publications, the selection of topics at the scientific meetings of diverse mental health groups, the popularity of CME credit courses nationwide that feature self psychology, the steadily increasing demand for training and for self-psychologically informed therapists all over the country—all attest to the increase in interest in and the spread of knowledge about self psychology. Closer to home, the expansion of the National Council for Psychoanalytic Self Psychology with its regional small study groups, the continuation of our own annual meetings with impressive attendance, the ensuing annual volumes of *Progress in Self Psychology*, the frequently appearing and eagerly bought books by self psychologists on self psychology—these developments are rightly considered by insiders as well as outsiders to be the most directly visible signs of activity on a promising track. But all this must be familiar to each of you. What you might not fully realize, however, is what has been happening worldwide.

As I thought of writing about the decisive increase in interest, enthusiasm, and actual knowledge of self psychology in Germany, some revival of interest in Holland and Switzerland, the efforts under way to make contact with a small group of analysts in England, the increasingly intensive teaching of self psychology and clinical supervision in Paris, the ongoing teaching of self psychology at the University of Budapest, the small active group in Italy, and the budding serious interest in the Scandinavian countries emanating from Oslo, it occurred to me how informative it would be to have representatives of each of these countries report to us at one of our conferences on what they have achieved in their respective countries thus far and on what they are contemplating for the future. Outside of Europe, the Israel Psychoanalytic Society, as well as other mental health professionals there, has become more actively inquisitive about self psychology. The Japanese have translated selected essays from the first two volumes of *The Search for the Self* (Ornstein, 1978). In Thailand there appear to be a lively interest and serious study of self psychology. Sydney has long been a stronghold of self psychology in Australia, and Perth, at the other end of that continent, is now uniting with New Zealand in organizing a psychotherapy society that puts self psychology into the center of its clinical and theoretical orientation. We are beginning to forge a link to China via Taiwan, where some self psychology literature will soon be translated into Chinese. The surprise is the extent to which an earlier definite but still limited interest in self psychology from Kleinian South America has escalated within the last two or three years. In Mexico this expansion has reached unexpected proportions: the Psychoanalytic Society in Mexico City observed the tenth anniversary of Heinz Kohut's death with a symposium on self psychology presented entirely by its own members. The details and special circumstances surrounding this increase of interest in self psychology from each of the countries I mentioned are fascinating and instructive, but we shall have to wait to learn about them on some future occasion.

I now turn to the second cluster of criteria, some of the intrinsic elements of the self psychology paradigm, to pursue the question of whether self psychology is on a promising developmental path or not. The answer—I do not want to keep you in suspense—is a resounding YES. And in the following pages I shall try to explain why.

The idea of a trajectory has been with me for quite some time, but I recall that Brandchaft (1986) supplied me with the word when he said the following in Toronto: "If in fact Heinz Kohut made it possible for us to see and understand more of human experience and the psychoanalytic process than before, it is important that this growing body of work follow its *trajectory* toward the realization of its own potential" (p. 246; italics added). What is this trajectory and how shall we know whether we are moving toward the realization of its potential? Is there only one well-defined and agreed-upon trajectory for self psychology or are there several competing ones, without much agreement between us about them? On these pages I only focus on Kohut's self psychology, but I shall return later to a brief discussion of the issue of multiple trajectories. In order to consider these questions I focus first on some aspects of the genesis of self psychology and then on some characteristics of its clinical and theoretical system as a whole in the hope of identifying what has put it and what may keep it on a promising trajectory.

SOME ASPECTS OF THE GENESIS
OF SELF PSYCHOLOGY

When I once asked Heinz Kohut what enabled him to move into new directions so soon after he began his analytic career, he paused for a moment and said that by the time he was in his early twenties he had read, digested, and made his own all that Freud had written and was thus able to move on from there. Subsequent conversations and various additional remarks in his writings expanded on this off-the-cuff response. Aspects of his own childhood experiences (about which he spoke at times with analytic reflection), his enormous erudition and wide general reading, and his extensive clinical experience—in other words, his own childhood and adult life-story—in combination with his unique talent for introspective-empathic observation and theorizing enabled Kohut, within a particular historical period in psychoanalysis and the surrounding Zeitgeist, to formulate his self psychology in various stages over a period of about 15 years.

The potential for such specific creative developments is perhaps innate and can be discovered in its then-unrecognized early manifestations throughout the period prior to its full fruition in a retrospective scrutiny, once enough relevant life history data become available. My own focus for tracing Kohut's developing ideas on the self has not been his life history but only his early psychoanalytic writings (and his frequent personal communications about them), which permit a step-by-step tracing of the evolving system of self psychology in the process of its gradual unfolding and articulation.

There are, however—on this we would all agree—two thoroughly intertwined aspects of the development of Kohut's ideas whose respective contributions will have to be considered separately in any comprehensive study in order to enable us to put self psychology some day into a proper historical perspective. One aspect relates to the "nuclear program" laid down in Kohut in response to his endowment and the specific life experiences within his family and the Viennese, as well as the broader European, culture of his time. This is undoubtedly the source or wellspring of his unique contributions. The other aspect relates to the influences of the contexts in which Kohut actually worked—the narrow one of Chicago; the broader one of psychoanalysis as a whole; and the even broader one of the spirit of his time, the Zeitgeist—all of which codetermined the form and content of his scientific work.

I shall make some brief comments on these contexts to exemplify what I mean. Hartmannian ego psychology and Alexander's biologizing and sociologizing of psychoanalysis had a clearly acknowledged impact on the timing and form of Kohut's (1959) well-known methodologic-epistemologic essay, "On Introspection, Empathy and Psychoanalysis." Kohut was convinced that these influences were distorting the essence of psychoanalysis. The deeper emotional and intellectual roots of the main points of the essay converge on Kohut's view of reality (external as well as internal reality), namely, that it is in principle unknowable and that we can only grasp aspects of it on the basis of the specific operation(s) we apply to it in the process of our inquiry. Hence the fundamental importance of the method, as reflected in the subtitle of the essay: "An Examination of the Relationship Between Mode of Observation and Theory." Kohut grew up with this modern, postpositivist, view of reality. It had become so much a part of him that he took it for granted and incorrectly assumed that all psychoanalysts shared it. It had become a foundation of his thinking and it informed his view of psychoanalysis as an empirical science. And since Kohut was thus not a radical empiricist, holding that we could ultimately know reality as it actually existed out there, his notion of psychoanalysis as an empirical science could still accommodate, without apparent contradiction, the postpositivist "constructionist" (i.e., hermeneutic, or interpretive) view of reality, in which the observer had a direct and definite impact on the observed and in which a jointly forged reality emerged as a result.

The 1959 essay thus established the psychoanalytic method afresh[1] and shifted its epistemology more decisively away from conventional, positivist science, of which medicine, psychiatry, and even psychoanalysis were a part. The essay also marked the actual beginning—although with some latency period in its wake—of Kohut's later systematic study of the self and its disorders. The latency period provided him, as president of the American Psychoanalytic Association, with experiences regarding the "group self" of the association, and these gave an immediate external impetus to his recognition of the need to study the vulnerabilities of the self as he observed them there and also in his clinical practice.

I regard Kohut's 1959 essay as a significant part of the "genetic endowment" of self psychology, a part of its "nuclear program." What I mean is this: What Kohut established in the methodologic-epistemologic realm—like it or not—significantly determined the path on which he put the future development of self psychology. I will not recount the details of the essay and what followed it. It should be enough to remark that these methodologic–epistemologic innovations began to transform psychoanalysis from a 19th-century mechanistic, objectivist-positivist theory into a 20th-century constructivist-contextualist one. Kohut's brand of psychoanalysis was therefore,

---

[1] I use the phrase *afresh* deliberately because Kohut's own early claim and that of other self psychologists that he merely restated or reemphasized the psychoanalytic method as it was originally proposed by Freud is not borne out by my reading of the pre-Kohutian literature and Kohut's own writings. Not everyone agrees with this assessment, so further efforts to sort this out are necessary.

even before any of its further developments, already on a promising, avant-garde path.[2]

Let us now take a quick look at some of the characteristics of the clinical–theoretical system Kohut proposed a few years later to see the further outlines of the trajectory of self psychology and to see if it is indeed in the process of fulfilling its potential.

SOME CHARACTERISTICS OF THE CLINICAL AND THEORETICAL SYSTEM OF SELF PSYCHOLOGY

Kohut's method and epistemologic stance proved extremely fruitful. Jointly and inseparably, these have led to a new paradigm in psychoanalysis. This is now past history. The method and the epistemology in which this paradigm is embedded have created an open clinical–theoretical system. From within this open system, with its core concepts of the selfobject and the selfobject transferences, we are able to maintain a continuous dialogue with the patients of today, as well as with the surrounding culture, and to become ever more attuned to both. Out of this ongoing dialogue we can fill in, expand, and modify the details of the basic paradigm until it has fulfilled its potentialities and can give way to a new one. His method and epistemology might be the most enduring part of Kohut's entire system, not to mention the clinical insights it has helped us attain, which I think are considerable and at this point appear quite durable.

As you know, self psychology first emerged out of Kohut's focus on what he called "the leading psychopathology of our time." It was this aspect of *The Analysis of the Self* (Kohut, 1971) that spoke to all who immediately grasped his message. It was the thrust of his approach from the outset to be in tune with and understand, as well as explain, the psychopathology *and* the psychology of our time, just as Freud understood and explained the leading psychopathology and the psychology of the Victorian age. Kohut decisively moved further toward this goal with *The Restoration of the Self* (Kohut, 1977), which encompassed the whole spectrum of psychopathology, and continued in this direction in all his subsequent writings.

Self psychology thus became psychoanalysis at its best. We no longer assumed that we could find "the truth" about the human condition, valid for all times and throughout all cultures; that was a mirage. We now had a more modest agenda but one no less

---

[2]It should be noted that there were other successful efforts to transform psychoanalysis into a postpositivist, pure psychology, notably those of George Klein, Roy Schafer, Paul Ricoeur, and Jacques Lacan, among others. However, except for Lacan, the others have not proposed a new paradigm for psychoanalysis.

important or less encompassing: a renewed and intensified focus, using the method of empathy, on individual subjective experience within the selfobject transferences and use of clinical findings beyond the clinical setting to study men and women in history.

Had Kohut only captured the essence of the psychology and psychopathology of our time, his permanent place in the annals of psychoanalysis would already have been assured. But I believe he did much more. And this is where I see self psychology on a promising trajectory and in the process of fulfilling its potentialities—without an end in sight yet! (Kohut was fond of saying that we have barely scratched the surface thus far.)

The clinical concept of the selfobject transferences and the developmental concept of selfobject needs and experiences—that is, the vicissitudes of the selfobject phenomena throughout life—are the foundational constructs of self psychology from which all the rest derives. These concepts have, in turn, further anchored psychoanalysis in the postpositivist, constructivist reality and have thereby restored to it its erstwhile revolutionary power in the human sciences. Let me explain: these concepts have led us to view the self, among other things, as an open system, one that is not delimited by the physical boundaries, the skin, of the person. Thus, the self is open to include others or to be included in the self of others. This view has permitted us to transcend the concept of transference as a phenomenon played out between two well-demarcated selves each of whom is the recipient of projections and introjections in the transference-countertransference experience within the closed system of each participant in the analytic process. The new psychoanalysis has, Kohut held, turned away from focusing on macro-events within the life cycle as the key pathogenic elements and focuses instead on the micro-experiences surrounding them. It has also turned away from regarding the macro-structures of id, ego, and superego as adequately accounting for subjective experience and pathogenesis. The new approach rivets our analytic attention on the micro-structures of self-experience, the level on which development and the treatment process can be more adequately accounted for.

Self psychology is on a promising trajectory because it is open to an ever-deepening grasp of the psychology and psychopathology of our time, as well as in harmony with the contemporary postpositivist, contextualist, constructivist philosophy of science.

No one among us—whichever trajectory he or she follows—seems to doubt the central significance of the concepts of the selfobject and the selfobject transferences. But among the various trends within self psychology, about which much more can be said than can be included here, different clinical and theoretical elements are stressed, leading to different emphases and therefore to different trajectories.

Let me, therefore, mention a few of the consequences I consider important, even at the risk of talking about the very familiar. (1) Although Kohut's thinking in the 1959 paper replaced the awkward psychobiological concept of the drives with a psychological concept of subjective drivenness, it was only the selfobject concept that clearly established a substitute motivational (developmental and clinical) context and could therefore more meaningfully and persuasively do away with classical drive theory and pave the way for a substitution of it with an affect theory congenial to self psychology.[3] The previous psychoanalytic paradigms, bar none, have not achieved this transformation sufficiently, even if some could be viewed, retrospectively, as having inched toward it. The second step was largely missing; these paradigms did not offer a compelling substitute for drive theory derived from the transference. (2) The selfobject concept brought together within the self external and internal reality more felicitously than did previous approaches and thereby put contextuality (the idea of meaning as established in context) in the center of the psychoanalytic theory and treatment process. In this connection the idea of a one-person, versus a two- or three-person, psychology, initiated by Rickman and taken over by Balint as a corrective measure, appears to me now as sociologizing the analytic context. Of course, there are two persons in the analytic consulting room (and often three in fantasy), but the selfobject concept retains the focus on the inner experience of each participant, an experience that always includes the other or others. Self psychology does not slight the "interpersonal," but it has a psychoanalytic intrapsychic view of it. This intrapsychic view of self psychology may be considered by an external observer as a one-person system and may be misinterpreted as disregarding the interpersonal unless we understand the full implications of the selfobject concept. (3) This selfobject concept, in fact, refocused our attention on the transforming impact of lived experience, which, mediated through fantasy formation, is responsible for the establishment of health or illness. This concept is therefore a key element in the psychoanalytic treatment process, which views cure as being brought about by a new lived experience — with or without insight as the curative instrument. Mind you, the treatment is always conducted with the steps of understanding and explaining (in varied proportions as the individual context demands),

---

[3]See, for instance, the affect theories of Basch (1975, 1976) and of Stolorow, Brandchaft, and Atwood (1987).

but insight and relationship can no longer be meaningfully separated. The argument of insight versus the relationship as the curative element is no longer relevant. There is no significant therapeutic relationship without insight, and no curative insight is possible without a significant therapeutic relationship. You see how ingrained certain loaded phrases are: if I want to be more pedantically accurate, to avoid the ambiguity within psychoanalysis of the term *relationship*, I should say that there is no significant therapeutic experience without insight and no curative insight without a significant therapeutic experience. All of psychoanalysis is a psychology of relationships on some level, but that does not differentiate one psychoanalytic approach from another. The term *relationship*, without further qualifying features that separate and differentiate the various kinds of psychoanalyses, is too ambiguous. This differentiation is what Kohut accomplished, but he did not stop there. Rightly or wrongly, he drastically revamped the motivational system of psychoanalysis and proceeded to elaborate on those structures that genetically codetermine the particular quality of relationship patients and analysts are capable of sustaining. This is why I view the self psychological version of psychoanalysis as a structural theory par excellence.

There are, of course, many other implications to the selfobject concept that I have mentioned here, but I now turn my attention to summing up and answering my questions more directly.

Obviously, there are multiple trajectories of self psychology today. In this age of constructivist reality it could not be otherwise. We know that method and epistemology, as well as the specific theories these have spawned, at first expand and then inevitably limit our horizon. That is contextualism, whether we can fully accept it or not.

We may now ask, Is Kohut's empiricism an irreconcilable contradiction to the constructivist view of reality or not? I could not easily decide. I asked Arnold Goldberg in order to obtain some consensual validation for my perception that Kohut appeared to have been on the fence on this issue, like most of the rest of us. Goldberg agreed without hesitation. Then I asked him if he thought that Kohut would have moved more decisively toward constructivism during the last ten years if he were still in our midst. "Oh yes, without any doubt," Goldberg said, to my great relief. But I found myself unable to let go of what Kohut's modulated, benign empiricism has provided for us as clinicians in his various clinical and theoretical formulations. Nor, I thought, could other analysts fully move toward constructivism. Read the volumes of *Progress* and note the language most of us are using and the fondness we have for grand theories. I know I do. So I have worked out a tentative solution, at least for the time being. An empiricism that does not claim that there is a reality out there that is ultimately knowable, an empiricism that considers theories not as verities but as instruments of further observation, can perhaps be viewed as a "constructivist empiricism." There is one added demand: that our empirical findings and theories be regarded as a significant part of our own context and be as completely open to scrutiny as whatever the patient brings to the analytic situation. It is this attention to the negotiability of our contributions to the analytic situation that will keep us and our theories open to change and truly attuned to the subjectivity of the patient. (This tentative solution suggests to me that we shall have to clean up our epistemologic act sooner or later more decisively.)

In the meantime, self psychology continues to fulfill its intrinsic potential, as evidenced by the ongoing contributions by self psychologists to an understanding of the curative process and of other clinical and developmental problems. Self psychology continues to have great impact on further developments of brief as well as long-term psychotherapy, and it has finally caught the attention of some feminist psychologists and other feminist writers—with mutual benefit to both fields—to name only a few areas for additional expansion.

To conclude, let me encapsulate my message by referring to what McHugh and Slavney (1983) call the four separate domains of psychiatry: the concept of disease, the concept of dimensions, the concept of behaviors, and the concept of the life story. Only the latter interests us here. These authors maintain that very different, incompatible epistemologies prevail in these various realms, thus creating all the conceptual confusion in psychiatry today. They would not hesitate to commit themselves to a constructivist approach without reservation because they have the other domains in which radical empiricism might reign supreme. They call life story reasoning the method appropriate to the domain of psychodynamics. They claim that the hermeneutic (narrative) approach is central to our domain. They see Freud as an imaginative, original storyteller whose life story reasoning revolutionized our understanding of individual human beings. It is storytellers who touch our lives most deeply. And McHugh and Slavney elaborate richly on what Freud's main oedipal story line is all about. That story line has enthralled Western man and woman ever since it was first told by Freud (and, of course, without full awareness even before). I believe Kohut was also a remarkable storyteller, one who reworked and renamed Freud's story of pleasure-seeking Guilty Man and subsumed it under the umbrella of his own original story of fulfillment-seeking Tragic Man. Guilty Man since then is no longer a separate story but one made more cohesive and more intelligible as an aspect of Tragic Man. Contextualism at its best.

As a storyteller Kohut astounded a number of us many years ago when we were listening with him to a case presentation none of us could make much sense of. It was a Saturday afternoon as I recall, and most of us left the meeting quite discouraged. We reconvened the next morning, not knowing where to pick up the pieces. Kohut stepped up to the blackboard and offered us a most cohesive, encompassing story that illuminated every aspect of the confusing life story of the day before. Of course, we had no immediate way of testing the validity or the reliability of Kohut's story, but the aesthetic experience we all had was exhilarating. The story has continued to make sense to many of us, and many of us have greatly embellished that story since then. But the original story remains the core until it too will be subsumed under the umbrella of a new story, whose outlines we cannot yet fathom.

I say it without apology—even if it sounds like I have not yet transcended my idealization of Heinz Kohut even after all this time—that I have never met a storyteller like him, before or since!

REFERENCES

Basch, M. F. (1975), Toward a theory that encompasses depression: A revision of existing casual hypotheses in psychoanalysis. In: *Depression and Human Existence*, ed. E. J. Anthony & T. Benedek. Boston: Little, Brown, pp. 202–227.

_____ (1976), The concept of affect: A re-examination. *J. Amer. Psychoanal. Assn.*, 24:759–777.

Brandchaft, B. (1986), British object-relations theory and self psychology. In: *Progress in Self Psychology, Vol. 2*, ed. A. Goldberg. New York: Guilford Press, pp. 286–296.

Kohut, H. (1959), Introspection, empathy and psychoanalysis: An examination of the relation between mode of observation and theory. In: *The Search for the Self, Vol. 1*, ed. P. H. Ornstein. New York: International Universities Press, 1978, pp. 205–232.

_____ (1971), *The Analysis of the Self*. New York: International Universities Press.

_____ (1977), *The Restoration of the Self*. New York: International Universities Press.

McHugh, P. R. & Slavney, P. R. (1983), *The Perspectives of Psychiatry*. Baltimore: The Johns Hopkins University Press.

Ornstein, P. H., ed. (1978), *The Search for the Self: Selected Writings of Heinz Kohut 1950–1978, Vols. 1 & 2*. New York: International Universities Press.

Stolorow, R. D., Brandchaft, B. & Atwood, G. E. (1987), *Psychoanalytic Treatment—An Intersubjective Approach*. Hillsdale, NJ: The Analytic Press.

Interpretation

Chapter 2

The Role of Interpretation in Therapeutic Change

Ernest S. Wolf

Of all the various procedures that in their totality make up the psychoanalytic process, interpretation stands at the most pivotal center. Other aspects of the analytic interaction, such as providing a comfortable, undisturbed analytic setting or creating an appropriate analytic ambience, are, in essence, just preparatory for the moment when the right interpretation will result in a modification of the analysand's psychic life. My definition of interpretation is a very wide one. It includes all those intentional activities of the analyst that in their totality bring about a modification of the analysand's psyche. The modification brought about may be for the better (i.e., therapeutic), but it may fail or even be antitherapeutic. The activities that are included in my definition are verbal statements and any other consciously directed interventions by the analyst, including those apparent noninterventions or omissions of an action that are the cause for a modification in the analysand's mental world. Clearly, all interpretations are experiences and are effective by virtue of their being experienced as goal-directed interventions from the side of the analyst.[1] Thus, I would exclude those experiences that accidentally or nonintentionally emanate from the analyst. In this discussion I want

---

[1]There is no good reason to exclude nonverbal experiences from the experiences that are constructed by the analyst to bring about modifications in the analysand. Such a restriction of the concept of interpretation would miss many, if not most, of the effective interventions by the analyst.

to highlight the interpretative process as understood and guided by the principles of a self-psychologically informed psychoanalysis.

Interpretation has always been one of the most discussed aspects, and is sometimes the most controversial, of the whole analytic procedure. The reason for this intense interest is that the interpretation reflects not only the analyst's technical methods and proficiency but also his or her theoretical commitments, personality, character, and attitude toward the analysand. One might say that looking through the interpretation is like opening a window into the core of the analytic process, revealing analyst as well as analysand in their depths. Many factors combine to shape the analyst's interpretation. However, there is little agreement as to which of these is the most important. Perhaps the majority of our colleagues hold that the theoretical commitment of the analyst is the decisive particular that will determine the outcome of the analysis. Others will underline the primary importance of the analyst's attitude toward the analysand, insisting that this orientation toward the patient is mainly determined by the analyst's character and personality. It is universally accepted, therefore, that all analysts should undergo some analytic therapy of their own during their preparation for analytic practice, though this therapeutic analysis is euphemistically labeled a "training analysis." Presumably, the training analysis will make the prospective analyst aware of any tendencies that might be inimical to proper analytic functioning and will neutralize those tendencies.

Most self psychologists would probably agree with their more traditionally minded colleagues that the theoretical orientation of the analyst is of decisive importance. This seems as it should be since the reason for adopting a theoretical posture is precisely one's conviction of its scientific truth as well as its therapeutic efficacy. It is also generally assumed that committing oneself to a theory is a rational act in which one carefully weighs the pros and cons of competing methods and conceptualizations. I wish to dissent from this easy view (Wolf, 1991) by suggesting that it is the analyst's personality-determined philosophical orientation and value system that is reflected in the choice of a theoretical commitment. I believe that a certain vulnerability of the self to its own excitements leads to a self-protective posture of the analyst that favors structure, distance, laws, truth, and scientific reasoning. Freud's emphasis on intrapsychic dynamics and the associated emphasis on abstinence, neutrality, and denial of gratification in treatment may well have been motivated by an anxiety-driven need to keep his passions and those of his followers in check. On the other hand, I think that a stronger self, one that is less vulnerable to its affects, can afford a posture of flexibility, emotional closeness, spontaneity, and empathic responsiveness. Kohut's reliance on empathic immersion and elucidation of subjective experiences led him to downgrade abstinence and abandon neutrality in favor of establishing an identification with the interests of the analysand. Finally, allowing "optimal responsiveness," as advocated by Bacal (1985) and Terman (1988), to replace the deprivation imposed by strict nongratification is evidence for the maturity and relative freedom from anxiety of contemporary analysts.

SOME HISTORICAL NOTES

As a child of the 19th century, psychoanalysis carried from birth some of the ideological struggles of the times. These contradictory tendencies were heightened by the double rootedness of early contributors in both a humanistic and a medical background. Like a child who manifests signs of its parental heritage, psychoanalysis presents an uneasy mixture of classic rationalism with romantic idealism. Any science aims for encompassing explanations of the observed data. In the natural sciences the point of view of the observer versus the observed is relatively uncomplicated; ideally, the conclusions are not tainted by the personal prejudices of the investigators. Not so in the sciences that study humans. Here the complications multiply. The observer often has a significant impact on the observed merely by making the needed observation. Pure unambiguous observations are difficult to make even if one makes allowances for the unavoidable interactions between observer and observed. Inevitably, there also are conflicting interests that color the data. The observer and the observed do not look at data from the same point of view; consequently, they frequently perceive the same event very differently. Objectivity in the study of human beings is not a given as it is in the natural sciences, where the observer's potential emotional involvement and distortions can easily be controlled. But no amount of control can eliminate human subjectivity. The point of view of observer or of observed, from inside or from outside, always remains a decisive determinant. This is also true of the observer of other human beings who in order to be true to his scientific training attempts to divorce himself from his own subjectivity in making his so-called objective observations. The very effort to be objective and nonparticipating, like a natural scientist, perverts his intentions. Does that mean psychoanalysis is not a science? On the contrary, to the extent that psychoanalysts are aware of the special conditions and limitations of their observations they are true scientists. However, their science of psychoanalysis is not a natural science. Neither is it a humanistic endeavor like history. It is a science of the human, different from both the *Naturwissenschaften* and the *Geisteswissenschaften*.

These considerations are of special importance when discussing the role of interpretation in psychoanalysis. The dictionary defines *interpretation* as an "explanation of what is obscure," but I find this definition rather obscure as far as psychoanalysis is concerned because it leaves out the person to whom the explanation/interpretation is addressed. Does the explanation serve to make sense to the observing analyst or does it serve to enlighten the analysand or is it primarily in the service of communicating to the professional community? Is it designed to enhance the analyst's experience of himself as a scientist or is it designed to bring the saving truth to the analysand or is it designed to produce mutative effects on either, both, or on the analytic process in which they are participating?

FREUD: THE AMBIVALENCE OF THE INVESTIGATING PHYSICIAN

From their very beginning the theories and methods created by Sigmund Freud were caught in a dilemma derived from their creator's basic conflict of identity, that is, the conflict between being an investigative scientist or a physician attempting to heal. If we could have asked Freud about this dissonance of primary aims, he most likely would have insisted on being the scientific observer whose researches were of therapeutic benefit to his analysands mainly as a by-product. He repeatedly stressed the importance of understanding and elucidating the psyche of his analysands while disparaging therapeutic ambition. Indeed, the very word chosen for his activity, *psychoanalysis*, alludes to serious observation and study rather than to modifying actions. His career upon completion of his medical training was in neurological research, and it was not until growing family responsibilities forced him into active medical practice that he moved from the laboratory into the consulting room. It seems he disliked being a doctor. Yet, as a compassionate and humane person Freud was not indifferent to the suffering of his patients. Furthermore, he knew that his patients came to him to be succored and healed and not because they wanted to advance his research ambitions. As a man with a strong sense of truth and justice he therefore felt obligated to do the very best in his powers to help them.

However, the conflict between the scientist and the healer has remained a source of hidden unease in psychoanalysis, as in all of medical practice. Some analysts seem more identified with the exploring tradition, as represented by Freud; others seem more in sympathy with the accent on the patient, as represented by Freud's closest friend and collaborator, Sándor Ferenczi. The difference between these two analytic postures is delicate and mostly unconsciously determined by the analyst's personal history, personality, and, perhaps, training. I believe that some of the controversies that have arisen among psychoanalysts, historically as well as currently, are an expression of these subtle differences. In this connection it is interesting to read what Ferenczi wrote to Freud in 1930:

> I do not share, for instance, your view that the therapeutic process is negligible or unimportant, and that simply because it appears less interesting to us we should ignore it. I, too, have often felt "fed up"[2] in this respect, but overcame this tendency, and I am glad to inform you that precisely in this area a whole series of questions have now come into a new, a sharper focus, perhaps even the problem of repression [Dupont, 1988, p. xiii].

In his diary Ferenczi was more direct and outspoken about Freud's therapeutic attitudes:

> One learned from him [Freud] and from his kind of technique various things that made one's life and work more comfortable: the calm, unemotional reserve; the unruffled assurance that one knew better; and the theories, the seeking and finding of the causes of failure in the patient instead of partly in ourselves. The dishonesty of reserving the technique for one's own person; the advice not to let patients learn anything about the technique; and, finally the pessimistic view, shared with only a trusted few, that neurotics are a rabble[3] . . . [Dupont, 1988, p. 185].

Ferenczi goes on to state his own views:

> This was the point where I refused to follow him. Against his will I began to deal openly with questions of technique. I refused to abuse the patient's trust in this way, and neither did I share his idea that therapy was worthless. I believed rather that therapy was good, but perhaps we were still deficient, and I began to look for our errors.

Indeed, Ferenczi's openly experimental clinical attitude appears more correct scientifically than Freud's theory-bound dogmatism.

---

[2]In English in the original.
[3]Ferenczi's characterization is called "not implausible" by Gay (1988, p. 529), who documents various instances of Freud's use of "rabble" (*Gesindel*).

It is against this historical background that I want to examine the formulation and the clinical usage of the concept of interpretation in psychoanalytic treatment. One of the earliest elucidations of the process of therapeutic interpretation can be gleaned from Freud's discussion of the psychotherapy of hysteria (Freud, 1895, pp. 281–283). It is a most interesting essay because it illustrates Freud's ambivalent struggle between the scientist and the humanist, as well as something about himself in the roles of therapist and researcher. He does not in this work use the word *interpretation (Deutung)*, perhaps because he had reserved the term *Deutung* for the interpretation of dreams, which was already occupying him.

In this article Freud is still rather authoritarian in his approach, and he mentions the pressure technique to elicit pathogenic recollections against the patient's often stubborn resistance. He writes, revealingly; "It is of course of great importance for the progress of the analysis that one should always turn out to be in the right vis-à-vis the patient, otherwise one would always be dependent on what he chose to tell one" (p. 281). And: "The principle point is that I should guess the secret and tell it to the patient straight out; and he is then as a rule obliged to abandon his rejection of it" (p. 281). Freud then becomes the scientific investigator: "We may reckon on the intellectual interest which the patient begins to feel after working for a short time. By explaining things to him, by giving him information about the marvellous world of physical process . . . we make him himself into a collaborator, induce him to regard himself with the objective interest of an investigator" (p. 282). But then Freud goes on to confess his human involvement:

> One works to the best of one's power, as an elucidator (where ignorance has given rise to fear), as a teacher, as the representative of a freer or superior view of the world, as a father confessor who gives absolution, as it were, by a continuance of his sympathy and respect after the confession has been made. One tries to give the patient human assistance, as far as this is allowed by the capacity of one's own personality and by the amount of sympathy that one can feel for the particular case [p. 282-283].

Summarizing, Freud states, "Besides the intellectual motives which we mobilize to overcome the resistance, there is an affective factor, the personal influence of the physician, which we can seldom do without, and in a number of cases the latter alone is in a position to remove resistance" (p. 283).

But we can sense Freud's uneasiness at having given up the purely intellectual, scientific posture, for he goes on, almost apologetically, "The situation here is no different from what it is elsewhere in medicine and there is no therapeutic procedure of which one may say that it can do entirely without the co-operation of this personal factor" (p. 283).

As psychoanalysis gained adherents from diverse nonmedical branches of the academic community, Freud began to worry about what we commonly call "wild analysis." He mentioned having the impression that some of his colleagues thought the procedure an easy one that could be practiced offhand: "I conclude this from the fact that not one of all the people who have shown an interest in my therapy and passed definite judgments upon it has ever asked me how I actually go about it" (Freud, 1905, p. 261).

Indeed, Freud (1910) published an article, "Concerning Wild Analysis," in which he expressed his misgivings. A few years later, in "Recommendations on Analytic Technique," he gave technical advice to those of his colleagues who cared to read about his therapeutic posture. Obviously writing for those who did not possess the self-discipline and scientific neutrality that he himself displayed, Freud (1912) now reversed his former humanistic approach in which he recognized the ubiquitous necessity of a human factor, and wrote the following:

> I cannot advise my colleagues too urgently to model themselves during psycho-analytic treatment on the surgeon, who puts aside his feelings, even his human sympathy, and concentrates his mental forces on the single aim of performing the operation as skillfully as possible. Under present-day conditions the feeling that is most dangerous to a psychoanalyst is the therapeutic ambition [p. 115].

And further: "The justification for requiring this emotional coldness in the analyst is that it created the most advantageous conditions for both parties" (p. 115).

I am not sure that Freud really believed that the analyst's coldness creates the most advantageous conditions. Rather, I think he was inspired by fear of public ridicule and humiliation at the hands of his "wild" colleagues. Freud made an effort to protect his brainchild, psychoanalysis, by resisting, at least in his public writings, his own and his colleagues' tendencies toward an interactive and warmly human relationship with patients. However, as revealed by some of the analysands who published memoirs of their therapy with him, Freud remained the compassionate and empathically attuned physician within the privacy of his own consulting room. Unfortunately, in his publications he continued to exhibit the surgeonlike posture that became the model for future generations of analysts and analytic students. Rather than analyze Freud's anxiety motivated resistance to a full analytic relationship, most of his followers heeded his words, not his actions. In so doing they colluded with their hero's anxiety by copying their idealized mentor's defenses even in the relative safety of their own consulting rooms.

INTERPRETATION AND THERAPEUTIC AMBIENCE

Interpretation is a rather awkward and even misleading word for an activity that would be better referred to as an explanatory process. It is often loosely applied to every voluntary verbal participation by the analyst in the psychoanalytic treatment. Menninger (1958) thought it a presumptuous term that gives young analysts the wrong idea about their main functions, which he defined as quiet observation, listening, and occasional commenting (p. 129). Glover (1949) recognized two distinctive interpretative processes: "Interpretation can be either positive, when the unconscious content giving rise to the difficulty is communicated to the patient, or exploratory, when the unconscious emotions (usually anxiety and/or guilt) causing the hitch are ventilated" (p. 315).

Greenson (1967) thought, like Glover, that the role of the interpretative process was to make the unconscious conscious: "To interpret means to make an unconscious phenomenon conscious. More precisely, it means to make conscious the unconscious meaning, source, history, mode, or cause of a given psychic event. This usually requires more than a single intervention" (p. 39). Greenson thought of interpretation as essentially the analytic procedure par excellence: "The most important analytic procedure is interpretation; all others are subordinate to it both theoretically and practically. All analytic procedures are either steps which lead to an interpretation or make an interpretation effective" (p. 37).

Kohut (1984) was a great admirer of Glover, from whose writings he said that he had probably benefitted more than from those of any other psychoanalyst, with the exception of Freud (p. 93). I think it was Glover's "in-tuneness" with his analysands that impressed Kohut. However, he found himself in total disagreement with Glover's dismissal of the therapeutic effect of what Glover termed "inexact" interpretations. Glover found a nonpsychoanalytic explanation for the apparent effectiveness of inexact interpretations; he proposed that it is the nonspecific suggestibility of the analysand that leads to pseudosuccesses in such instances. It was a hallmark of

Kohut's approach to his analysands that he always paid serious attention to what his patients told him, having learned not to dismiss the patient's experiences too easily. If the patient reported a therapeutic success after an inexact interpretation, Kohut was very reluctant to label such an improvement a pseudosuccess unless he had independent evidence of the patient's need to hide his misery. He believed that inexact interpretations, like incomplete interpretations, could still be useful and effective explanations that would fall within the definition of interpretation if they had positive therapeutic consequences. One is therefore not surprised to hear that in his last lecture a few days before he died Kohut (1981) gave what is probably the most pithy of his definitions of the role of interpretation in the therapeutic process of psychoanalysis: "Analysis cures by giving explanations" (p. 532).

SELF-PSYCHOLOGICAL PRINCIPLES AND INTERPRETATION

The following case vignette illustrates the interpretation of a fear of the therapeutic situation, a fear that is often misleadingly called a resistance. I also attempt to contrast a theory-bound approach to an empathic approach.[4] The next vignette from the middle part of analysis illustrated a disruption/restoration sequence evoked by the therapist that was associated with a therapeutic gain.

Vignette: "Resistance" Interpretation

Quite a number of years ago a patient came to me because of chronic depressions, hypochondriasis, occasional sexual impotence, and, contrastingly, periods of sudden excitement during which he would spend money rather loosely. This pattern had disturbed the patient for many years but several attempts at psychotherapy, with and without drug therapy, had failed. On the recommendation of a friend he now wanted to try psychoanalysis. Since I feared a cyclothymic process or at best a borderline condition, I was reluctant to start analysis, but sensing that the pathology was primarily narcissistic, I

---

[4]The dichotomy theory vs. empathy can easily be misleading. There can be no collection of any data without a prior theory that guides the recognition of relevant data. The collection of empathic data must be guided by a theory, often unacknowledged, that gives meaning to empathic observations. In my use of the rhetorical dichotomy of theory vs. empathy I am trying to downgrade conclusions that are essentially derived from the manipulation of concepts, usually psychodynamic formulations, that are far removed from clinical observations.

was eager to try the insights I had recently learned from Kohut's conceptualizations.

During the early weeks of the analysis the patient made sure that I learned in detail the manifestations of his depression and hypochondriasis and expressed his conviction that no one could help him. Occasionally he would mention his work, generalizing that he was performing very poorly but then giving specific instances where he had in fact accomplished certain tasks with unusual skill and speed, leaving his competitors way behind. I cannot ignore my reaction to this patient because it became an important aspect of my recognizing and interpreting his fears. I felt annoyed by the long, repetitious, seemingly never-ending recital of his depressive and hypochondriacal suffering, particularly when this was combined with his assuring me of my therapeutic impotence. I thought that he had to be very angry with me (and probably with his family also) for he tried to make me (and them) suffer also. I speculated that his aggression was mobilizing and that he was defending himself against his hostile impulses by making himself helplessly sick, crying for help, and developing all kinds of debilitating hypochondriacal symptoms. Yet by making me and others suffer while assuring us of our inability to do something, he was hurting our self-esteem and impairing our ability to act. Thus, he was acting out his hostile aggression.

I interpreted none of this at that time because I thought such an interpretation based on a psychodynamic theory and not on my empathic immersion would have little effect. Indeed, I sensed it would make him more defensive. I now believe that such a theory-bound interpretation is likely to be incorrect. Instead, I told the patient that he was confronting me with my therapeutic impotence because he feared he could not be helped. He was looking for reassurance of my therapeutic prowess and interest in him. Not being helped would be a most painful disappointment for him, and therefore he hoped that I would deny his assertion that I could not help him. I told him that he was afraid I was not really interested in him and would sooner or later turn away from him like others had done and that he felt it necessary to tell me in great detail of his suffering to make sure I really could appreciate how much he suffered, how really sick he was, how much he needed me. And, I added, since he felt deeply humiliated by his neediness, he felt it necessary to report some unusual accomplishments so that I would not lose respect for him. Following these explanations he seemed to relax a little, and there was some diminishment of his defensiveness. We both felt more at ease and the analysis proceeded.

Of course, these interpretations are incomplete because they do not yet include the genetic background. In other words, a complete interpretation has to be a piece of personality dynamics seen not only in the context of the here and now but also as a part of a life history that articulates with and makes sense of what is known about the person's developmental history.

Vignette: Interpretation of Disruption Precipitated by Therapist

Mr. G, a middle-aged lawyer, entered analysis complaining of anxiety and depression that were at times so overwhelming that he could not concentrate on his work. He was also aware of the fact that in spite of his professional training and judgement he tended to become excessively and personally involved with his clients. He was the fourth and youngest child of successful upper-middle-class parents. Father was a busy corporate executive who expected much from his children without, however, devoting much time or directly relating to them. Although the patient had been a superior student, he felt he had not lived up to father's expectations, especially on the athletic field. His mother seemed to have been an unreliable source of emotional support, sometimes appearing too concerned and anxious and at other times too busy and distant. In the analysis Mr. G's need for a constant, reliable relationship to a mirroring and confirming selfobject manifested itself, for example, in symptomatic reactions to even the most minor changes in his regular schedule of four appointments per week. Concomitantly, his intense need to idealize me was reflected in his gradual and mainly unconscious imitation of my style of dress and speech as well as in concern mixed with depressive affect when he imagined that some other patient was my favorite and would be thought by me to be more worthwhile than he. During the week preceding the sequence of sessions I am using to illustrate how a disruption of the transference became a working-through episode, the patient had changed a Friday hour to the same time on a Tuesday. On the following Monday he talked at length about the struggle at his office to get rid of an unsatisfactory employee. Then he commented on how much more convenient the new Tuesday appointment was than the Friday sessions. While listening to these comments, I picked up my appointment book and made a brief notation. I do not ordinarily take notes during analytic sessions, and the patient heard me moving around. Suddenly, he fell silent. After a while I suggested that my writing had disturbed him. He was not sure, although he admitted that he was aware of the noise and had become annoyed. Still, he doubted that his silence was connected to this; he just felt he had nothing more to say.

On the next day Mr. G reported a surge of angry feelings after leaving my office. It had made him furious to think that I was writing and not really listening to him. His fury had mounted as he felt ignored and yet was helpless to do anything about it. Reminding himself that my transgression was relatively minor had not controlled the mounting tension, and that night he slept fitfully. He remembered a brief dream fragment: He is at a friend's house and in animated conversation with him when the friend's wife comes in and then walks out with her husband into another room, leaving the patient alone. I agreed with the patient that in the dream he felt ignored and left out, just as he had in our previous analytic session when he noticed my writing. Further associations led directly to memories of his parents, particularly to incidents when the parents were so caught up in their own interests that he felt similarly shunted aside, ignored, and neglected.

My matter-of-fact acceptance without either feeling or acting apologetic for having precipitated the experience of affects reminiscent of his response to childhood events helped the patient in lessening his self-blame for being so sensitive as to lead to a disruption. His success in conveying to me how he felt and how he experienced my lack of attention reduced his feelings of helplessness and thus ameliorated his narcissistic rage. His recall of the overwhelming intensity of similar affects during his childhood also increased his acceptance of his own genuine need for a different response from his parents then and from me now. At the same time, he gradually came to feel, and finally to believe, that my understanding and acceptance of his needs now, even without gratification, was enough legitimation of his self. The intensity of the affect began to diminish, and the tension between us began to fade away.

Vignette: Interpretation of Analyst's Empathic Lapse

A young lawyer, in his third year of analysis, reported that his cat had just died. The cat had never been mentioned before, and rather perfunctorily, without any real feeling, I acknowledged the loss. A period of silence ensued and I said something like "Let's go on." More silence. I commented that the cat must have been quite important and that the loss must be very painful to the patient. Yes, the patient acknowledged, the cat—he used the cat's name—meant very much to him, but he did not think I could understand that. He sounded upset. During the next session he was still upset; I could tell by his coldly angry voice. I interpreted that he was angry with me for not having been more sympathetic. Yes, he agreed, he did not think I really cared, but, just like his mother, I acted as if I did. Mother would put on a great show of concern, especially when other people were watching, but the patient felt she didn't really care. I confirmed that I did not feel about pets the same way that he and many other people do, and I interpreted that he experienced my comments, like his mother's, as a pretense of concern.

In this example of a disruption one can discern elements of both here-and-now experience and of transference of the past into the present. Both aspects always participate. In this case the analysand first experienced his analyst as not empathic, as not understanding how he felt, and then he was reminded of similar painful and traumatic malattunements in his childhood. The transference of the expectation of not being understood made my lack of attunement a repetition for the patient of a childhood trauma; not only was I suddenly not available as a confirming selfobject experience in the present but I even seemed to the patient to endorse and sanction the validity of his mother's lack of empathy, as well as her need to pretend. I, for my part, had thought myself well attuned to the patient. I knew about mother's pretending to feelings she did not have, but I had never before been aware that the analysand had any particular interest in pets. My perfunctory response seemed an appropriate acknowledgment. In fact, it *was* an appropriate acknowledgment, from my point of view. But not so from the patient's perspective. He unquestionably experienced a lack of empathy and understanding. The analyst must recognize and acknowledge the patient's perspective because by so doing he restores the patient's experience of a bond with the analyst and he provides the patient with an experience of having effectively communicated to the analyst.

Generally speaking, it is an apparent consequence of such malattunement that patients feel alone and overwhelmed by affects of anxiety, frustration, anger, humiliation, helpless rage, or hopeless depression. It is useful to remember that the disruption of the therapeutic relationship is associated with crushed self-esteem; that is, a devastating sense of "badness" characterizes the disrupted state of the analysand. Why is this so? Within the frame of a self-psychologically oriented treatment we conceptualize that the loss of attunement, the disjointed communication, is experienced as a loss of intimacy, that is, as a threat to the attachment of analysand to analyst. Or, in selfobject terminology, we could say that the experience of a selfobject bond is lost and with it the experience of a cohesive self. Indeed, numerous observations over many years allow us to assert with a high degree of reliability that a selfobject bond—whether of a mirroring or idealizing or alter-ego variety—is a necessary condition for a self state that is experienced as being whole, cohesive, balanced, and energetic. During a disruption the self-experience of the analyst will qualitatively include similar feelings, if he allows himself to become aware of them, though one may reasonably hope he will be able to resist the regressive and fragmenting pull of the disruption more effectively than the patient can.

DISCUSSION

The role of interpretation in psychoanalysis depends on the function it is intended to perform. In the initial phases of an analysis the patient's fear of the mysteriously dangerous analytic process and fear of the unknown analyst combine to restrict and distort his associations no matter how faithfully he has promised to associate freely. During this phase the role of interpretation is to free the patient of these fears, some of which are conscious and some of which are unconscious. In accordance with traditional Freudian precepts, interpretation should start from the surface, that is, from what the analyst surmises are the analysand's conscious and most highly charged fears. Conscious ideas and misperceptions can often be successfully relieved by verbal interventions that are designed to communicate elucidating and explanatory ideas for the analysand's perusal and possible acceptance. Unconscious attitudes and anxieties transferred from past experiences are much more difficult to modify. Simple dynamic explanations about what is going on unconsciously are usually ineffective even if they make good sense to the patient. Insight contained in a verbal statement rarely reaches the analysand's unconscious. It is necessary to provide an experience for the analysand that is contrary to the unconscious expectation. Since the unconscious expectation is derived from an early childhood experience, it leads the analysand to anticipate a relatively authoritative, parental, guiding, and judging role for the analyst. The experience of a proper analytic ambience that eschews the authoritarian milieu of old-style (old country) nursery schools and kindergarten has the best chance of counteracting the unconscious expectation. A consistent, benign, listening, and nonmoralizing analyst will blunt the fears and raise the analysand's hopes of finally being understood by someone who cares. As the analyst gets to know his patient better, he can gradually address the specific fears, the so-called resistances. I want to stress, however, that it is not analysands' fear of their own impulses, sexual or aggressive or otherwise, that motivates their resistance. It is fear that past experiences with the surround will be repeated.

Similar considerations should govern the management of the disruptions that characterize the middle phase of an analysis. From the patient's point of view these disruptions as a rule are precipitated by some act of omission or commission of the analyst. The therapist suddenly is experienced as not caring or not listening or being mostly concerned with his own agenda. During this middle phase a unique dynamic situation exists that facilitates such disruptions. The therapeutic ambience has diminished the patient's fears, and the repressed archaic needs for selfobject responsiveness become mobilized. The availability of the therapist as a caring and understanding selfobject expedites the establishment of a selfobject bond with the therapist. This newly established intra-analytic selfobject tie strengthens the self and usually manifests itself as an increasing feeling of well-being as the analysis progresses. The sudden disconnection of this selfobject tie is correlated with some disorganization of the self and associated symptoms, usually anger, anxiety, and depression. The role of interpretation now is to repair the selfobject tie and through it to restore the therapeutic process. And again, just as with the so-called resistance interpretations, the verbal form of the explanation, that is, the content communicated, is much less important than the experience evoked by the interpretation. Among the experiences of the analysand elicited by a well-managed interpretation is the experience of having brought about a modification in the analyst's behavior: the analyst has admitted that he did something to precipitate the patient's perception of him, a perception that caused the disruption. Thus the analyst implies he is more than a mere commenting observer; he is a responsibly acting and interacting participant. That relieves the patient of much of his pain and humiliation. Having brought about the analyst's admission of his part of the responsibility for what happened, the patient has an experience of having been efficacious, an experience quite in contrast to the expectation of always feeling helpless and impotent, as he did in childhood.

In summary, therefore, the role of interpretation is manifold, depending on the need of the analytic process. The role may be to lower fears or it may be to provide experiences of efficacy or it may be to communicate insights by explanations. All three are important and it would only be evidence of an intellectual bias were I to assign special importance to the provision of insight.

Let me say in concluding that my downgrading of the verbal aspect of interpretations and insight does not mean that interpretations are less important than we have always thought. Since merely knowing something often has no effect on either thought, affect, or behavior, it has always been mysterious why insight should be such an important therapeutic factor. Now we can dynamically explain how the experience evoked by interpretations and explanations strengthens the very fabric of the self via the strengthening of the selfobject tie between analyst and analysand. Our therapeutic approach has become that much more rational and effective.

REFERENCES

Bacal, H. (1985), Optimal responsiveness and the therapeutic process. In: *Progress in Self Psychology, Vol. 1*, ed. A. Goldberg. New York: Guilford Press, pp. 202–227.

Dupont, J., ed. (1988), *The Clinical Diary of Sándor Ferenczi*. Cambridge, MA: Harvard University Press.

Freud, S. (1895), Studies on hysteria. *Standard Edition*, 2. London: Hogarth Press, 1955.

———— (1905), On psychotherapy. *Standard Edition*, 7:257–268. London: Hogarth Press, 1953.

———— (1910), Concerning "wild analysis." *Standard Edition*, 12:221–227. London: Hogarth Press, 1958.

———— (1912), Recommendations to physicians practising psycho-analysis. *Standard Edition*, 12:109–120. London: Hogarth Press, 1958.

Gay, P. (1988), *Freud: A Life for Our Time*. New York: Norton.

Glover, E. (1955), *The Technique of Psychoanalysis*. London: Baillière, Tindall & Cox.

———— (1949), *Psycho-Analysis*. London: Staples Press, 2nd ed.

Greenson, R. (1967), *The Technique and Practice of Psychoanalysis*. New York: International Universities Press.

Kohut, H. (1981), On empathy. In: *The Search for the Self, Vol. 4*, P. Ornstein. New York: International Universities Press, 1991.

———— (1984), *How Does Analysis Cure?* ed. A. Goldberg & P. Stepansky. Chicago: University of Chicago Press.

Menninger, K. (1958), *Theory of Psychoanalytic Technique*. New York: Basic Books.

Terman, D. (1988), Optimal frustration: Structuralization and the therapeutic process. In: *Progress in Self Psychology, Vol. 4*, ed. A. Goldberg. New York: Guilford Press, pp. 113–125.

Wolf, E. (1992), On being a scientist or a healer: Reflections on abstinence, neutrality, and gratification. *The Annual of Psychoanalysis,*, 20:115–129.

Chapter 3

Thoughts on the Nature and Therapeutic Action of Psychoanalytic Interpretation

Robert D. Stolorow

The most general statement that can be made about a psychoanalytic interpretation is that it is an act of illuminating *personal meaning*. Since meaning is something that exists only within a world of subjective experience, all psychoanalytic interpretations, as Kohut (1959) eloquently demonstrated, must be informed by the psychoanalyst's empathy, which provides access to the patient's world of experience. Thus, any discussion of the nature and therapeutic action of psychoanalytic interpretation must begin with a consideration of the thorny question of what constitutes the essence of analytic empathy.

In an important paper delivered at the Eleventh Annual Conference on the Psychology of the Self in Washington, D.C., Brandchaft (1988) voiced certain concerns and caveats about the conflation of two uses of the concept of empathy appearing in Kohut's later writings. In one usage, consistent with his original pathbreaking essay (1959) on the subject, Kohut (1982) describes empathy as a "mode of observation attuned to the inner life of man" (p. 396), an *investigatory stance* that constitutes the "quintessence of psychoanalysis" (p. 398). In a second usage he depicts empathy as a "powerful emotional bond between people" (p. 397) and claims that "empathy *per se*, the mere presence of empathy, has . . . a beneficial, in a broad sense, a therapeutic effect—both in the clinical setting and in human life, in general" (p. 397). The same term, *empathy*, is being used to designate

---

This chapter is dedicated in loving memory to Dr. Daphne S. Stolorow.

both a mode of psychological investigation and a mode of affective responsiveness and bonding.

In agreement with Brandchaft (1988), I have come to believe that such conflation of usages contains serious potential pitfalls, as do a number of otherwise valuable formulations, such as Bacal's (1985) concept of optimal responsiveness and my (1983) own previously proposed conception of optimal empathy. Many people who become psychoanalysts have in their childhood histories a common element of having been required unduly to serve archaic selfobject functions for a parent (Miller, 1979), a requirement that is readily revived in reaction to patients' archaic states and developmental longings. When empathy is equated with an ideal of optimal human responsiveness and at the same time rightfully claimed to lie at the heart of the psychoanalytic process, this can exacerbate the analyst's countertransference dilemma, which takes the form of a requirement to provide the patient with an unbroken selfobject experience uncontaminated by painful repetitions of past childhood traumata—a requirement now invoked in the name of Kohut, Bacal, or Stolorow. As Brandchaft (1988) observes, when an analyst comes under the grip of such a requirement, the quintessential psychoanalytic aim of investigating and illuminating the patient's inner experience can become significantly subverted.

Considerations such as these have led my collaborators and me (Stolorow, Brandchaft, and Atwood, 1987) to reaffirm Kohut's (1959) original conceptualization of analytic empathy as a unique investigatory stance. We have characterized this stance as an attitude of *sustained empathic inquiry*, an attitude that consistently seeks to comprehend the meaning of a patient's expressions from a perspective within, rather than outside, the patient's own subjective frame of reference. I suggest that we restrict the concept of analytic empathy to refer to this distinctive investigatory stance and use some other term, such as *affective responsiveness*, to capture the "powerful emotional bond between people" (p. 397) that Kohut (1982) believed can also produce therapeutic effects. By making this suggestion, I do not mean to imply that analysts should routinely inhibit their natural affective responsiveness, although under some circumstances it might be desirable to do so. However, an essential ingredient of the analyst's attitude of empathic inquiry is his commitment continually to investigate the *meaning* of his affective responsiveness, or its absence, for the patient. After all, what is affective responsiveness for the goose might be something quite different for the gander. What the analyst experiences as affective responsiveness the patient may experience as a covert seduction or a promise that revived archaic longings will literally be fulfilled in a concretized form. On the other hand, an analyst's emotional reserve can at times be experienced by a patient as a yearned-for haven of safety in which his own experience can be articulated free from the requirement to adapt to another's affectivity. Whether or not the analyst's affective responsiveness will itself have a beneficial or therapeutic effect will depend on its meaning for the patient.

I wish to stress that our emphasis on inquiry does not mean that the analyst is constantly asking questions. On the contrary, the analyst uses all the means at his disposal to facilitate the unfolding and illumination of the patient's subjective world, which may include prolonged periods of silent listening and reflection, in which the analyst searches his own world of experience for potential analogues of what the patient is presenting to him. Such analogues may be drawn from multiple sources, such as the analyst's own childhood history, his personal analysis, his recollections of other patients' analyses or of case reports by other analysts, his readings of great works of literature, his knowledge of developmental research, and his studies of psychoanalytic theories. It is my view that psychoanalytic theories vary greatly in their capacity to enhance empathic access to the patient's subjective world and that differing psychoanalytic theories often address fundamentally different realms of experience. When *any* theoretical system is elevated to the status of a metapsychology whose categories are presumed to be universally and centrally salient for all persons, then I believe such a theory actually has a constricting impact on analysts' efforts to comprehend the uniqueness of their patients' psychological worlds.

I also wish to emphasize that the attitude of sustained empathic inquiry is not to be equated with an exclusive preoccupation with conscious elements in a patient's experience, a common misconception voiced by self psychology's critics. Indeed, empathic inquiry may be *defined* as a method of investigating and illuminating the principles that *unconsciously* organize a patient's experiences. Such unconscious principles become manifest, for example, in the invariant *meanings* that the analyst's qualities and activities recurrently come to acquire for the patient. Such meanings may contain defensive purposes, and failing to investigate unconscious defensiveness when a patient has shown a developmental readiness for such analysis is *not* empathy (Trop and Stolorow, 1991).

I prefer the concept of sustained empathic inquiry to the commonly used phrase *prolonged empathic immersion* (Kohut, 1977) partly because the former, as I have indicated, underscores the analyst's investigative function. In addition, I believe that the idea of empathic immersion contains another potential countertransference pitfall, wherein the analyst feels required to immerse himself completely in the patient's experience, banishing his own psychological organization from the psychoanalytic dialogue so that he can gaze directly upon his patient's subjective world with pure and presuppositionless eyes—surely an impossible feat for even the most gifted of analysts. Such a requirement defies the profoundly intersubjective nature of the analytic process, to which the analyst's organizing principles, including those enshrined in the theory through which he attempts to order the analytic data, make an inevitable and unavoidable contribution.

My collaborators and I (Atwood and Stolorow, 1984; Stolorow et al., 1987) have conceptualized the development of psychoanalytic understanding as an intersubjective process involving a dialogue between two personal universes. Hence, the process of arriving at a psychoanalytic interpretation entails making empathic inferences about the principles organizing the patient's experience, inferences that alternate and interact with the analyst's acts of reflection upon the involvement of his own subjective reality in the ongoing investigation. Thus, the attitude of sustained empathic inquiry, which informs the analyst's interpretations, must of necessity encompass the entire intersubjective field created by the interplay between the differently organized subjective worlds of patient and analyst.

Having elucidated my view of the empathic stance that forms the basis for constructing psychoanalytic interpretations, I turn now to the primary focus of this chapter: conceptualizing the therapeutic action of psychoanalytic interpretation. My emphasis on the therapeutic effect of interpretation, as opposed to noninterpretive elements within the therapeutic interaction, parallels and complements my reaffirmation of the investigative function of analytic empathy. I hope, thereby, to provide an answer to those critics—Mitchell (1988), for example—who mistakenly portray self psychology as attributing therapeutic action primarily to the analyst's "affective tone and its emotional impact" (p. 294) rather than to the analyst's interpretations.

There has been a long-standing debate within psychoanalysis over the role of cognitive insight versus affective attachment in the process of therapeutic change (see Friedman, 1978, for an excellent historical review of this controversy). In recent years the pendulum seems to have swung in the direction of affective attachment, with a number of authors, each from his own theoretical viewpoint, emphasizing the mutative power of *new relational experiences* with the analyst: Kohut (1971, 1977, 1984), who spoke in terms of the establishment, disruption, and repair of selfobject ties; Modell (1984), who emphasizes the holding functions of the analytic setting; Emde (1988) and P. Tolpin (1988), who view the emotional availability and engagement of the analyst as correcting for early deficits; and Gill (1982), Weiss and Sampson (1986), and Fosshage (1992), who stress the new interpersonal experiences with the analyst as disconfirming transference expectations (for earlier versions of this position see also Strachey, 1934; Alexander, 1950; Stone, 1957; Fairbairn, 1958; Loewald, 1960). It is my view that once the psychoanalytic situation is recognized as an intersubjective system, the dichotomy between insight through interpretation and affective bonding with the analyst is revealed to be a false one (Stolorow et al., 1987; Stolorow, 1991). The therapeutic impact of the analyst's accurate transference interpretations, for example, lies not only in the insights they convey but also in the extent to which they demonstrate the analyst's attunement to the patient's affective states and developmental longings. The analyst's transference interpretations, in other words, are not disembodied transmissions of insight *about* the analytic relationship; they are an inherent, inseparable component *of* that very bond. As Atwood and I (1984) stated:

> Every transference interpretation that successfully illuminates for the patient his unconscious past simultaneously crystallizes an elusive present—the novelty of the therapist as an understanding presence. Perceptions of self and other are perforce transformed . . . to allow for the new experience [p. 60].

It is not so much, I would now add, that existing psychological structures are thereby changed as that alternative principles for organizing experience gradually come into being.

Kohut (1984) divided the interpretive process into two phases, a first in which the analyst conveys an empathic *understanding* of the patient's emotional experience and a second in which the analyst offers an interpretive *explanation* of that experience. I have not found this formulation especially congenial because it seems to me to separate the affective and cognitive components of the analyst's investigative activity, components that I believe are indissociable. Instead of the two discrete phases proposed by Kohut, I envision a continuum of interpretations of increasing cognitive compexity, with *both* the analyst's affect attunements *and* cognitive inferences playing a part at every point along the continuum. Despite my reservation, however, I find Kohut's formulation of the interpretive process to be extremely valuable in that it makes explicit what is implicit in all of his writings, namely, that if an interpretation is to produce a therapeutic

36   Stolorow

effect, it must provide the patient with a *new experience of being deeply understood*. This emphasis on the therapeutic benefit of new selfobject experiences provided by the analyst's communications of empathic understanding has been usefully amplified by a number of contributors to the self psychology literature (Ornstein and Ornstein, 1980; M. Tolpin, 1987; Bacal, 1990; J. Miller, 1990; Wolf, 1990; Lindon,1991).

But now, in an apparent reversal of my earlier position, I wish to point out a potential pitfall of this emphasis on the newness of the selfobject experiences provided by the analyst's empathic communications: the danger of neglecting the contribution of the *patient's* psychological organization—what Bacal (1990) describes as the patient's "creative phantasy" (p. 369)—to the therapeutic impact of the analyst's interpretations (see also Brandchaft, 1991). To the current emphasis on new relational experiences, I wish to add the essential therapeutic contribution of something old, something derived from the patient's psychological depths, namely, the *specific transference meaning* for a particular patient at a particular point in the analysis of the experience of being understood, a meaning that itself will eventually need to be investigated and interpreted (Gill, 1982). It is my central thesis here that such specific transference meanings constitute a crucial ingredient of the therapeutic action of psychoanalytic interpretations and that this applies both to transference interpretations and to interpretations of extratransference material (see A. Ornstein, 1990).

Winnicott (1954) claimed that "whenever we understand a patient in a deep way and show that we do so by a correct and well-timed interpretation we are in fact holding the patient" (p. 261). Winnicott here seems to assume that the experience of being understood has a single transference meaning, the feeling of being held, that applies universally to all patients across the board. In contrast, I envision a vast multiplicity of possible transference meanings, with the specific meaning of the analyst's attuned interpretations being determined by the particular developmental needs and longings mobilized in the transference at any given juncture. Let me illustrate with a brief vignette.[1]

Stuart sought analysis at the age of 26 to find relief from tormenting states of obsessional rumination that regularly followed injurious experiences that made him feel intensely vulnerable, anxious, overwhelmed, and confused. The older of two children, he

---

[1] I am indebted to Dr. Elizabeth Asunsolo for providing me with the clinical material for this vignette.

described his father as a passive presence in the home, seemingly controlled by his wife and appearing weak and helpless in the face of her frequent outbursts of rage. In relation to himself, Stuart experienced his father as distant, uninterested, and emotionally unavailable. The patient described his mother as anxious, unhappy, and frequently overwhelmed, and also as intrusive and "controlling [his] identity." He felt he had to function as a "substitute husband" for her and to be a "father" to his younger sister, to "set an example for her" by suppressing his own emotional reactions to events within the family. He was always aware of his mother's emotions, he said, and felt responsible for comforting her when she was upset. Being organized around her neediness made him feel "special" to her, but his specialness had come at the price of a constant requirement to be "big" and "strong" in order to take care of her and maintain her emotional equilibrium. When he brought his own difficulties to her in the hope of a comforting response, she would become frustrated and overwhelmed and invariably tell him to leave her alone.

The most profound emotional truth of Stuart's childhood was his sense of being totally alone with painful experiences, both within and outside the family. He felt a complete absence of a strong, idealizable figure who could protect him and help guide him through painful situations; hence, he turned to his own excellent mind to find a sense of control and safety. Omnipotent thought became his substitute for the missing idealizable parent, setting the foundation for his later obsessional symptomatology.

As might be expected in light of this history of profound emotional neglect and abandonment, the early months of Stuart's analysis centered around his fears of exposing his needs to his female analyst. He felt that he had to be big and strong and brave in order to please the analyst, and he expected her to desert or punish him for expressing any wish to be taken care of. He feared that the analyst, like his mother, would be overwhelmed by his needs and painful feelings and that she would become injured and even "destroyed" if he were to voice any angry reactions to her disappointing him. Gradually and conflictually, Stuart began to acknowledge his growing attachment to the analyst, along with the disruptive impact of separations from her, which evoked severe anxiety and an intensification of his obsessional brooding. After about 18 months of analysis, he was able to articulate a deep yearning for the analyst to provide complete protection from painful affect.

Around this time, the analyst's accurate interpretations of the meanings of the patient's painful emotional experiences, both within and outside the transference, began to produce remarkable effects. Here is a sampling of his reactions to interpretations that provided him with the experience of being understood:

> I feel so good. You're an expert, taking care of me. I feel happy, protected, in the right place.

> I feel protected by you. I have a resource, so I'm able to feel sad and uncertain.

> Oooh! I'm feeling really happy. You're helping me, giving me direction. You're calm and strong, not frivolous like my mother. This is big-time help!

> I feel so good here, hearing your sweet voice behind me. You know things; you're clear and logical. You're in charge of the situation, and I feel protected, less vulnerable.

Following therapeutic moments such as these the patient would experience states of calm of increasing duration, and his obsessional preoccupations would diminish and even disappear. His anxiety and obsessional thinking would return, of course, in reaction to misattunements and separations, although less so as the treatment progressed, and his disruptive reactions, wherein the analyst became the emotionally abandoning mother of his childhood, still needed to be analyzed. But what I wish to stress here is that at this point the powerfully ameliorative impact of the analyst's attuned interpretations and of the patient's consequent feeling of being understood derived from the profound transference meaning that both had come to acquire for him. They materialized the analyst as the deeply longed-for, calm, strong, knowing, and protective mother so sorely absent during his childhood. To the extent that the patient now felt protected by an idealizable parent, the illusory protection afforded by the activity of his own mind became unnecessary and dispensable.

Similar observations can be made about the therapeutic effect of the transference meaning of interpretations when other selfobject needs are in the foreground. For a patient immersed in a primary mirror transference, the experience of being understood can evoke a sense of being deeply treasured by the analyst, of having attained a position at the very center of the analyst's world. In the context of a twinship transference, the analyst's understanding can be organized as evidence of the patient having found the yearned-for soul mate whose experiential sameness promises to alleviate lifelong feelings of painful singularity. Interpretations of defensiveness, in some instances, can establish the analyst in the transference as an idealizable, benign adversary (Lachmann, 1986; Wolf, 1988), facilitating the patient's demarcation of self-boundaries. All such transference experiences, as Kohut (1971, 1977, 1984) repeatedly emphasized, reanimate stalled development and thereby fuel the process of therapeutic transformation.

Anyone who has conducted an analysis from a self psychology perspective has witnessed the enormous therapeutic benefits of analyzing ruptures in selfobject transference ties. Throughout his writings, Kohut (1971, 1977, 1984) explained these therapeutic effects by invoking his theory of optimal frustration leading to transmuting internalization, an explanation that has been questioned by a number of self-psychologically minded authors (Socarides and Stolorow, 1984/1985; Bacal, 1985; Stolorow et al., 1987; Terman, 1988). How might the therapeutic action of analyzing disruptions be explained according to the thesis I have been developing here?

Most patients who come to us for analysis have, as children, suffered repeated, complex experiences of selfobject failure, which I conceptualize schematically as occurring in two phases. In the first phase a primary selfobject need is met with rebuff or disappointment by a caregiver, producing a painful emotional reaction. In the second phase the child experiences a secondary selfobject longing for an attuned response that would modulate, contain, and ameliorate his painful reactive affect state. But parents who repeatedly rebuff primary selfobject needs are usually not able to provide attuned responsiveness to the child's painful emotional reactions. The child perceives that his painful reactive feelings are unwelcome or damaging to the caregiver and must be defensively sequestered in order to preserve the needed bond. Under such circumstances, as my collaborators and I (Socarides and Stolorow, 1984/85; Stolorow et al., 1987) have stressed, these walled-off painful feelings become a source of lifelong inner conflict and vulnerability to traumatic states, and in analysis their re-exposure to the analyst tends to be strenuously resisted.

In light of this developmental formulation, how might we conceptualize the therapeutic impact of analyzing disruptions of selfobject transference ties, that is, transference repetitions of experiences of primary selfobject failure? In conducting such an analysis, the analyst investigates and interprets the various elements of the rupture from the perspective of the patient's subjective frame of reference—the qualities or activities of the analyst that produced the disruption, its specific meanings, its impact on the analytic bond and on the

patient's self-experience, the early developmental traumata it replicates, and, especially important, the patient's expectations and fears
of how the analyst will respond to the articulation of the painful
feelings that follow in its wake (Stolorow et al., 1987). I believe that it
is the transference meaning of this investigative and interpretive
activity that is its principal source of therapeutic action in that it
establishes the analyst in the transference as the secondarily longed-
for, receptive, and understanding parent who, through his attuned
responsiveness, will "hold" (Winnicott, 1954) and thereby eventually
alleviate the patient's painful emotional reaction to an experience of
primary selfobject failure. The selfobject tie becomes thereby mended
and expanded, and primary selfobject yearnings are permitted to
emerge more freely as the patient feels increasing confidence that his
emotional reactions to experiences of rebuff and disappointment will
be received and contained by the analyst. Concomitantly, a developmental process is set in motion wherein the formerly sequestered
painful reactive affect states, the heritage of the patient's history of
traumatic developmental failure, gradually become integrated and
transformed and the patient's capacity for affect tolerance becomes
increasingly strengthened.

There is an additional transference meaning of the analyst's
attuned interpretive activity that I believe may contribute a therapeutic element in all analyses but is especially important in the
treatment of patients who have suffered severe developmental derailments in the articulation of perceptual and affective experience.
These are patients often prone to fragmented, disorganized, or
psychosomatic states, for whom broad areas of early experience failed
to evoke validating attunement from caregivers and, consequently,
whose perceptions remain ill-defined and precariously held, easily
usurped by the judgments of others, and whose affects tend to be felt
as diffuse bodily states rather than symbolically elaborated feelings.
In such cases the analyst's investigation and illumination of the
patient's inner experiences, always from the patient's perspective,
serve to articulate and consolidate the patient's subjective reality,
crystallizing the patient's experience, lifting it to higher levels of
organization, and strengthening the patient's confidence in its validity. The analyst thereby becomes established in the transference as
the missing and longed-for validator of the patient's psychic reality, a
selfobject function so fundamental and basic that my collaborators
and I (Trop and Stolorow, 1991; Stolorow, Atwood, and Brandchaft,
1992) believe that its appearance in analysis deserves to be designated
by a specific term: the "self-delineating selfobject transference."

I would like now to place my discussion of the therapeutic action of psychoanalytic interpretation within the broader framework of the conceptualization of transference that my collaborators and I (Stolorow et al., 1987) have previously proposed. In this formulation the transference, viewed as the product of unconscious organizing activity (Stolorow and Lachmann, 1984/1985), is seen to consist of two basic dimensions: In one dimension are the patient's yearnings and hopes for selfobject experiences that were missing or insufficient during the formative years. In the other dimension, which is a source of conflict and resistance, are his expectations and fears of a transference repetition of the original experiences of selfobject failure (A. Ornstein, 1974). All well-conducted analyses, we have suggested, are characterized by inevitable, continual shifts in the figure–ground relationships between these two dimensions of the transference as they oscillate between the foreground and background of the patient's experience of the analytic bond, shifts and oscillations that are profoundly influenced by whether or not the analyst's interpretive activity is experienced by the patient as being attuned to his affective states and needs. When the analyst's interpretations are experienced as unattuned or misattuned, foreshadowing a traumatic repetition of early developmental failure, the conflictual and resistive dimension of the transference is frequently brought into the foreground, while the patient's selfobject longings are driven into hiding. Attuned interpretations, by contrast, evoke, strengthen, and expand the selfobject dimension of the transference, and herein, I have argued, lies a principal source of their therapeutic effects.[2]

In closing, I wish to emphasize that by bringing to focus the therapeutic impact of the transference meanings of psychoanalytic interpretations, I do not discount the existence of other sources of therapeutic action, including those that may derive from enhancements of the patient's self-reflective capacity (Brandchaft and Stolorow, 1990) or from the meanings of noninterpretive elements within the therapeutic process. I do hope to have demonstrated that the therapeutic action of psychoanalytic interpretation is something that takes form within a specific intersubjective interaction to which the psychological organizations of both analyst and patient make distinctive contributions. The analyst, through sustained empathic inquiry, constructs an interpretation that enables the patient to feel deeply

---

[2]Sometimes disruptions can occur that are quite confusing to the analyst: because of unrecognized shifts in the patient's psychological organization, interpretations that were once experienced within the selfobject dimension of the transference suddenly become assimilated into the repetitive/conflictual/resistive dimension, producing unexpected exacerbations of the patient's suffering and manifest symptomatology (Trop and Stolorow, 1991).

understood. The patient, from within the depths of his own subjective world, weaves that experience of being understood into the tapestry of his unique, mobilized selfobject yearnings, enabling a thwarted developmental process to become reinstated. Psychoanalytic interpretations, I am contending, derive their mutative power from the intersubjective matrix in which they crystallize.

REFERENCES

Alexander, F. (1950), Analysis of the therapeutic factors in psychoanalytic treatment. *Psychoanal. Quart.*, 19:482-500.
Atwood, G. & Stolorow, R. (1984), *Structures of Subjectivity*. Hillsdale, NJ: The Analytic Press.
Bacal, H. (1985), Optimal responsiveness and the therapeutic process. In: *Progress in Self Psychology, Vol. 1*, ed. A. Goldberg. New York: Guilford Press, pp. 202-226.
_____ (1990), The elements of a corrective selfobject experience. *Psychoanal. Inq.*, 10:347-372.
Brandchaft, B. (1988), Critical issues in regard to empathy. Presented at the Eleventh Annual Conference on the Psychology of the Self, Washington, DC, October 16.
_____ (1991), Countertransference in the analytic process. In: *The Evolution of Self Psychology*, ed. A. Goldberg. Hillsdale, NJ: The Analytic Press, pp. 99-105.
_____ & Stolorow, R. (1990), Varieties of therapeutic alliance. *The Annual of Psychoanalysis*, 18:99-114. Hillsdale, NJ: The Analytic Press.
Emde, R. (1988), Development terminable and interminable: II. Recent psychoanalytic theory and therapeutic considerations. *Internat. J. Psycho-Anal.*, 69:283-296.
Fairbairn, W. R. D. (1958), On the nature and aims of psycho-analytical treatment. *Internat. J. Psycho-Anal.*, 39:374-385.
Fosshage, J. (1992), Self psychology: The self and its vicissitudes within a relational matrix. In: *Relational Perspectives in Psychoanalysis*, ed. N. Skolnick & S. Warshaw. Hillsdale, NJ: The Analytic Press.
Friedman, L. (1978), Trends in the psychoanalytic theory of treatment. *Psychoanal. Quart.*, 47:524-567.
Gill, M. (1982), *Analysis of Transference, Vol. 1*. Madison, CT: International Universities Press.
Kohut, H. (1959), Introspection, empathy, and psychoanalysis. *J. Amer. Psychoanal. Assn.*, 7:459-483.
_____ (1971), *The Analysis of the Self*. Madison, CT: International Universities Press.
_____ (1977), *The Restoration of the Self*. Madison, CT: International Universities Press.
_____ (1982), Introspection, empathy, and the semicircle of mental health. *Internat. J. Psycho-Anal.*, 63:395-407.
_____ (1984), *How Does Analysis Cure?* ed. A. Goldberg & P. Stepansky. Chicago: University of Chicago Press.
Lachmann, F. (1986), Interpretation of psychic conflict and adversarial relationships. *Psychoanal. Psychol.*, 3:341-355.
Lindon, J. (1991), Does technique require theory? *Bull. Menn. Clin.*, 55:1-21.
Loewald, H. (1960), On the therapeutic action of psychoanalysis. *Internat. J. Psycho-Anal.*, 41:16-33.
Miller, A. (1979), *Prisoners of Childhood*. New York: Basic Books, 1981.
Miller, J. (1990), The corrective emotional experience. *Psychoanal. Inq.*, 10:373-388.

Mitchell, S. (1988), *Relational Concepts in Psychoanalysis*. Cambridge: Harvard University Press.

Modell, A. (1984), *Psychoanalysis in a New Context*. Madison, CT: International Universities Press.

Ornstein, A. (1974), The dread to repeat and the new beginning. *The Annual of Psychoanalysis*, 2:231–248. New York: International Universities Press.

_____ (1990), Selfobject transferences and the process of working through. In: *The Realities of Transference*, ed. A. Goldberg. Hillsdale, NJ: The Analytic Press, pp. 41–58.

Ornstein, P. & Ornstein, A. (1980), Formulating interpretations in clinical psychoanalysis. *Internat. J. Psycho-Anal.*, 61:203–211.

Socarides, D. & Stolorow, R. (1984/1985), Affects and selfobjects. *The Annual of Psychoanalysis*, 12/13:105–119. New York: International Universities Press.

Stolorow, R. (1983), Self Psychology: A structural psychology. In: *Reflections on Self Psychology*, ed. J. Lichtenberg & S. Kaplan. Hillsdale, NJ: The Analytic Press, pp. 287–296.

_____ (1991), The intersubjective context of intrapsychic experience. *Psychoanal. Inq.*, 11:171–184.

_____ Atwood, G. & Brandchaft, B. (1992), Three realms of the unconscious and their therapeutic transformation. *Psychoanal. Rev.*, 79:25–30.

_____ Brandchaft, B. & Atwood, G. (1987), *Psychoanalytic Treatment*. Hillsdale, NJ: The Analytic Press.

_____ & Lachmann, F. (1984/1985), Transference: The future of an illusion. *The Annual of Psychoanalysis*, 12/13:19–37. New York: International Universities Press.

Stone, L. (1957), Book review of *Psychoanalysis and Psychotherapy* by F. Alexander. *Psychoanal. Quart.*, 26:397–405.

Strachey, J. (1934), The nature of the therapeutic action of psychoanalysis. *Internat. J. Psycho-Anal.*, 15:127–159.

Terman, D. (1988), Optimum frustration: Structuralization and the therapeutic process. In: *Learning from Kohut*, ed. A. Goldberg. Hillsdale, NJ: The Analytic Press, pp. 113–125.

Tolpin, M. (1987), Discussion of "The Analyst's Stance" by M. Black. *The Annual of Psychoanalysis*, 15:159–164.

Tolpin, P. (1988), Optimal affective engagement: The analyst's role in therapy. In: *Learning from Kohut*, ed. A. Goldberg. Hillsdale, NJ: The Analytic Press, pp. 160–168.

Trop, J. & Stolorow, R. (1991), A developmental perspective on analytic empathy. *J. Amer. Acad. Psychoanal.*, 19:31–46.

Weiss, J. & Sampson, H. (1986), *The Psychoanalytic Process*. New York: Guilford Press.

Winnicott, D. (1954). Withdrawal and regression. In: *Through Paediatrics to Psycho-Analysis*. London: Hogarth Press, 1958, pp. 255–261.

Wolf, E. (1988), *Treating the Self*. New York: Guilford Press.

_____ (1990), Clinical responsiveness: Corrective or empathic? *Psychoanal. Inq.*, 10:420–432.

Chapter 4

Interpretation in a Developmental Perspective

Frank M. Lachmann
Beatrice Beebe

Historically, the role of interpretation in psychoanalytic treatment was consonant with a model of development in which the child needed to be enticed out of its autistic-narcissistic shell through the influence of reality as mediated by parents. The infant was believed to be unaware of its surroundings, protected by a stimulus barrier against impingements from the external world, and responsive only to inner urges of hunger, pain, aggressive discharges, and libidinal needs. Early development consisted of a laborious process of distinguishing between id and ego, inside and outside, fantasy and reality. For an adult patient to be able to utilize interpretations, considerable sophistication in having made these distinctions was necessary. Psychotic and narcissistic patients were unenticeable and hence unanalyzable. The analyst's interpretations had to strengthen the patient's relationship to reality and lessen the regressive pull of the id, with the observing ego functions remaining relatively intact.

The advent of empirical work on infancy, reformulations of the concept of transference, and the clinical–theoretical contributions of self psychology challenged the traditional model of development and its role in explaining the therapeutic action of psychoanalysis. Self psychologists have demonstrated that patients previously regarded as unanalyzable turn out to form analyzable selfobject transference. The analyst's interpretive activity is now understood to include a range of therapeutic endeavors. According to Wolf (this volume) it includes "all (the) intentional interventions by the analyst, verbal and non-verbal, that modify the analysand's psyche." According to Stolorow (this volume), "the therapeutic action of psychoanalytic interpretation . . . takes from within a specific intersubjective interaction to which the psychological organization of both analyst and patient make distinctive contributions." Together Wolf and Stolorow recognize the totality of the analytic relationship in its effect on the patient's psyche. They emphasize the emotional availability and responsivity of the analyst and the effect of a loss of such attunement on the therapeutic relationship. They consider affect to be a quality of the dyad and note that breaches in the affective tie result in a loss of intimacy. The threatened connection between the analysand and the analyst then requires attention so that ruptures can be restored. For Stolorow this attunement is organized within the patient–analyst interaction, an intersubjective field. Wolf emphasizes that the analyst must continuously provide and maintain an ambience in which the patient can experience the freedom to reflect upon his anxieties. The contributions to the curative process made by the patient–analyst interactions are recognized by both Stolorow and Wolf.

In the evolution of psychoanalysis the importance of affect, the moment of affective urgency (Strachey, 1934; Fenichel, 1938–1939; Greenson, 1967), has been recognized as optimal for the making of interpretations. There has always been a concern that interpretations would fall prey to the patient's resistive, intellectualizing processes. Self psychology and the contributions by Wolf and Stolorow provide a clinical guide for avoiding this pitfall through their emphasis on monitoring the patient's reactions and attending to ruptures in the selfobject tie.

In addition, the clinical illustrations offered by Stolorow and Wolf permit us to consider interpretations from the developmental perspective we have been studying (Beebe and Lachmann, 1988a, b; Lachmann and Beebe, 1989). Our perspective on the therapeutic action of interpretations differs from the one employed by traditional psychoanalysis and is consistent with the clinical theory of self psychology.

In the case described by Stolorow, the analyst interpreted the patient's obsessional symptomatology as derived from his need for idealizable parents. The patient's excellent mind and the omnipotence accorded to his thoughts shielded him from the danger of experiencing his need for his unavailable father and overanxious mother. The interpretation had an immediate effect on the patient's experience of the analytic situation. In the past the patient needed to defend against the expectation that his yearnings for his parents would be unmet. In contrast, he could now permit his yearnings for the analyst to emerge.

The patient's responses describe the change in his state. From feeling bad about himself he felt "good . . . taken care of . . . happy . . . protected." From an experience of jeopardy, feeling he was in the hands of a parent who needed him to be the expert, he changed to a state in which he felt relieved of this prematurely imposed burden. He said to his analyst, "You're an expert."

In his first case illustration Wolf described a patient who elaborated upon his depression and sudden bursts of excitement. His pervasive state was one of helplessness, hopelessness, and a dread of being left alone to this fate. Wolf's interpretation addressed this sense of hopelessness and included his impression that the patient wished to have these expectations disconfirmed. Wolf indicated that this was not a complete interpretation because genetic material was not included. If we follow the model presented in Stolorow's case, we might include in the interpretation a recognition that in the past, in contrast to the current analytic relationship, the patient had found it necessary to conceal his reactive disappointment and anger. Nevertheless, even without the genetic material and solely on the basis of the interpretation that his superficially hostile facade concealed his fear of being given up on, the patient's state changed and he felt "relaxed." With additional genetic material, additional affective and bodily states could have been revived, and transformed as well.

Interpretations potentially organize a heightened affective and cognitive moment; a visceral and kinesthetic shift may be experienced, as well as a cognitive reorganization involving surprise and novelty (Reik, 1935; Wolf 1991). Both the Stolorow and the Wolf examples dramatically illustrate these changes in the patient's self-state. We use these two illustrations to propose that the interpretive process entails self-state transformations.

Our use of the term *self-state* draws on contributions from two sources: Stern's (1983, 1985) and Sander's (1983) discussions of state transformation and the self-regulating other and Kohut's (1980, 1984) discussion of self states, as they are seen in self-state dreams.

Stern's (1985) use of the term *self-regulating other* refers to the caregiver who regulates the infant's states of arousal, affect intensity, and security of attachment. "The infant is with an other who regulates the infant's own self experience" (p. 102). *State* refers to the variations in sleep and wakefulness that occur as the infant passes between crying and alert periods; between quiet activity, drowsiness, and sleep; between wet discomfort and dry comfort; and between hunger and satiation. However, these states of alertness, arousal, activity, and sleep are socially negotiated, a product of the mutual regulation system (Sander, 1983). Sander suggests that the earliest self is organized around the infant's recognition of recurrent, predictable transitions of state, in particular, interactive contexts. Thus, early state transformations are related to both self-regulatory capacity and the expectation that the mutual regulatory system will facilitate or interfere with these transformations.

In psychoanalytic theory state changes have generally been associated with drive satisfactions. For example, being fed when hungry is assumed to lead to libidinal attachment of the infant to the hunger-drive-satisfying object. The caretaker's ministrations to the infant, whether through feeding, diapering, or soothing, are assumed to strengthen the infant's attachment to the caretaker.

Various clinicians and researchers (e.g., Ainsworth et al., 1978; Bowlby, 1980; Stern, 1983, 1985) have proposed a contrasting view. They hold that there are numerous interactions that promote attachment between infants and their caretakers that have nothing to do with drive gratification. The interactions that promote attachment are mutually regulated, reciprocal exchanges in which each partner influences the other on a moment-to-moment basis. Stern (1983) categorizes these mutual regulations as state sharing (e.g., mutual cooing) and self–other complementarity (e.g., a ball pushed back and forth between the infant and the caretaker).

The caretaking ministrations that occur during feeding, changing, and calming, Stern (1983) argues, are represented by the infant as state transformations. However, Stern places state transformations in a different category from state sharing and complementarity: "The experience of being hungry, getting fed, and going blissfully to sleep does not, even when associated with a particular person, lead to subjective intimacy with the feeding person, unless accompanied by self–other complementing and state sharing" (p. 79). We hold that these caretaking ministrations dramatically transform self-states. With the advent of symbolic capacities and increasing elaboration upon one's subjective experience, self-states in the child and adult include the domain of the self in a psychological sense. Post-infancy self-state transformations may increase a sense of control, mastery, or agency.

Psychopathology can be reflected through a kind of dream, delineated by Kohut (1984) as a self-state dream, in which the imagery is an undisguised or only minimally disguised depiction of the dreamer's sense of self. Self-states may be depicted in dreams as "an empty landscape, burned-out forests, decaying neighborhoods . . . an airplane out of control that wildly flies higher and higher" (Kohut, 1980, p. 508). These dreams herald self experiences such as aimlessness, depression, hypomania, fragmentation, despair, or hopelessness.

The analyst's understanding and recognition of the self-state constitutes an interpretation and contributes to the selfobject tie.

Our use of *self-state* is broader than Stern's inasmuch as we extend this perspective into adult life. Like Stern, however, we distinguish affect, cognition, and arousal. How each of these aspects of self-state is affected will differ from one person to the next. Our use of the term is not confined to the dream imagery. Dreams provide a glimpse into a person's self-state, but moods, symptoms, and transference manifestations may reflect self-states as well.

We use the term "self-state" to propose that it is at this level of psychological organization that psychoanalysis exercises its therapeutic action. And it is at this level that interpretations exercise their therapeutic effect. We do not confine the impact of interpretations to affect alone. Affect provides a significant dimension of the transformational experience but it is not its totality. Affects are encoded in a meaningful, symbolically rich context. The fact that an analyst's formulations contain elements of surprise (Reik, 1935) and novelty to the patient that are instrumental in the transformative experience illustrates the indispensable role of cognition as well. We include cognitive, affective, and somatic dimensions of experience as aspects of the self-state and its transformations.

Affects and moods reflect self-states, dream imagery conveys their pervasive presence, and psychopathology or a sense of well-being arises from them. These mediators of self-states may reach awareness and be accessible to self-reflection and empathic inquiry by an analyst. "Feeling different" may accompany the transforming experience.

It is in this context that we refer to Brandchaft's (1988) and Stolorow's (1991) emphasis on distinguishing between empathy as a mode of investigation and empathy as a description of a mode of responsiveness. As discussed by Stolorow, the analyst's sustained empathic inquiry may be experienced by a patient in a variety of ways; we propose that one of these is as a sharing of states.

In his second and third illustrations Wolf described treatment incidents in which the analytic ambience was disrupted, in one instance by the meaning the patient gave to the analyst's jotting down a note and in the other instance by the meaning for the patient of the analyst's perfunctory acknowledgment of the death of the patient's cat. For these patients there was a disruption of both the ongoing shared state and of the back-and-forth interaction between analyst and patient.

These two illustrations differ significantly from Wolf's first case and from Stolorow's case, which utilize interpretations par excellence. In the case of the patient who relaxed after the interpretation and the patient who could permit his longings for the analyst to be expressed, the dramatic self-state transformation became foreground. Although the selfobject tie and the relational dimension were critical at the moment of transformation, we are proposing that an enhanced sense of self took precedence. These interpretations par excellence "modified the analysand's psyche" (Wolf, 1991). In Wolf's second and third examples the nature of the therapeutic interaction was different. The analytic ambience was disrupted and the specific focus of the interpretation was to reestablish the ruptured selfobject tie. It is this tie, rather than the self-state, that is retained in the foreground.

In early development, state transformations (e.g., from crying to calming or from hunger to satiation) are socially negotiated, a product of the mutual regulatory system (Sander, 1983). They contribute both the self-regulatory capacity and the mutual regulatory system. In adult treatment, interpretations transform self-states with respect to such dimensions as intactness–fragmentation, depletion–vitality, and freedom of the self-regulatory range. Self-state transformation is crucial for an understanding from our developmental perspective of the therapeutic action of interpretation.

We propose that the interpretive process involves all three aspects of the self-with-other (Stern, 1983) but that its therapeutic action lies in the transformation of the self-state, with state sharing and complementarity in the background. In our use of Stern's concepts we do not assume direct linear translations between infant and adult organizations. We use infant research to provide evocative metaphors and organizing principles. Thus, the two vignettes in which Wolf restored ruptures are instances in which state sharing and complementarity are prominent but these vignettes do not illustrate the heightened and poignant affective and cognitive reorganizations that accompany the transformation of the self-state. In Wolf's first case and in Stolorow's case the self-state became a foreground experience, as reported by each patient and observed by each analyst.

An interpretation may be influential because it provides an experience of mutuality through self–other complementarity or a sense of merger through the sharing of an intimate moment. We include here the patient's experience of the analyst's empathic inquiry and analyst–patient interactions such as rupture and repair of the selfobject tie. However, interpretations par excellence must in addition, as Wolf noted, "modify the analysand's psyche" through self-state transformations.

Self psychology is often misunderstood and misrepresented as requiring only empathic activity on the part of the analyst. Both Wolf and Stolorow have emphasized the importance of interpretation and have distinguished it from the centrality of sustained empathic inquiry. Empathic inquiry will be represented by the analysand as part of the mutual regulatory system of self-with-other, patient-with-analyst. As Stolorow pointed out, the meaning of being the center of the analyst's empathic inquiry will be determined by the patient's individual organizing themes. These themes will be subjective elaborations of self-with-other. Being the subject of empathic inquiry is often experienced by a patient as feeling understood, being understandable, and expecting to be understood. However, empathic inquiry is not all that the analyst contributes to the analytic process. Both Stolorow and Wolf have outlined the critical role of the analyst's interpretive activity.

The analyst's interpretive activity transforms the patient's self-state. It contributes the patient's capacity to reorganize his state—usually in a positive direction. Interpretations are optimally effective when the patient experiences the alteration in self-state against a background of the tie to the analyst. We propose that these moments accrue to the patient's self-regulatory capacity. As a consequence of the self-state transformation the range and freedom of the self-regulatory capacity is enhanced, internal reorganization occurs, and the state of the self is shifted along the dimension of fragmentation-intactness toward greater cohesion and along the dimension of depletion–vitality toward a richer affective repertoire.

There are two implications that we draw from these proposals. First, treatments that only lead the patient toward interpretations or, on the other hand, treatments that emphasize only the therapeutic relationship, supplying "empathy" or providing a "holding environment," may fail to offer the patient the possibility of the transformations of self-state through interpretation. For the patient, this dimension of experience contributes to, elaborates, and affirms self-regulation. Second, treatments that emphasize interpretation without attention to the patient's subjective experience fail to offer the patient the possibility of self-with-other state sharing and complementarity. These are required for the transformations of self-state through interpretation. Interpretations without the sustained self-object tie, or interpretations that rupture the selfobject tie (Lachmann and Beebe, 1992), can be experienced as shattering the sense of self.

Self-state changes are mutually organized events that transform and reorganize experience and promote self-regulation, vitality, and cohesion. The process of interpretation derives its effectiveness from its transformation of the patient's subjective states. The chapters by Wolf and Stolorow contain excellent illustrations of such self-state transformations: interpretations par excellence.

REFERENCES

Ainsworth, M., Blehar, M., Waters, E. & Wall, S. (1978), *Patterns of Attachment: A Psychological Study of the Strange Situation*. Hillsdale, NJ: Lawrence Erlbaum Associates.

Beebe, B. & Lachmann, F. M. (1988a), Mother–infant mutual influence and precursors of psychic structure. In: *Frontiers in Self Psychology: Progress in Self Psychology, Vol. 3*, ed. A. Goldberg. Hillsdale, NJ: The Analytic Press, pp. 3–25.

——— ——— (1988b), The contribution of mother–infant mutual influence to the origins of self and object representations. *Psychoanal. Psychol.*, 3:305–337.

Bowlby, J. (1980), *Attachment and Loss, Vol. 3*. New York: Basic Books.

Brandchaft, B. (1988), Critical issues in regard to empathy. Presented at the 11th Annual Conference on the Psychology of the Self, Washington, DC, October 16.

Fenichel, O. (1938–1939), *Problems of Psychoanalytic Technique*, trans. D. Brunswick. New York: Psychoanalytic Quarterly Press, 1941.

Greenson, R. R. (1967), *The Technique and Practice of Psychoanalysis*. New York: International Universities Press.

Kohut, H. (1980), Selected problems in self psychological theory. In: *The Search for the Self, Vol. 4*, ed. P. Ornstein. Madison, CT: International Universities Press, 1991, pp. 489–523.

——— (1984), *How Does Analysis Cure?* ed. A. Goldberg & P. Stepansky. Chicago: University of Chicago Press.

Lachmann, F. M. & Beebe, B. (1989), Oneness fantasies revisited. *Psychoanal. Psychol.* 6:137–148.

——— (1992) Representational and selfobject transferences: A developmental perspective. In: *Progress in Self Psychology, Vol. 8*, ed. A. Goldberg. Hillsdale, NJ: The Analytic Press, pp. 3–15.

Reik, T. (1935), *Surprise and the Psychoanalyst: On the Conjecture and Comprehension of Unconscious Processes*. New York: Dutton, 1937.

Sander, L. (1983), To begin with: Reflections on ontogeny. In: *Reflections on Self Psychology*, ed. J. Lichtenberg & S. Kaplan. Hillsdale, NJ: The Analytic Press, pp. 85–104.

Stern, D. (1983), The early development of schemas of self, of other, and of "self-with-other." In: *Reflections on Self Psychology*, ed. J. Lichtenberg & S. Kaplan. Hillsdale, NJ: The Analytic Press, pp. 49–84.

——— (1985), *The Interpersonal World of the Infant*. New York: Basic Books.

Strachey, J. (1934), The nature of the therapeutic action of psycho-analysis. *Internat. J. Psycho-Anal.* 15:127–159.

Chapter 5

Commentary
on Papers by Stolorow
and by Wolf

Robert J. Leider

In other chapters of this section Stolorow and Wolf consider the role of interpretation in therapeutic change. Both follow a similar expository path. Each provides a definition of interpretation, describes its role in the therapeutic process, compares its role with that of other elements in the therapeutic situation, and attempts to delineate the factors he considers essential to the curative process. In addition, as a subsidiary topic, both comment on the relation of theory to observation and understanding.

Unfortunately, I cannot do justice here to the topic or to the many ideas presented by Stolorow and Wolf. I will, therefore, not note the many points on which I agree but, rather, in the hope of stimulating further thought, will focus on those with which I disagree. I will select salient topics, compare the views of Wolf and Stolorow, and offer some comments of my own.

THE DEFINITION OF INTERPRETATION

Stolorow begins by saying that a psychoanalytic interpretation is "an act of illuminating personal meaning." He makes it clear that he, at least theoretically, differentiates interpretation from other, noninterpretive, elements within the therapeutic situation. Wolf, on the other hand, uses a much broader definition of interpretation, one that includes not only verbal statements but *all* intentional activities intended to bring about a modification of the analysand's psyche.

Stolorow's definition is consistent with the customary meaning of interpretation, that of Wolf is not.[1]

Wolf does not explicitly delineate his reasons for adopting such an all-inclusive definition, but two major considerations apparently inform his thinking: first, the belief that an affectively responsive environment is essential for therapeutic change and, second, the conviction that a distant, detached translation of unconscious meaning is not therapeutic.

Though I agree with Wolf on the importance of those factors to the therapeutic process, in my opinion they neither warrant nor justify the broad definition of interpretation he advanced. Wolf himself finds it difficult to adhere to his broad definition and reverts to the more usual narrow definition when he states that "interpretation is a rather awkward and even misleading word for an activity that would be better referred to as an explanatory process."

Wolf's definition interferes with efforts to understand the therapeutic process for at least two reasons: First, redefinition of a word for which there is a customary meaning confounds clear communication. Second, Wolf's definition conflates two elements of the therapeutic process considered by many to be separate and to have separate therapeutic effects.[2]

EMPATHY AND THEORY

Stolorow and Wolf both follow Kohut (1959) in recognizing empathy as the means by which we gain access to the inner world of another human being. However, they differ markedly in the role they accord theory in empathic observation.

Stolorow views theory as a guide that helps direct attention, organize observation, and facilitate recognition of the subjective experiences of the patient. And he emphasizes that "theories vary in their capacity to enhance empathic access to patients' subjective worlds." Stolorow is in agreement with Kohut (1984), who also believed that theory permitted the observer (the quattrocento painter,

---

[1]Some authors (e.g., Bibring, 1954; Greenson, 1967) use the term *interpretation* to refer to the illumination of unconscious meaning and use *clarification* to refer to illumination of preconscious connections and meanings. However, it is recognized that interpretations are most effective when aimed at material on the verge of conscious recognition. The distinction between clarification and interpretation is thus diminished and is, in fact, ephemeral.

[2]Stolorow suggests that a false dichotomy is introduced by attempting to separate the effects of insight from those of affective responsiveness. However, even if that is correct, *words* that differentiate them are required for discussion and examination of that view.

the contemporary psychoanalytic clinician) to perceive formerly unrecognized configurations or, at the very least, to increase his
awareness of the significance of configurations he had but dimly
perceived" (p. 176).

Wolf, on the other hand, is suspicious of theory and concentrates
on its potential misuse. He asserts that theory is more often determined by the personality and philosophical and moral value systems
of the therapist than by rational criteria such as scientific truth or
therapeutic efficacy and that it may be used to buttress rationaliza-
tions designed to avoid the therapist's own anxiety. With these
assertions Wolf places those who differ with him in the uncongenial
position of having to prove that defensive factors are not the main
determinants of the theoretical position they advance.

Wolf also fears that theory leads to experience-distant formulaic
interpretations. To illustrate this point, he describes a clinical
vignette intended to show how empathic understanding led him to
avoid a "theory-bound" interpretation (of hostile, aggressive wishes)
and helped him to make a different, better interpretation. Probably it
did.

But that example does not expose theory as the impediment to
empathic understanding Wolf considers it to be; rather, it demonstrates that it is essential to have the right theory. What happened
was that, consciously or unconsciously, Wolf realized than an interpretation based on classical drive theory was wrong—that is, that it
did not fit the patient's subjective state. Wolf's interpretation was not
based on empathy alone but on empathy informed by a *different*
theory, one more relevant to that patient and his problems.

Clinical judgment is not based on empathic perception uninformed
by theory. Empathy provides access to the inner state of another.
Theory informs, but need not restrict, lines of empathic inquiry; it
permits prediction and explanation of our observations, and it guides
our technical interventions. But—and this is most important—when a
patient's responses do not match our expectations, we do not force
them to do so; rather, we strive to fashion a new theory that better
articulates and better explains the subjective experience of the patient.

INTERPRETATION AND THE PROCESS OF CURE

Both Stolorow and Wolf devote a considerable part of their discussions to the process of cure. Wolf delineates several facets of
interpretation (interpretation of resistance, of disruptions of self-
cohesion and selfobject transferences, and of background genetics)

and several experiential, effective, noninterpretive elements that he
deems central to the therapeutic process. After considering the
relative importance of *verbal explanation* and of *new experience*, he
concludes that (1) the contents communicated by an interpretation are
much less important than the experience it evokes and that (2) the
main role of interpretation is to repair the selfobject tie to the
therapist, thereby restoring the therapeutic process. In other words,
it is necessary to provide the patient with a new experience contrary
to, and more beneficial than, his unconscious expectation.

Wolf asserts that in downgrading the importance of the verbal
aspects of interpretation and insight he does not mean to imply that
interpretation is less important than previously thought. Perhaps not.
But for Wolf the importance of interpretation rests on the restoration
of a selfobject bond. In his view interpretation is important only
insofar as it provides an experience of being understood; explanation
and cognitive elaboration (the customary meaning of interpretation)
have no specific effect on intrapsychic organization and are of no
special import.[3]

Wolf's position raises several questions: Is the only effect of an
interpretation, a good explanation, the reestablishment of a selfobject
bond with the therapist? When a patient says, "Gee, I never realized
that before, that makes sense out of it," are we to doubt that
statement, ignore his pleasure and sense of mastery, and discount his
belief that the interpretation provided a new, integrating perspective?
I think not!

Stolorow, on the other hand, distinguishes the therapeutic effects
of interpretive and noninterpretive elements in the treatment situation and disagrees with those who would attribute *primary* therapeutic effect to the therapist's affective tone and its emotional impact.
In fact, Stolorow takes considerable pain to disavow any obligation to
provide the patient with a selfobject experience uncontaminated by
painful repetitions of past childhood traumas, a requirement he states

---

[3]Kohut, on occasion, expressed a view similar to Wolf's. For example: "The
beneficial structural transformations occurring in a successful analysis do not take place
as the result of insights" (1977, p. 30). But, after a period of indecision, *Kohut renounced
that view.*

Kohut's final statement was that empathy alone is not curative, that the therapeutic
process requires a phase of understanding, sometimes very protracted, *necessarily*
followed by a phase of explanation (1984, pp. 104–108). He considered this so
important that in his last public address he made a special effort to emphasize it when
he said, "Analysis cures by giving explanations—interventions on the level of interpretation; not by 'understanding' " (1981, p. 532).

is often invoked in the name of Kohut himself or other self psychologists.

The effects of insight and interpretation cannot, in Stolorow's opinion, be separated from the effects of affective bonding; they are inextricably interwoven. For him the therapeutic process is a continuum in which both affective attunement *and* cognitive inference play a part at every point.

Were this Stolorow's final position I would be in almost complete agreement with him. But he continues and, in my opinion, confounds the matter by saying the following:

> It is the transference meaning of this investigative and interpretive activity that is its principal source of therapeutic action in that it establishes the analyst in the transference as the secondarily longed-for, receptive, and understanding parent who . . . will . . . eventually alleviate the patient's painful emotional reaction to an experience of primary selfobject failure [emphasis added].

This is a position with which I do not agree and which, I believe, conflicts with his earlier statements.

The statement that the principal effect of an interpretation is its transference effect—that is, the establishment of the analyst as a receptive and understanding parent—gives no weight to the effect of verbal description, articulation, and genetic explanation in changing the patient's subjective reality and raising its level of cognitive and affective organization.

In my view, the effects that accrue from verbal explanation, interpretation, and cognitive insight are separate from, and as essential to the curative process as, the effects that accrue from empathic attunement, "understanding," and the emotional responsiveness of the therapist. Separation of these factors, of the effects of explanation from those of feeling understood, does not introduce a false dichotomy into an intrinsically inseparable amalgam of therapeutic process, as Stolorow asserts.

Insight and affective responsiveness *are* separable strands of the treatment situation. The therapist's affective attunement and responsiveness make it possible for patients to recognize and differentiate the unconscious expectations they transferred to the present situation. The therapist's explanations and interpretations facilitate that recognition and foster a new integration on a different level of intrapsychic organization.

To borrow a metaphor from Stolorow, affect attunement and

interpretation are like the warp and woof—each separate and essential—from which is woven a tapestry of therapeutic transformation.

REFERENCES

Bibring, E. (1954), Psychoanalysis and the dynamic psychotherapies. *J. Amer. Psychoanal. Assn.*, 2:745–770.

Greenson, R. R. (1967), *The Technique and Practice of Psychoanalysis, Vol. 1*. New York: International Universities Press.

Kohut, H. (1959), Introspection, empathy and psychoanalysis: An examination of the relationship between modes of observation and theory. *J. Amer. Psychoanal. Assn.*, 7:459–483. Also in: *The Search for the Self, Vol. 1*, ed. P. Ornstein. New York: International Universities Press, 1978, pp. 205–232.

_____ (1977), *The Restoration of the Self*. New York: International Universities Press.

_____ (1981), On empathy. In: *The Search for the Self, Vol. 4*, ed. P. Ornstein. New York: International Universities Press, 1991, pp. 525–535.

_____ (1984), *How Does Analysis Cure?* ed. A. Goldberg & P. Stepansky. Chicago: University of Chicago Press.

Sex and Gender

Chapter 6

Sex, Gender, and Sexualization: A Case Study

Estelle Shane
Morton Shane

In this chapter our focus is on the many varieties of sexual experience conceptualized in the psychoanalytic literature and required for a more complete understanding of that aspect of human motivation. Thus, we address not just sex, sexuality, and sexualization but, more precisely, sex, sexuality, and sexualization as well as gender, gender self, gender identity, and core gender identity. The truly voluminous literature on this topic will be addressed only as it pertains to and illuminates the treatment of a young woman whose sexual development had been greatly compromised by self pathology.

Kathy K came into treatment six years ago at the age of 24, following her move to Los Angeles. Kathy's decision to leave the East Coast, where she had lived all her life and where she had attended college and graduate school, was occasioned by the remarriage of her father, a remarriage she experienced as a betrayal and as a narcissistic blow. Kathy's mother had committed suicide several years before, when Kathy was in her last year of college. Mrs. K had exhibited severe emotional difficulties throughout Kathy's life, difficulties related, presumably, to the fact that she had been in a concentration camp as a young woman, an experience she could neither talk about nor forget. All Kathy could say about her mother's trauma was that in some way it involved sexuality: her mother's youth and beauty had led somehow to her being spared extermination by the Nazis. Kathy felt that it was her mother's Holocaust experience that had prevented her from discussing sexual issues—or, for that matter, *any* issues concerning female development—with her daughter; such matters came to Kathy through books, through her father, and through school. Moreover, nothing was known of Kathy's mother's childhood nor of her family; apparently, no one from her family except Mrs. K herself had survived the Holocaust, and the matter was a forbidden topic in the household.

Kathy's father was a consulting engineer, and Mr. K's own father and mother had died in an automobile accident shortly after his marriage. Mr. K was an only child and, from what Kathy described, had lived a lonely, emotionally deprived life. Mother and father had had no friends to speak of, and quite early, Kathy, also an only child, was given the message that the small family should stick together. Yet the parents were not involved with one another either. Their relationship was not characterized by arguments but, rather, by a coldness between them that extended to their having separate bedrooms from early on. Kathy knew, because they had often told her so, that her parents had remained together because of her; her father, especially, had depended upon her, as she depended upon him, for emotional closeness and support. In fact, her father's remarriage after her mother's suicide came as a shock to Kathy that even exceeded the impact of her mother's taking her own life. After all, Kathy had known her mother was depressed and was accustomed to her mother's turning away from her; she had not known that her father was involved with someone else and had not anticipated *his* abandonment.

What characterized Kathy's childhood, then, was a mother who from the beginning was cold, distant, self-preoccupied, and depressed. In addition, Mrs. K was harshly critical of her only child, complaining that Kathy was fat, selfish, and self-centered and predicting regularly that no one could ever like her, let alone love her. Kathy's father, on the other hand, had been deeply committed to her, deeply involved with her, and always supportive of her needs. Kathy, then, turned to her father for the developmental necessities her mother could not provide, particularly the phase-appropriate affect attunement, stimulation, and modulation required for adequate development of her self. Both the expression of her sexuality and the unfolding of her gender identity had been compromised.

Kathy had been referred to me (E.S.) by a male analyst from the East Coast who had seen her for about three months in twice-a-week psychotherapy to provide help with her reactions to her mother's suicide. The referring analyst had recommended more intensive work, and I, after seeing Kathy several times, concurred with that recommendation. Kathy suffered from low self-regard and a feeling of being different from, and inferior to, everyone else, especially in the area of her sexual life. For example, she told me with considerable shame that she had never had a sexual or romantic experience. Moreover, she described, also with shame and in great confusion, masturbation fantasies predominantly concerned with her having intercourse with women, fantasies in which she played the male role, accompanied by a vague sense of having a penis. This flawed sense of gender self would seem to reflect, at least in part, the depth and intensity of the poor relationship Kathy described having with her mother. We can surmise that her fantasy of herself as a man making love to a woman was a persistent effort to repair and strengthen this failed primary selfobject bond. Thus, Kathy's masturbatory fantasies were not just expressions of sensual sexuality but were, in addition, *sexualizations* motivated by her frustrated attachment needs.

The concept of sexualization as an important motivational force was first put forward by George Klein (1969) when he used the term *sexualized*, as opposed to the term *sexual*, in an effort to call attention to the fact that sensuality serves not just for the experience of pleasure or pleasurable discharge in itself but serves just as often to achieve essentially nonsexual aims. Klein noted that the individual may be drawn toward sensual pleasure because it gives comfort, alters reality, or manufactures a sense of pride in oneself; genital sex, therefore, may be used defensively and adaptively for self-reparative and self-sustaining functions.

The noun *sexualization* and the adjective *sexualized* were not invented by George Klein, however. He could easily have borrowed them from either Freud or Hartmann, among others, but Klein provided a new meaning, different from any in use before. For Freud, and then Hartmann and the ego psychologists, an experience was seen as sexualized if it took on sexual meanings not inherent in the activity per se. For example, if seeing, using one's eyes, takes on sexual meaning, the activity of looking becomes sexualized and it may become forbidden. In the same way, Hartmann introduced the terms *aggressivization* and *aggressivized activity* to evoke the suffusion of innocuous thought or behavior with aggressive energy or meaning. Because classical analysis conceives of only two drives, or two basic motivations, much neutral activity becomes explainable in sexual terms or in aggressive ones. Thus, Kathy's fantasy of assuming the male role in relation to a woman, in light of her frustrated relationship with her mother, would not be conceptualized in classical theory as a sexualization of the frustrated attachment tie to the mother, as we are viewing it here, but, rather, would be seen as a sexually motivated and, undoubtedly, aggressively tinged sexual displacement from father to mother in a negative oedipal configuration partly fixated on a preoedipal level. The important point we want to make is that the motivation to be uncovered in Kathy's fantasy in classical terms would still be to achieve sexual pleasure, however broadly defined. What George Klein introduced as totally new in clinical psychoanalytic understanding with his construct of *sexualized* activity is the concept of sex being used to express many self-motivations *other than* sexual pleasure per se (even if that sexual pleasure is conceptualized in the broad Freudian sense of sexuality experienced on oral, anal, and phallic narcissistic, as well as genital, levels.) His term is the same as Freud's and parallels Hartmann's, but his *meaning* is totally different from theirs.

Kohut, seeming to elaborate on Klein's idea and focusing primarily on the attachment motivation so central to self psychology, advanced the concept of sexuality (when "grossly expressed," to use Kohut's words, as in the subjective experience of being driven) as representing a breakdown product of a fragmenting self. What Kohut accomplished through this reconceptualizing shorthand was the explanation that sexuality can be heightened and made more urgent in the service of establishing a connection to the needed and heretofore frustrating selfobject, thereby restoring cohesion to a shaky self. In Kathy's case, then, the masturbation fantasy of a genital connection to a woman carried with it an even greater need, that of an archaic selfobject bond necessary to maintain her self.

But aside from the presenting symptoms already described and aside from the masturbation fantasies the significance of which she, in any case, mostly disavowed, what urgently motivated Kathy to seek treatment with me at the outset was her recognition that the relationships she had established with particular girls throughout college and then into graduate school were strange, unsatisfying, and quite disturbing to her. Once having left home for college, Kathy had begun to attach herself to one special girl after another, girls from whom she felt she could not separate. Her entire existence seemed to depend upon being in the presence of that significant person, and she suffered untold jealousies and rages when she was frustrated in that wish. Each girl began her relationship with Kathy as a friend but eventually withdrew as Kathy's demands upon her became insupportable. Each in turn would protest in more or less clear terms that she could not provide Kathy with what Kathy seemed to need and still maintain her own sense of independence. Yet Kathy remained unable to free herself in subsequent relationships from her demandingness, despite the fact that she had come to acknowledge that her urgent need would invariably drive away the specially chosen friend. One can easily recognize here the peremptory, archaic selfobject quality to these involvements.

Kathy's history and her sense of the nature of her suffering convinced me that analysis was the treatment of choice, but Kathy was not in a financial position to follow this recommendation, even with the low fee offered. As it happened, Kathy, discovering that I was scheduled to attend a conference in the city in which her father lived, set up a meeting between us with the clear hope that her father, upon meeting with me, would become convinced that analysis was the appropriate treatment for her and would provide the necessary finances. Kathy herself had just arrived in Los Angeles, having recently dropped out of graduate school after a semester after completing a bachelor's degree program in physics. At the time, therefore, Kathy was in no way able to support the analysis on her own.

In the meeting with me Kathy's father supplied details of Kathy's life that confirmed the picture the patient had already presented. Furthermore, he described, albeit rather imprecisely, a genital variation in Kathy discovered at birth: an enlarged clitoris necessitated that her anatomical and hormonal development be monitored. Nothing untoward turned up, and by early adolescence Kathy had been pronounced completely normal. Nevertheless, there had been, and there still remained, a hint of anxiety in him (which Kathy's mother had also felt) over his daughter's physical *sexual* development, and then, later, over her psychological *gender* development. (Here we use Stoller's clarifying distinction between sex and gender, which we will refer to shortly. See Stoller, 1985, p. 6.) Kathy's father worried about the fact that Kathy had never had a relationship with a boy, either in high school or, insofar as he was aware, in college, and he wondered whether this lag in emotional development was related to the reputed variation in her genital anatomy. Further, Mr. K explained to me that Kathy had been told nothing regarding her possible sexual abnormality. Finally, he agreed to support Kathy's analysis, albeit at a substantially reduced fee. Once back in Los Angeles, I shared openly with the patient the information provided by her father. Kathy responded with anger that this too had never been discussed with her. In regard to her father's disclosure, Kathy remembered having appointments with doctors, her puzzlement as to why she was going (yet, as with all else sexual, no one explained anything to her), and the fear and humiliation that the examinations always engendered in her. In all, her father's report confirmed Kathy's long-standing self-image of being, as she said, "a puzzle piece that somehow did not fit," of being "different from everyone else, neither boy nor girl but some alien being in between."

The serendipitous meeting with Kathy's father obviously introduces important issues and clinical complications most germane to this case and to this overall topic. First, information came from outside the dyad, imposing on the patient new facts about her life that had not previously been disclosed, at least not directly. Second, the information suggested possible biological, hormonal, and anatomical influences on the patient's female development. Third—and, as it turns out, most important—the information revealed an inevitable, unavoidable influence on the development of the patient's core gender identity and consequent confused sense of femininity. We will take these in order.

The first issue is somewhat apart from the topic of sex and gender and will therefore be addressed mainly parenthetically. Here we have an instance of important historical data—historical truth, if you will—coming in between analyst and analysand, data not introduced introspectively, subjectively, or vicariously introspectively; not arrived at through a hermeneutic understanding of the patient; and not a creation of narrative truth (see Shane and Shane, 1980). We can question, therefore, whether these are analytic data in any pure sense, at least in an adult analysis; yet the data must inevitably influence analysand and analyst, their relationship, and their mutual reconstructions of the patient's infancy and childhood.

The second issue, that of new information about the patient's anatomical, hormonal, and sexual development, and the third issue, that of her gender development, require some clarification, best provided by Robert Stoller's (1985) work on sex and gender. His distinctions have been generally useful and are applicable here. According to Stoller, sex refers to a *biological* realm of multiple dimensions, which include chromosomes, external genitals, the internal sexual apparatus, hormonal states, secondary sex characteristics, and the brain. Gender, on the other hand, refers to a *psychological* state, masculinity versus femininity, with all the variations in between. Stoller then invents the term *gender identity* to refer to the entire psychological realm, the sense of being feminine versus the sense of being masculine, or, as in Kathy's case, the sense of being confused in terms of one's gender. Stoller further elaborates with the concept of *core gender identity*, which develops very early in life; consolidates probably by age two or three; and, once fixed, responds little if at all to any efforts to change it. Stoller describes core gender identity as "a conviction that the assignment of one's sex was anatomically and, ultimately psychologically correct" (p. 11). The assignment of one's sex begins very early in life, actually before birth, if the parents know, or believe they know, the sex of the fetus, and is done mainly by one's parents in conformity with its sexual biology, though ultimately, it is speculated, everyone with whom the individual comes in contact, from birth on, contributes to some degree to the individual's sex assignment. It is well known that girl infants are handled differently from boy infants, are talked to differently, are responded to with differing expectations, and so on.

It is clear that Kathy, upon entering treatment, suffered from a confused sense of gender identity. What the external information provided by the father did in the analysis was to shed some light on the development and formation of her core gender identity and to supply us with data from which we could infer possible sources of the core gender identity confusion with which she presented. We cannot know if there were any contributions to Kathy's psychological difficulties that stemmed from the arena of her *sexual* (i.e., anatomical-biological) development. We *do* know that although her clitoris was reportedly enlarged at birth, she was pronounced free of any permanent anatomical or hormonal anomalies by the consulting endocrine experts by the time she was 12.

In terms of gender, as opposed to sex, it is relatively easy to surmise that both parents were disturbed and confused to some degree about how firmly they could assign their child the role of feminine little girl, and, as we will see, there were important psychological sequelaé, which would have been apparent with or without the father's information.

For our purposes here, then, this case is illuminated by distinctions made in the literature among sex, gender, gender identity, core gender identity, and gender self. In self psychology, *gender self* tends to remain too global a term. We believe there is a need to consider a primitive gender self (or a core gender self) as well as a mature gender self, matching, more or less, Stoller's core gender identity and gender identity. As to Stoller's contention that core gender identity is fixed at age two or three and remains resistant to any change, the successful analysis of Kathy's gender confusion leads us to postulate that though core gender identity may be irreversible, core gender *identity confusion* or core gender *self-confusion* is not. That is, the *core gender* pathology in Kathy's case was embedded in *self* pathology. On the basis of this case, along with another case of core gender confusion (analyzed by M.S.), we postulate, first, that gender confusion is often linked to self pathology and, second, that it can best be ameliorated by a self-psychologically informed psychoanalysis.

Once in analysis, Kathy rather quickly developed a relationship with me most accurately characterized as an archaic mirroring selfobject transference. That is, her particular response to the analytic situation was to elevate the experience to one of central importance in her life, to bask in the analyst's presence, and to express her deep satisfaction at being so closely and exclusively attended to. She told me that for the first time in her life her needs were not frustrated, and her wish was that the analysis would go on forever. These good feelings emerging in the analytic dyad seemed somehow to influence her self-image: after only five to six months of analysis Kathy's feeling that she was different from others, of some unknown, uncertain gender, neither boy nor girl, man nor woman, gradually receded. An important moment for Kathy during this phase of treatment was when I told her, in an attempt at genetic reconstruction encompassing many details of her life narrative, that I imagined she had never experienced a woman who both recognized and appreciated her femininity. (It was following this reconstruction, which carried with it a tacit, unplanned, yet unavoidable acknowledgment on my part of the patient's actual femininity, that Kathy began having for the first time masturbation fantasies about men, beginning with a particular man whom she had met and with whom she had developed a close friendship. Later in the analysis, four years later, Kathy noted that when she attempted in a moment of feeling humiliated to create a masturbation fantasy on the old model, so comforting as well as exciting to her in the past, of being a man with a woman whom she admired, she found that she had lost completely the capacity to do so; she noted ruefully that she was now "forever fixed in [her] femininity.) Kathy went on to reflect that while being with me made her feel like a girl, she did not yet feel like a woman. She remarked also about another change in herself: in the past she had always felt empty, dark, and hollow inside, but now she was aware of a new vision, namely, that her analyst was the light that illuminated her darkness and that clarified and defined her self. Here one can see most clearly the inevitable interrelationship between Kathy's confused gender self and her overall self pathology; as one responds to treatment, it seems, so does the other. We can conceptualize this beneficial response to being in analysis as both the delineation of an archaic transference and as a development-enhancing, optimally responsive gratification deriving from it.

As the analysis progressed, what emerged in this archaic transference formation was a high level of expectation that the analyst be there, almost literally at the patient's beck and call. Kathy resented and resisted adamantly any threatened interruption in my attentions to her; even now, after six years of treatment, when asked to change an hour to another day, Kathy can still take extreme umbrage, as if the times of her particular hours are exclusively hers, never to be tampered with by any requirement so unimportant as alterations in my schedule. Once this phase of the analysis began, Kathy would watch the clock intently and argue vigorously about minutes she felt she had coming to her, though she herself recognized that at times the appointment extended some minutes *beyond* the allotted time. She would threaten to tie herself to the couch or to refuse to leave at the end of the hour and wondered insistently what I would do in such a case. She longed for me to take her home or invite her to my house on weekends and half expected, as if her reality-testing capacity were compromised, that such a thing might actually happen, that I might really extend the hour, be dissuaded from a planned vacation, or offer her an invitation for brunch. What the patient expressed was a sense that she was, as she said, "merged" with the analyst, with each being a part of the other, each participating in the other's life, and therefore not to be separated. Kathy's experience suggests the archaic nature of her transference, evoking the concept of symbiosis, and while symbiosis itself is not, in our minds, a phase in normal development, such a case demonstrates that the experience of symbiotic merger is real enough in analysis and in pathological states. For Kathy, as will be seen, the working through of the archaic transference mitigated this sense of merger.

Through our continued work together, we came to understand, with some surprise to the patient, that the feelings of oneness that Kathy experienced with me and her sense of entitlement about me were very close to the feelings that she had had in relation to her father throughout their life together. She had learned early to turn to her father for a steady, reliable, always available presence when she needed comfort and soothing. Each night he would sit by her bed and listen avidly to all she had to say. When she awoke in the middle of the night, she had only to call to him, and he would without hesitation come and stay with her, even through her teens and even when she was not frightened but only wanted his company. Apparently, Kathy's mother did not object, at least not to Kathy's knowledge, but merely remained a silent, though disapproving, presence in the background. Kathy contrasted this long and idyllic period in her relationship with her father, where her possession of him seemed exclusive, to what occurred between them after her mother's suicide, when she was in graduate school. Her father had already remarried. Kathy recounted with strong and righteous indignation that upon visiting the newly wedded pair, she was outraged when her stepmother announced that she was going to bed and her father got up and followed her, rather than remain behind and talk to Kathy. Kathy felt profoundly betrayed by her father and afterward found she could no longer function in school; she began to cut classes and to avoid work. It was following this experience that she left the East to come to Los Angeles. Since that time, despite father's willingness to support her treatment, relations between Kathy and her father (and stepmother) have been cool and distant.

We see evidence here, and it will be elaborated on later, of an unresolved Oedipus complex, not surprising given Kathy's lifelong experiences with her father. He had served as a replacement for her mother in her early years, but his attentions throughout Kathy's life were obviously not adequately attuned to her developmental needs. We speculate that his frustrations in his relationship to his wife led him to be overly solicitous and probably unconsciously seductive in phase-inappropriate ways, which nevertheless did compensate Kathy, at least in part, for her mother's more global lack of response to her. Kathy's departure for college disrupted the sustenance her father had provided for her, which she then attempted, in vain, to replace with special friendships in college, and later, more satisfactorily, in her relationship with her analyst.

A particularly clear example of the patient's transference expectations for a consistent, unyielding, attentive presence is revealed in the way in which she responded to anticipated separations from me. The prospect of my first long vacation, one year after her analysis began, filled Kathy with horror and indignation. She could barely acknowledge that vacations were to be expected, and she would not allow herself to conceive of the possibility of my having either needs or a life of my own. Kathy reasoned that if I really understood her and how much she needed me, it could only be considered cruel on my part to leave her, a deliberate infliction of pain and misery. Each vacation was experienced as a disruption in the treatment process, to be anticipated, argued about, and guarded against; and then, once gotten through, the sense of disruption had to be overcome. It was through these complaints preceding and following interruptions that Kathy came to understand that my leaving her without her protesting bitterly would make her feel as if she didn't exist at all. That is, the protest itself—and, as the patient articulated, the longer and more vehement the better—helped to define her very selfhood (a phenomenon evoking Lachmann's and Wolf's adversarial selfobject relationship). Kathy remembered that she could never argue with her mother, who would respond, on those rare occasions when Kathy dared to do so, with the silent treatment, lasting for days and making

Kathy feel, as she said, as if her very essence were destroyed. Kathy's discovery, finally, during one protracted phase of arguing in the analysis, that her protests allowed her to feel alive was of enormous relief to her. She began to tolerate separations better, to provide substitutes for me in my absence, and to preserve a sense of liveliness, cohesiveness, and self-constancy without me.

During the fourth year of Kathy's analysis, the earlier feelings of delight at being so perfectly understood, admired, and cared for by me were much tempered. Kathy lamented the fact that it was no longer so easy for her to maintain the illusion that I was a part of her, or she a part of me, despite her struggles to convince herself that some day she would be able to feel that way again. She dated the beginning of this sense of separateness to a period that preceded one of my dreaded absences from her; it came to her as if in a flash that my plans were made neither to spite her nor to please her but without her in mind at all. For a short period Kathy actually believed that this was, as she repeated often, the way it ought to be, that my separation and independence from her allowed her to hope for a similar independence for herself. At times Kathy would revert to symbiotic longings or, as she put it, to the more familiar illusion that she and I were working toward a "re-merger." But try as she might, she could not reclaim that feeling. She explained to me that in the past she would bask in my presence, a pleasure that was interrupted only by my absences on weekends and vacations. But with each experience of separation, it became clearer to her that she could no longer reclaim the comforting illusion of oneness. She sadly stated that while all of her life she had sought a relationship like the one she finally had with me, this most perfect relationship was, ironically enough, to be her last. She knew that she was losing me and that she would never be able to replace me with another, as she had done so often in the past, not because of my uniqueness but because of the inevitable changes she was already experiencing in herself.

During the fifth year in analysis Kathy had a significant dream in which she was being introduced to the wife of Steve, an attractive man with whom she worked and who was included in many of her masturbation fantasies. Steve's wife too was quite attractive, and in the dream Kathy felt the sting of jealousy. Then she inadvertently looked into a mirror and *realized*, as if for the first time, that she had sideburns and a mustache. She was shocked but at the same time knew that while she herself had never before seen the mustache and sideburns, this facial hair had come as no surprise to Steve and to his wife, who, she realized, had always seen her that way. The dream ended with Kathy thinking, "I must get rid of these."

In her associations Kathy immediately said that the mustache and sideburns stand for her fat, for her being overweight and unfeminine. She then talked about the party she had gone to the night before at Steve's house, where, in reality, she had met his wife for the first time. As she was dressing for the party, she had looked down at her bare feet and then her glance moved up her legs. She thought: "I've seen these feet before; I've seen those legs before. They are like my father's." She went on to note in her associations that sometimes when she looks at her arms, she sees her father's arms; that she sits like her father does, with her wrist on her forehead and her elbow on the table, when she is trying to solve a problem; and that she twirls her hair the way her father does. She throws a ball like her father does too. I perceived Kathy's associations to the dream as indicating an increased awareness of her previously repressed and disavowed identification with her father, an identification that had contributed significantly to her gender confusion and that had defended her from the painful competition with more attractive women. At this point, I reminded Kathy that it was her father who had taught her to play ball, and that it was her father with whom she would sit each afternoon after school as they worked together, Kathy on her homework and he on his reports. Indeed, I told her, she had needed her father to learn from. She must have learned many skills from him—how to work, how to play, and how to be with another person—and in the process may have picked up his habits as well. In addition, she had wanted (and at the same time had disavowed her wish) to be like a man; she wanted to acquire her father's strength and his masculine power for many reasons. She wanted to be close to her father; she wanted to be like her father; and, indeed, she even wanted to become her father. Kathy responded that she knew she had often felt like a man and that she understood now how connected to her father these manlike wishes and feelings were. But also she knew that in reality she looked like her father: he, her idealized father, was fat and she was fat too whereas, in contrast, her demeaned mother was thin. Then Kathy said, with sudden resolve, "I had better lose some weight."

This dream and the accompanying insight proved to be a key step in the patient's dieting for the first time in her life, in her losing weight, in her exercising, in her dressing attractively, and in her attracting the attention of the men around her. That year Kathy, close to age 30, began dating for the first time, had some preliminary sexual experiences, and then settled in on one relationship for a time. As she prepared to separate from me for that summer vacation, she noted that for the first time she didn't mind my leaving, so long as I intended to come back. As Kathy said, she had work to do, friends to see, and an interesting man to date. The archaic wish for symbiosis was apparently resolved in the transference, as the following statement, a kind of summary made by the patient in the last session before vacation, suggests: "When I first saw you, I had a feeling of emptiness inside myself, that something was missing in me, which I needed to fill with you. I then became preoccupied with keeping you there at the core of me, but lately I have been more aware of my own presence inside myself and less aware of yours."

That summer vacation marked the end of the patient's fifth year in analysis. At the first meeting in the fall she reported a dream: She and I were sitting facing one another, looking at one another's earrings. Mine were diamonds, whereas hers were just plastic. We decided to exchange earrings, but then it turned out that I really had no intention of giving up my own earrings; I kept *both* pairs, hers and mine, and Kathy had none.

Kathy associated to the unusual summer she had dating men and to her fear that I would be angry and jealous, first, because she was no longer so involved with me and, second, because she would be competitive with me for the attention of men, even for Mort, as she referred to my husband. She was young, I was old; she would ultimately win, I would ultimately lose. And as a result, I would be angry, feel hateful, and abandon her in response. I connected this fear of punishment and abandonment owing to her sexual attractiveness to men, and particularly to my husband, with Kathy's mother's sullen, silent disapproval of her father's obvious preference for Kathy. Nevertheless, neither Kathy's own insight nor my genetic interpretation served to alter the sense of danger Kathy felt. As a result of these feelings of sexual attraction and attractiveness and fear of my disapproval and consequent withdrawal, Kathy began to put back some of the weight she had lost. Currently, the analysis concerns this oedipal struggle, with all of its underlying gender self ramifications.

Kathy knows now that being obese is not just her mother's label for her and that dieting can change that condition, whereas failure to diet can reverse that direction, all of which was heretofore denied by Kathy, who had felt and insisted in the past that when she "got better" she would "get thinner," a cryptic reference to her unconscious belief that when she got better she would feel more like her mother, more like a woman. Also for the first time, she recognizes that there is a relationship between greater diligence and better performance; the application of this recognition, combined with her inherent capability and intelligence, has led to significant advancement in her employment. Finally, she has understood that better social responsiveness on her part leads to closer, more gratifying friendships.

We have presented this case to clarify the interrelationships among issues pertaining to sex, sexuality, and sexualization, as well as to gender, gender self, gender identity, and core gender identity, and to point to the connection between these issues and self pathology.

REFERENCES

Freud, S. (1905), Three essays on the theory of sexuality. *Standard Edition*, 7:135–243. London: Hogarth Press, 1953.

Hartmann, H. (1964), *Essays on Ego Psychology*. New York: International Universities Press.

Klein, G. S. (1969), Freud's two theories of sexuality. In: *Psychology versus Metapsychology*, ed. M. M. Gill & P. S. Holtzman. New York: International Universities Press, 1976, pp. 14–70.

Kohut, H. (1977) *The Restoration of the Self*. New York: International Universities Press.

———— (1984), *How Does Analysis Cure?* ed. A. Goldberg & P. Stepansky. New York: International Universities Press.

Lachmann, F. (1986), Interpretations of psychic conflict and adversarial relationships: A self-psychological perspective. *Psychoanal. Psychol.*, 3:341–355.

Shane, M. & Shane, E. (1980), An integration of developmental theories of the self. In: *Advances in Self Psychology*, ed. A. Goldberg. New York: International Universities Press.

Stoller, R. J. (1985), *Presentations of Gender*. New Haven, CT: Yale University Press.

Wolf, E. (1988), *Treating the Self*. New York: Guilford.

Chapter 7

Primary Failures
and Secondary
Formations:
Commentary on the
Shanes' Case Study
of Kathy K

Paul H. Tolpin

Although I differ with the Shanes' formulation of one aspect of Kathy K's pathology, I have little disagreement with the essentials of their understanding of the case. And, certainly, I can only express complete pleasure with the fluency and effectiveness of their presentation.

My comments, then, will address what I consider to be the problematic formulation, the role of the Oedipus complex in Kathy's pathology, and I will also comment on the role of sexualization, about which Kathy's case provides much relevant material. But both of these will be considered within the context of the larger issue of the relationship between primary developmental lacks and injuries in childhood self–selfobject experiences and the secondary psychological formations that are often used to make up for and ameliorate the painful consequences of primary deficiencies.

Recall that at the end of the fifth year of analysis and shortly before an upcoming vacation interruption Kathy summarized the crux of her therapy with an unusually insightful observation. She said, "When I first saw you, I had a feeling of emptiness inside myself, that something was missing in me, which I needed to fill *with you* [my emphasis]. I then became preoccupied with keeping you there at the core of me, but lately I have been more aware of my own presence inside myself and less aware of yours." In a few straightforward words Kathy described both the primary psychological fault in her development—the lack of an essentially positive, self-solidifying

75

experience with her mother—and the gradual repair of that lack in the analysis. The inner experience of repair was beginning to feel more reliably part of her and not just on loan from and dependent on the analyst.

Without the new sense of herself, Kathy was a desperately unhappy woman who had revealed with considerable shame that she had never, with anyone at all, had a romantic or sexual experience. In relation to her peers Kathy had apparently lived a rather isolated personal life interrupted by successive short-lived, highly intense, and overly demanding relationships with several girlfriends during college and graduate school. With each new girlfriend Kathy's entire existence seemed to be centered on the current friendship, but her embittered rages, when the friend found her tenacious demands becoming intolerable, inevitably led to a termination of the relationship. I believe this repeated sequence of events epitomizes Kathy's desperate attempts to fill in what she felt was missing in her. That missing emotional something was experienced as a void at the core of her, a void too terrible to bear. She reexperienced that same feeling in the analytic transference when her feeling of "oneness" with the analyst was disrupted. That sense of emptiness and that desperate need to somehow obliterate the intolerable experience of it were manifestations of Kathy's primary pathology: a deficit in her core self-structure. This brings us to a related issue, the Oedipus complex and what role it played in Kathy's psychological life.

Recall Kathy's outrage and sense of profound betrayal when her stepmother decided to go to bed and Kathy's father followed after her. Kathy collapsed psychologically: she was unable to function at school, she cut classes, she avoided work. Shortly after, she left the East and moved to Los Angeles. Was this series of events evidence of an unresolved Oedipus complex? At first glance it might reasonably appear to be so. But wait. Recall also how Kathy's father's devoted, affectionate attention to her had substituted in part for the missing involvement and affection of her mother, a concentration camp survivor, and a seriously damaged woman, who was self-absorbed, cold, angry, and chronically depreciating. Understandably, from early on Kathy had turned to her father for the love, the responsiveness, and the feeling of invigorating life that flowed from him, that vitalized her, and that she desperately longed to make a reliable part of her inner self-experience.

Did Kathy's deep attachment to her father arise from the developmental level of object loss and rivalry one might expect to see at the height of the oedipal period? In disagreement with the Shanes, I don't believe the Oedipus complex is the most useful clinical formulation here. As I see it, it is not love for her father, rivalry with her mother, and the consequent fear of the loss of mother's love that is Kathy's central problem. No, the problem is, rather, the deep underlying fragility of her self-organization, an organization born of her unfortunate mother's depression, her relative emotional absence, and her crushing criticalness. All this and more led to Kathy's desperate need for an exclusive relationship with someone who could make up for the basic emotional deprivation, the lack of normal positive selfobject responses, she had had to endure and had somehow survived.

Again, Kathy's crucial problem was the feeling of painful emptiness, her longing for the supportive, organizing presence of an engaged and loving other. Kathy's father was the loving other of her childhood. He had been her only hope and she could not bear the loss of him. The comment of a very self-aware patient of mine is relevant here. In summarizing a currently dominant transference experience and its momentous effect on her, she said, "Without the us, there is no me." I suggest that Kathy felt similarly about her father, not because he went off to bed with another woman but because at the moment of his leaving she had no "us"; she felt utterly deserted—as she had with her special girlfriends—and she realized that she had lost an essential part of her self, the something missing in her that she said she needed "to fill with" the analyst.

While the traditional concept of the Oedipus complex may be a useful clinical shorthand for both the expectable and the pathological experiences of the oedipal period, I believe its elevation by Freud to a position of such signal importance in normal and pathological development was misguided. However useful it may be for the understanding of some pathologies, its compelling manifest theme can overshadow more critical developmental disturbances that should be recognized as more relevant. In certain types of psychopathology, such as Kathy's, the oedipal drama is not a primary issue, if it is an issue at all (in some cases it may be a secondary formation), and can distract us from appreciating more basic and pervasive affective disturbances in development. (See Kohut, 1977, pp. 228–237, for his discussion of the Oedipus complex and the oedipal phase.)

Another issue: What about Kathy's identification with her father? While dressing for a party she looked at her legs and suddenly thought they looked like her father's. At other times she noticed the same thing about her arms and was aware of the similarities in how she and her father sat, fingered their hair while in thought, threw a ball, and so on. She realized how much she wanted to be like her father and how sometimes she even felt like a man. Recall how she used to fantasize about having intercourse with another woman during which she, Kathy, took the male role while vaguely imagining she had a penis. In their discussion of these issues the Shanes recognize how Kathy's need to maintain her necessary tie to her father took a variety of forms. At one time it took the shape of what, from a classical point of view, has been considered a perversion (not the Shanes' term or mine), at another time the form of confusion of gender, and at still another a sense of entitlement in relation to her analyst (as when Kathy insisted on being given what she wanted when she wanted it, on her terms, and not on the analyst's).

But what I want to emphasize here is that these examples are only the tip of the proverbial iceberg. They are the manifest forms of Kathy's pathology. Constructed from bits and pieces of childhood life experiences, they are indicative of an individualized mixture of past gratifications and moments of security and a variety of injuries or lacks. These past experiences are later expressed by way of symbolic concrete enactments or metaphorical thoughts, but the manifest forms are secondary.

For example, Kathy's fantasy of being like her father—behaving like him posturally, having legs like his, having a penis as he did—can be understood as a concretized form of her desire to experience within herself the life force that she felt emanated from him. This desire was expressed in a sexualized form in the fantasy of having a penis with which she could experience an erotically invigorating connection with a responding other; with that fantasy she was at least briefly saved from the effect of her devitalized and devitalizing mother. Her deepest feelings, as the Shanes suggested, were centered on the dread of reexperiencing the cold absence and the critical anger of her childhood mother, whose own private horrors greatly interfered with her ability to respond positively to her child's need for the manifold varieties of affectionate attachment that lead to the development of a securely cohesive self. Kathy attempted to make up for the lack of those essentials by assuming her father's vitality through overt manifestations, physical and otherwise. Later in treatment, when she was unable to sustain that borrowed vitality on her own, she imperiously demanded, out of desperation, that the analyst maintain that steady-state feeling in her by being available at all times.

The point I am trying to make here—and I hope it does not come across as reductionistic—is a simple one: Just as we must recognize our patients' defensive retreat from experiencing the pain of their depths while we, at appropriate moments, decipher and clarify for them the unique origins of the overt features of their pathology, so too must we keep in mind that broader, more basic vulnerabilities in the formation of the core self underlie and provide the nurturant soil for the development of the more conspicuous, attention-calling and attention-getting symptomatology. But it is the primary deficits, the failures in good-enough parenting, that we must ultimately recognize and attempt to remedy if we are to achieve more substantive results from our analytic efforts. In addition, we must remain aware of the salutary effect of innate temperament, talents, and skills; useful defenses and adaptive, compensatory structures; family values, traditions, and available social possibilities. In various combinations all of these can shift the often expected outcome of damaging developmental experiences by ameliorating the failures of early selfobject experiences and by providing psychological avenues that can lead to more adaptively successful personality organizations. These various built-in tendencies and fortunate life experiences often play a critical role in the outcome of our therapeutic efforts.

Finally, I want to summarize the essential thrust of my argument by quoting some relevant thoughts of Martin Buber (1957) on the subject of a basic human need[1]:

> Man wishes to be confirmed in his being by man, and wishes to have a presence in the being of the other. The human person needs confirmation. . . . Sent forth from the natural domain of species into the hazard of this solitary category . . . he watches for a Yes which allows him to be and which can only come to him from one human person to another. It is from one man to another that the heavenly bread of self-being is passed [p. 104].

I believe the Shanes have made a similar statement and recommendation, and except for our differences about the role of oedipal issues in Kathy's pathology we are in agreement in our understanding of this case.

REFERENCES

Buber, M. (1957), Distance and relation. *Psychiatry,* 20:97–104.
Kohut, H. (1977), *The Restoration of the Self.* New York: International Universities Press.

---

[1]I want to thank Dr. Louis B. Shapiro for calling my attention to Buber's observations.

Chapter 8

Sharing Femininity— An Optimal Response in the Analysis of a Woman by a Woman: Commentary on the Shanes' Case Study of Kathy K

Howard A. Bacal

In their chapter, Sex, Gender, and Sexualization: A Case Study, Estelle and Morton Shane address the multiple (biological and psychological) determinants of gender confusion but focus on the inadequate selfobject experience that underlies it. They illustrate this with a case in depth. The Shanes' study of the treatment of Kathy K by Estelle Shane is a tour de force of explication of complexity in brief. In a chapter whose range and content easily justify a discussion many times its length, we are offered an impressive account of a successful self-psychological therapy of a case of gender pathology along with a remarkably thorough consideration of the multiple determinants that may have affected the patient's aberrant sexual development.

I will direct my comments to their main focus: the nature of the patient's self pathology, how it contributed to her core gender identity confusion and her difficulty in proceeding with heterosexual relationships, and their understanding of the therapeutic process that is curing her.

The Shanes' central understanding of Kathy K is that she turned to her father for selfobject responsiveness to compensate herself for the experience of unmanageable selfobject failures in her early relationship with her mother.

The archaic mirroring selfobject relationship that Kathy established with her analyst seemed primarily an attempt, now with the analyst, to resume the paternal selfobject relationship of childhood, a connection she traumatically lost when her father remarried, a loss, we are told, that affected Kathy more than the earlier suicide of her mother. There was some evidence to suggest that the strength of Kathy's reaction to the father's remarrying derived also from behavior toward her that had inappropriately stimulated her expectations of a relationship that went beyond that of father and daughter.

While this formulation makes sense, I am also impressed by Kathy's need to correct her sense of self-defect through the experience of a relationship with a *woman* who would meet specific selfobject needs. As much as the father compensated her for what she felt deprived of by the mother, it was not enough; it lacked some quality. In effect, Kathy had been trying to obtain what she needed from women friends, who understandably could not tolerate the archaic nature of her selfobject demands.

In a paper entitled "Technical Problems Found in the Analysis of Women by a Woman Analyst: A Contribution to the Question 'What Does a Woman Want?'" Enid Balint (1973) discusses the cases of two of her female analysands whose mothers were either depressed or withdrawn. The main preoccupation of these patients was the satisfaction of their depressed mothers' archaic needs, a preoccupation that also manifested itself in the transference. Because their attempts to satisfy their mothers entailed unconscious identification with a penis, their pleasure in their genitals was compromised and a satisfying sexual life of their own was impeded. Balint recognizes, as do the Shanes, the challenge in following the threads of these patients' instinctual life as they relate to the struggle of the self to maintain the needed tie to the object. She suggests that what

> women want both in their relationship with men and with women [is] to use that primitive structure in human relations, namely the capacity for mutual concern (Balint, 1972). Owing to its primitive nature it can only be satisfactorily expressed by the body itself. . . . The vagina is that part of a woman's body which is felt to be the most important area with which to express mutual concern with men (this does not exclude the rest of her body). However, in her relation to women she is at a loss to know how to express it unless she has herself introjected and identified with a satisfactory satisfying woman's body which satisfied her and which she felt she satisfied when she was an infant . . . unless a woman can experience mutual concern with women her relationship with men is likely to be impoverished [p. 200].

We know that Estelle Shane's patient was completely unsuccessful in "righting" her depressed, cold, and preoccupied mother, who repeatedly turned away from her, and that she turned to her father for the satisfaction of all her psychological needs. Yet there is evidence to suggest that the need for the mother's responsiveness lived latently in her unconscious. Kathy's masturbation fantasies of using a penis to make love to a woman might have been not only an expression of sensual sexuality, not only the sexualization of frustrated attachment needs, now directed to the father, but also the sexualized unconscious expression of her need to undo her primary feminine self-defect *by relating effectively to a woman*.

Kathy could not, with her body, offer the mother what she needed. Because of the deficit in her early psychosomatic experiences with the mother, along with the inadequate affirmation she received from both parents for the existence of a definite feminine self, she could not imagine achieving this with her female body. There is much evidence to indicate that Kathy wished to become like her admired father, but an unconscious motivation for this identification might have been the wish to give her mother in fantasy the only thing she felt or sensed the mother could value and be satisfied by: a male body. We must also note that Kathy's masturbation fantasy was operative while she was in analysis; thus, she also involved the analyst in what may have been her deepest selfobject need, namely, to stimulate, enliven, and satisfy, and be responded to in turn by, the analyst-as-mother.

Father saved the patient's psychological life, but he did not quite fill the bill. Kathy lacked the sense of a valued and valuable feminine self, which she could only have substantively got from the mother. I believe the Shanes imply this when they state that her masturbation fantasy "carried with it an even greater need, that of an archaic selfobject bond necessary to maintain her self."

Thus, I would understand Kathy's *improvement* as due to a significant extent to the meeting of an essential therapeutic need: the sense of a *relationship* with a woman (her analyst) who values what one woman can give to another at the very deepest levels, a relationship with a woman who knows, accepts, and enjoys her own femininity, both physically and emotionally, and who can enable the patient to experience her deeply within herself, "psychosomatically." Kathy virtually confirmed this at a later point when she, having lost the capacity to create the old masturbation fantasy and now "forever fixed in her femininity," noted "another change in herself, that in the past she had always felt empty, dark, and hollow inside, but now she was aware of a *new* vision, that her analyst was the light that illuminated her darkness and that clarified and defined her self." In effect, it was important to Kathy that her analyst appreciated that she "had never experienced a *woman* who both recognized and appreciated her femininity" (I have italicized the word *woman* here, as I believe that this was of no small importance for Kathy). I am curious why the therapist is apologetic for her response that accompanied this reconstruction, that is, her "tacit, unplanned, yet unavoidable acknowledgment . . . of the patient's actual femininity." It was after this that Kathy first started having masturbation fantasies about a man![1]

The emergence in Kathy of insistent primitive archaic needs,[2] which, when not met, led to significant disruption, was understood as reflecting feelings she had in relation to her father. Interestingly, however, they began to recede when she experienced herself as alive and distinct when arguing vehemently with the analyst, something she could never do with the mother. And while her dream about having a moustache and sideburns and having her father's feet and legs ushered in much insight about her extensive identification with her responsive, fat father, her successful resolve to then lose weight and become more feminine and attractive to men must surely have had at least something to do with her growing identification with the responsive,[3] slim, attractive woman analyst from whom she was at the same time struggling to differentiate herself.

I should like to offer a hunch about the dream of the earrings. I think the dream shows Kathy's struggle to achieve these aims in the face of her fear that the analyst will not wholly comprehend her conflicts about the wish to fully commit to being a woman. That is, I suspect that her pulling back from her progress arises not only from anxieties associated with *competitive* oedipal issues and fear of the analyst's anger and jealousy but also from residual fear that she might indeed become committed to being a woman, which is to say, more like her mother, who had nothing valuable to give to another woman.

---

[1] I am, of course, suggesting that the therapeutic effect of Kathy's *experience of the relationship with Estelle Shane*—which may have been mediated at times by interpretations—was considerably more powerful than any of the insights the patient undoubtedly garnered from the analyst's accurate verbal reconstructions.

[2] The patient's regression is to an archaic state most extensively studied by Michael Balint (1968), which he called "primary love." Balint termed its disruption the "basic fault."

[3] In further discussion, Anna Ornstein emphasized that the importance of the analyst's femininity was mediated to her patient not through identification but by an idealized woman's mirroring the confused little girl in her femininity. I would agree, in part, with Dr. Ornstein. As I indicated above, I believe it was important to Kathy that she received not only the interpretative recognition of a need but that she also experienced a woman responding with appreciation to her actual femininity. I would submit, however, that the patient's experience of her analyst's response facilitated a process of identification with her. I would add that it is not only idealization and mirroring that constitute the "corrective selfobject experience" for this patient (Bacal, 1990) but also the experience of another kind of relationship: the *enjoyment of sharing* what is felt to be valuable (in this case, to a woman). This may be regarded as a specific form of selfobject experience (Dr. B. Herzog, personal communication, 1991).

However, in order to value herself as a woman, she feels she must not only differentiate herself from her analyst but become more like her. In order to become more like her, the child in her needs to feel that it is all right with the analyst that Kathy share with her her most valuable possessions: all the earrings (her femininity) and the most desirable man.

REFERENCES

Bacal, H. (1990), The elements of a corrective selfobject experience. *Psychoanal. Inq.*, 10:347–372.

Balint, E. (1973), A contribution to the question "What does a woman want?" *Internat. J. Psycho-Anal.*, 54:195–201.

Balint, M. (1968), *The Basic Fault*. London: Tavistock.

Chapter 9

The Bad Girl,
The Good Girl,
Their Mothers, and
the Analyst: The Role
of the Twinship
Selfobject in Female
Oedipal Development

Diane Martinez

If there is one lesson that I have learned during my life as an analyst, it is the lesson that what my patients tell me is likely to be true—that many times when I believed that I was right and my patients were wrong, it turned out, though often only after a prolonged search, that *my* rightness was superficial whereas their rightness was profound.

Heinz Kohut (1984)

The theoretical understanding of the normal oedipal phase and the pathology that arises when the developmental steps of that period go awry have never been the primary focus of self psychology. In *The Analysis of the Self* (1971) Kohut discussed the role of narcissistic factors in the modification of phallic narcissism and the idealization of the superego but stated that development during and pathology derived from the oedipal phase were satisfactorily explained by classical theory. In *The Restoration of the Self* (1977) Kohut said that drive theory provides an incomplete but adequate basis for understanding the oedipal phase. In his depiction of the oedipal period from a self-psychological viewpoint, he emphasized the importance of *pride* and *joy* in the parents' response to the oedipal child's phase-appropriate sexual yearnings and competitive strivings for firming the child's independent self. Kohut speculated, "Could it not

The author wishes to thank Drs. Michael Basch, Anna Ornstein, and Morton Shane for their help with this paper.

87

be that we have considered the dramatic desires and anxieties of the oedipal child as normal events when, in fact, they are the child's reactions to empathy failures from the side of the self-object environment of the oedipal phase?" [p. 247]. In *How Does Analysis Cure?* (1984) Kohut outlined in more detail the sequence of events that he then saw leading to the development of the Oedipus complex. In this description the child enters the oedipal phase with the exhilaration that accompanies any forward developmental step. However, the child's strong and vital self becomes weakened if his or her phase-appropriate affection and assertiveness do not elicit proud mirroring responses from the parents but instead encounter parental preconscious sexual stimulation and/or hostile competitiveness. Kohut observed that such flawed parental responses may occur overtly or may manifest indirectly through prohibitive, rejecting, or withdrawing responses. In this situation the child's healthy affection and assertiveness become grossly sexual and hostile, with the final outcome being the pathological Oedipus complex. Here, then, the oedipal child's fears are not primarily of their drive experience or the possible consequences. Rather, he or she fears being confronted by a seductive (rather than affection-accepting) parent of the opposite sex or by a hostilely competitive (rather than pridefully pleased) same-sex parent. Only when these latter fears are realized do the fears related to drive experience become relevant. Kohut concluded that the set of conflicts called the Oedipus complex is not the primary cause of psychopathology but its result. He challenged others to differentiate between the self weaknesses and selfobject failures that lead to the drive phenomena encountered in narcissistic personality disorders and those that lead to the isolation and intensification of drives that underlie classical oedipal neuroses.

Appearing simultaneously with the publication of *How Does Analysis Cure?* were two papers presenting analyses in which the basis of the patients' pathology lay in selfobject failure during the oedipal phase. A. Ornstein (1983a) described the successful analysis of a man who developed an idealizing transference to her as a strong father who delights in his son's assertiveness and competitiveness. This selfobject transference arose in relationship to a deficit in the patient's self created by the father's inability to respond to his son's oedipal phase needs. In her discussion Ornstein addressed the process of identification in the resolution of the Oedipus complex from a self-psychological perspective. She stressed that the exchange of a pathological identification with a depressed father for a healthy one was not sufficient explanation for what transpired in the analysis. She contrasted the concept of identification with Kohut's concept of transmuting internalization, concluding that the grosser taking in of an aspect of another as a part of one's own psychic structure (the identification of classical theory) could only be regarded as defensive or compensatory. Ornstein stated that disappointments in the same-sex parent during the oedipal phase have special pathogenic significance because gender-linked values and standards (what is masculine and what is feminine) become relevant at this time. She proposed that the negative Oedipus complex, the longing for sexual closeness with the same-sex parent, is an effort to reengage the idealized same-sex parent as a "mirror-er" of phase-appropriate development. The erotization under these circumstances, she explained, represents the intensity of the child's longing. Ornstein felt that her recognition of this patient's need for her to function as a *paternal* selfobject was crucial and that the needed analytic process would not have occurred had she viewed his transference to her as a response defined by her being a woman.

Terman (1984–1985) described the analysis of a young woman whose problems derived from the failure of her mother to function as a selfobject for her oedipal development. As the analysis unfolded, the predominant transference was to a maternal oedipal selfobject. The need was for the analyst to mirror the patient's gendered sexual self. The patient feared that the analyst would be a rejecting, punishing mirror, as her oedipal mother had been. A turning point in the treatment was Terman's realization that he could not interpret the patient's fears on the basis of her conflicts over her impulses. Rather, he had to bear witness to the fact that her mother really had responded to her proud little girl with inappropriate anger. In his discussion Terman addressed the maturation of the grandiose self in the oedipal phase. He stressed that the very heart of the oedipal frustration is narcissistic: "One simply isn't 'big enough.' " A mirroring parental acceptance of the child's phase-appropriate grandiosity is required to decrease the distance between the oedipal child's idealized parental imago and the grandiose self. In this way, for example, the little boy's archaic aim of having his mother now is transformed into the realizable ambition of having a girl just like mother when he grows up. Terman proposed that the residue of this mirroring experience becomes the skeleton of the superego in its regulating capacity.

Detrick (1985) and Basch (1992) have both proposed that twinship is the most basic of the three selfobject experiences. However, there is far less in the literature on the role of twinship (or kinship, as Basch prefers) in development than on the mirroring and idealizing selfobject experiences. Kohut (1984) did suggest that there is a pivotal point in twinship selfobject development from ages four to six. Solomon (1991) stated that the preoedipal girl sorts out her anatomical realities and the meanings she will attribute to them via twinship experiences with both parents. Logically, the fundamental task of the oedipal phase of acquiring differentiated gender-specific traits would seem to call for an experience of twinship with the same-sex parent. Here, however, the concept of the transmuting internalization of these aspects of the self begins to potentially overlap with the concept of identification as it is used in classical theory to explain the resolution of oedipal conflict. Ornstein (1983a, b) explored this issue with regard to the mirroring and idealizing selfobject experiences with the same-sex parent. The same specific task remains to be done with the experience of twinship, as does the more general task of outlining the role of the twinship selfobject experience during the oedipal phase.

It is with the concept of self pathology as the core of oedipal problems that I have taken another look at two of my early analytic cases: one that "went wrong" when in my frame of mind at the time I "did everything right" and another that "went right" when I began to "do things wrong." Both women were diagnosed as having structural neuroses of the hysterical type and had documented trauma during their oedipal phase. The nature of this trauma could be more clearly appreciated than is often the case because remnants of their mothers' traumatic behaviors remained and/or were reactivated during the course of the analyses. My discussion is an attempt to make a general contribution to the self-psychological understanding of the oedipal phase in female development and to explore the specific role of the twinship selfobject experience during this time.

CASE 1: THE BAD GIRL

Marisol, a Mexican-American woman, was a single 30-year-old when she entered analysis. Our initial contact was my returning her call to my answering service. She did not recognize my name, although I returned her call within the hour. In explanation, she said she had "expected a man or at least an older woman with not soft a voice." Her reaction was, "Aha, it is a woman," as if she had suspected fate might deal her this particular blow. At our first meeting she complained of depression, low self-esteem and problems with men. She told me about her pattern of involvement with "unavailable" men, which she associated with her father's inability to let her grow up. She described feeling hopelessly bogged down in finishing her doctoral program in education. Her ultimate career goal was to develop programs for minority students.

Marisol was born to a farming couple in a rural area of Mexico, the second child of four. She described her early years as "happy"; in particular, she had a special relationship with her father, from which her mother felt excluded. When she was five, her father left for the United States. She recalled this as being a complete and traumatic surprise. Her mother was very distressed after his departure. She would repeatedly tell the children that their father was squandering money on women and alcohol and would never send for them. In fact, Marisol's father did send for her mother and oldest brother six months later. The three youngest children stayed behind with their punitive, controlling maternal grandmother. After another six months the parents sent for them. From this point Marisol described her experience and relationship with her parents in negative terms. The family was poor and lived in a public housing project. Because her parents were frightened by the environment, they were restrictive and intolerant of problems the children had that necessitated their dealing with any authority. From the time Marisol was eight until she was ten, her mother had frequent hospitalizations for an unexplained sequence of illnesses. The children were cared for by public aid housekeepers. Marisol recalled this as a time when they were poorly fed, dirty, and harshly punished. The only history Marisol felt was pertinent from her adolescence was a relationship with a man her parents attempted to "force upon" her when she had no such interest. She described her young adulthood as a series of battles with her parents over her autonomy. She had been involved in brief romantic relationships with men, some involving sex, but none had worked out. Her relationships with female friends were equally unsatisfactory; she felt alienated from other women, believing that they could not be trusted to be accepting or supportive.

During the first six months of the analysis Marisol was often late. She said it had to do with "giving in versus breaking the rules." She painted a picture of a dependent relationship as one in which she was at the whim of a depriving and punitive person. I interpreted to her that her "rebelliousness" was defending against feeling vulnerable with me. With this approach the material shifted to a concern for her adequacy as a woman. Marisol said she felt stuck in her life, "like in a pool of something heavy." Wishes to be a successful career woman with a husband and children painfully contrasted with her conviction that this could never happen to her. In her fantasy either other people resented her success or she failed. The only satisfaction she could envision for herself was "revenge, which tastes good compared to nothing." Although she said she really enjoyed sex, she felt guilty about it: "It's like getting away with something." Any reference Marisol made to me was followed by images of "tight-assed, girdled women" who thought they were too good for her. However, she would adamantly deny categorizing me in this way or holding any concern about her acceptability to me.

Upon my return from vacation 18 months into the analysis, Marisol wished aloud to be "a more sociable, spontaneous, confident person." She followed with, "I guess I could start by trying here." She reported dreams of being with her sister, which were remarkable to her because of the exquisite feeling of closeness between them. (In retrospect, these most likely reflected a budding twinship selfobject experience.) It was in this atmosphere that Marisol took a magazine from my waiting room without asking and tried to return it furtively the next day. When I brought it up, she said I was accusing her of stealing because she was "from the ghetto." I interpreted this act as revealing her competitive wish to have what was mine. Marisol found this interpretation highly insulting.

Gradually, Marisol could acknowledge being curious about me but denied it had any particular significance since she was always interested in people who, she said, "lead the life I'd like to live." She had a dream that took place in the women's rest room of my building: She was looking in the mirror and trying to put on lipstick. The harder she tried, the uglier she looked. Associating to the image of herself as ugly, Marisol said, "I've been *made* to feel that I am ugly. My mother has always used expressions like 'whore,' 'low class,' 'dirty' about me. When it comes to me, she is full of bitterness, hatred, envy, and jealousy." In response to my questions about this, Marisol began to tell me about what amounted to her mother's chronic paranoid distortions of reality. Marisol had been aware of this in her mother, but its meaning and impact on her had been disavowed until this time. In retrospect, we saw that her mother's distress during her father's absence and her later hospitalizations were almost certainly psychotic episodes.

These disclosures and conclusions, which emerged over a period of weeks, were accompanied by intense anxiety. A pattern of missing a session following one in which she told me "too much" or spoke positively about her own future emerged. I interpreted to Marisol that her progress unconsciously equaled being destructive to her parents. In contrast to much of what I had said, Marisol felt this made sense. What I failed to appreciate was the extent to which her progress consisted of her growing attachment to me; nor was I aware that my interpretations focusing on her drives were being experienced as an ugly reflection. My strategy with regard to the transference was to continue to suggest to Marisol that her now obvious comparison of herself to me was rooted in frightening, hostile, competitive feelings. She steadfastly maintained this was impossible: "You are in a completely different class; it would be like a dog racing with a horse." She concurred with my observation that she viewed herself as not measuring up but could never derive relief from my interpretation that this was a defense against her competitiveness.

Marisol chose as her dissertation topic the effects of having a teacher from a different cultural background, which, of course, was an issue for us. (I am not Hispanic and my name was not Martinez at this time.) I recall viewing this as hostile and devaluing of me— although, thankfully, I did not make that interpretation. Marisol reported a striking dream during this period:

> I was with my sister in a hotel. I went to what should have been my room, but the other lady hadn't left yet. When she did, it was in a hurry and she left her bath water. There was also a silver cup that said "Epsom Salt." I said to myself, "She wasn't as glamorous as I thought. She must have a skin disorder." I felt sorry for her and considered how I could get her things back to her. Then I got into the bathwater.

At the time, I focused on the devaluation of the lady (me) in looking at the dream. In retrospect, in this and numerous other examples, I see Marisol attempting to bridge the intrapsychic gap she experienced between herself and me. I had become a woman she wanted to emulate and by whom she wished to be accepted. I also was the yearned-for (twin) sister whose like presence made her journey more acceptable and less frightening. Her devaluation of me was an expression of this painful gap and a defense against her yearning. In other words, the transference was a selfobject transference with idealizing and twinship characteristics.

About two and a half years into the analysis Marisol discovered that her boyfriend was seeing another woman. His betrayal enraged her. I interpreted her anger at the other woman as a displacement of a negative maternal transference. In apparent response Marisol began to come 20 to 30 minutes late or miss sessions entirely. She tried to ignore everything I said (which was a healthy thing to do, given the circumstance). When I confronted her with this, she said, "My generalized hatred and contempt prevents me from relating to *anyone*." Her perception of me and the external world became frankly paranoid. She had irrational fears that she was pregnant and multiple other hypochondriacal concerns. Work on her dissertation, which had been going extremely well, stopped. Previously unreported memories of childhood with themes of malevolent "Anglo" authority figures and hurtful doctors and nurses came to Marisol at this time. I now see my failure, in the context of the intense selfobject transference, to recognize the profound humiliation at her boyfriend's betrayal as the precipitant of her fragmentation.

Not surprisingly, my interpretations of Marisol's "resistance" led to no improvement in the situation. I finally began to talk to her about the feasibility of continuing her analysis under the circumstances of her not coming to sessions. Her response was that she felt we had made progress with feelings about her family but that the issues now were with "society as a whole." She explained:

> What you think is important, I don't. I am filled with the pure unadulterated hatred of whites. I have no patience for Latinos, just pure contempt and disgust. I am still being rejected because I am a poor Mexican. That is what makes me rage inside. People who exploit and abuse me. Don't expect any love from me for a society that thinks I'm shit. I think they are shit. If I cannot use my analysis to vent my rage, there is no point to it.

I suggested that we continue to try to find a way to work with these issues, and Marisol agreed. However, she continued to come late or miss sessions altogether. Her functioning further deteriorated and she was in a continuous, alienated rage. Ultimately, I suggested that we switch to twice-weekly psychotherapy, as this would be a better approach to her difficulties. Although she was concerned about being "a failure," her primary reaction was relief, and there was an immediate improvement in her functioning.

Once we were sitting face-to-face, Marisol began to report other painful memories. In one such instance she tearfully recalled, "When I was about five, my mother tortured a cat until it died. She said it was a bad cat that killed its kittens. She tied it to a tree and beat it to death with a stick." She also related that her parents had physically hurt one another and the children after the move to the United States. I told Marisol that the childhood physical abuse had impaired her ability to trust and that this was at the core of the impasse in the analysis. I now see this interpretation as inexact in that it disregarded the "abuse" that Marisol had suffered in the analysis. As it turned out, Marisol stayed in therapy only a few more weeks. Once back to her baseline, she seemed to need to seal over the experience. Unfortunately, I have no follow-up.

I now think Marisol could have had a successful analysis. I

contributed to her nontherapeutic regression by being insensitive to her vulnerability to humiliation and to her healthy positive selfobject attachment to me. Kohut (1984) said that in psychoanalysis "it is not possible to reactivate traumatic situations of infancy and childhood to which the self had on its own responded constructively during its early development." He continued, "Even if the revival of these situations were feasible, moreover, no good purpose would be served if we could in fact bring it about" [p. 43]. Looking back, I see that my need in my early development as a psychoanalyst to make use of my theoretical orientation as a selfobject may in fact have reactivated Marisol's childhood traumatic situation, leading to the described profound fragmentation of her self.

CASE 2: THE GOOD GIRL

Paula was a 27-year-old who was engaged to be married when she was referred to me. Her internist suggested she might benefit from psychotherapy for what he diagnosed as functional abdominal pain. Paula told me there were indeed stressful situations in her life. She and her boyfriend had just decided to marry after living together for a year. However, this decision was reached only after she threatened to leave, making things tense between them. She had also recently been fired from a position in the prominent advertising firm where they met. Paula did not understand why this had happened and felt terribly humiliated.

Paula was the elder of two daughters in her upper-middle-class family. She described her homemaker mother as "goal-oriented and intelligent." She depicted her father as "loving"; although his job demanded long hours and extensive travel, Paula felt closer to him than to her mother. The only problematic aspect of her childhood, she said, was that her mother "discouraged expression of negative feelings." Paula felt "out of the mainstream" during her adolescence, a feeling she connected with twice having to change high schools owing to family moves; she compensated by putting her energies into her studies. Once in college she had a need to prove herself socially. She dated extensively but the relationships, many of which included premature sexual involvement, tended to end badly. Friendships with other women always seemed to result in some painful disappointment. After college Paula began graduate work but quickly lost enthusiasm for her studies. She briefly saw a psychiatrist for depressive feelings. He helped her to see that she had conflicts between what she felt she should do and what she wanted to do. Ultimately, she decided to leave school. Despite her mother's reassurance, Paula felt she had let her down by not completing her doctorate.

Paula knew she had a problem related to her career. She was bright and capable and had high ambitions. However, she had noticed that even when she achieved her goals, she felt empty and dissatisfied. Paula also knew that her boyfriend, as distinct from other men with whom she had been involved, had the potential to be a good husband. She both loved and admired him but felt she could not be as open emotionally or sexually as she wanted. In addition, he wanted children but she felt a deep reluctance to undergo a pregnancy and raise a child. After a few sessions Paula's abdominal pain disappeared and she felt enthusiastic about her upcoming wedding. However, it was clear she was struggling with some characterologic issues, and we decided to start an analysis.

Just before my first vacation Paula casually mentioned that her mother had suffered a "nervous breakdown" after the birth of her younger sister, when Paula was four. Her mother's symptoms had been those of a major depression with paranoid features. When I asked how she had failed to mention this previously, Paula said she had been conscious of it but it had never seemed important. I interpreted the timing of the revelation as having to do with the anticipation of my absence. Paula agreed but felt she probably wanted far too much.

Shortly after, Paula reported the following dream.

> A friend and I were to be married on the same day. We got up in the morning and had a fight. There was not enough time to prepare for my wedding. She had relatives to help her. I felt I was being punished for having gotten angry. She said, "How can you be mad? I had to put up all night with your rolling all over the bed. Isn't that enough?" It was like she had made a concession so I couldn't be angry.

Atypically, Paula had few and seemingly superficial associations to this dream. I suggested that she might have wanted more help from me in emotionally preparing for her recent marriage. While she agreed this made sense on an intellectual level, she was not in touch with the corresponding affects in relation to me.

As time passed, I emerged as an idealized figure whose approval Paula tried to win by being "good." Being good meant not complaining, arguing, making demands, or being angry. Paula ultimately said, "I've operated under the assumption that I had to portray an image you would like to get the most out of the sessions. I was transferring my expectations onto you without recognizing the origin." She associated this experience of me with her mother. Her mother's image of the perfect woman was that of a nun: passive, forgiving, asexual. Paula saw her mother as having striven to live up to this ideal herself, and Paula grew up feeling that the only way to please her mother was to be just like her. She reported a vivid dream in which she was a child and her adult husband followed her from room to room, interrupting her just as she started to enjoy herself in play. Her husband was a threatening figure in the dream, and her affect was of being somewhat frightened and very oppressed. I proposed that this was how she had experienced her mother's worried depression as a child.

A year and a half into treatment, as the aforementioned defensive position was being worked through, Paula's mother was hospitalized for a major depressive episode.[1] In response to this event Paula relived her intense anger at her mother and her associated sense of her own "badness." Paula's mother was also taking a look at what her previous depression had taken away from her mothering ability, and she was able to validate Paula's feelings and insights. The honest dialogue that developed between them was quite moving. Paula learned that her mother had become depressed when pregnant with Paula's younger sister to the point of being convinced that she would die in childbirth. Her treatment ultimately required electroconvulsive therapy. Paula's experience of her rigid, corporate work environment as controlling, devaluing, and "full of meaningless rules" brought her childhood affective experience of her mother's depression into full awareness. Elements of this experience also served to remind Paula of her maternal grandmother, who Paula learned had cared for her during her mother's hospitalization.

I had no success at making Paula's intense anger a part of her transference experience with me.[2] Like Terman's patient, Paula demanded that I be a witness to, rather than a participant in, this process. My pointing out suggestions of her anger toward me or

---

[1]Kohut (1977) noted that on occasion a patient's parent will manifest serious self pathology during the time the son or daughter is being emancipated from a merger with that parent.

[2]Kohut (1979), in describing Mr. Z's analysis during his exploration of his mother's psychopathology, concluded:

It is my impression that the comparative underemphasis of transference distortions in such cases is not a defensive maneuver but that it is in the service of progress. In order to be able to proceed with the task of perceiving the serious pathology of the selfobject in childhood, the patient has to be certain that the current selfobject, the analyst, is not again exposing him to the pathological milieu of early life [p. 13].

possible resistance to her experience of it would cause Paula to retreat to a less affectful interchange of the earlier "good girl" variety. In retrospect, I believe these interventions disrupted Paula's transference to me as a mirroring selfobject. In contrast, my simple reflection of her affective state or of her insights into how her past intruded on her present served to vitalize her self experience and to move the analytic work forward. Ultimately, we understood that my attempts to make myself the object of her feelings led her to experience me as her fragile, intolerant mother. I now see that these interventions corresponded too closely to Paula's mother's preoccupation with containing her own anixiety. Paula's earlier statement that her mother discouraged expression of negative feelings now took on deeper meaning. We understood that her characterologic "good girl" stance supported a desperately needed tie to her mother. I began to suggest to her that she feared involving herself deeply with me out of a fear of repeating her experience with her mother. This approach made sense to Paula:

> My mother put her worries on me and wasn't helpful with mine. I had to deal with things on my own as best I could. I shut her out of a lot of things because of this and so felt I was constantly rejecting her. I relied on myself for the answers. I got used to doing things a certain way. This control gave me a sense of identity and enabled me to get through times when mother was hammering into me things I didn't want to do. My identity is formed around the idea of "She doesn't know what she is doing." To lose that brings up vulnerable feelings. With mother it was all or nothing. I feel I have to trust you completely or not at all.

This approach freed Paula to negotiate and handle her anger at her job constructively. She developed a more balanced view of her mother and of herself in relation to her mother. Only then could she acknowledge that analysis could at times feel restrictive and controlling and ask for appointment times more compatible with her own busy schedule.

On the heels of this work, status and respect became important to Paula. Competing, however, seemed "unchristian." I simply addressed the extent to which she felt these healthy yearnings were unacceptable. Almost overnight, her competitiveness and assertiveness began to overtly manifest. She took on more responsibility at work and began running in organized races. Paula was delighted with her "new self." There were new memories from the time of her mother's illness. Paula recalled turning her attentions to her father then: "I would crawl into his bed for comfort, instead of my mother's." Apparently, her mother became uncomfortable with this and insisted it stop. Paula recalled feeling responsible for her mother's "red eyes." I suggested that she had attached her mother's unhappiness to her developmentally appropriate competitive and sexual fantasies and that this had led her to reject these aspects of herself. As a result of this work Paula began to make moves toward fulfilling her career goals. She took a course to prepare for the Graduate Record Exam (GRE) and applied to graduate school. Simultaneously, she sought and received a promotion at work.

Given our earlier experience, I was reluctant to try bringing Paula's competitiveness into our relationship, but old theories die hard. After a session in which she expressed particularly intense competitive feelings with other females, Paula pulled a muscle by being too vigorous in an exercise class. I could hold back no longer. I commented that with all her growing she might be comparing herself to me. She, without missing a beat, responded, "It would be so nice to have my own business like you do, not to have to conform." These feelings had not been unconscious, only unspoken. Encouraged, I continued over the next few days to focus on her competitive feelings toward me. In doing so, I again disrupted the selfobject transference in which an idealizing component had become discernible. Paula became less enthusiastic and this time came up with a variety of "good girl" reasons to consider decreasing the frequency of her sessions. Her associations led to thoughts of her mother's problems with intrusiveness: "With my mother it was a feeling like she didn't have a life of her own. Her attention was overwhelming. Not the kind of support I needed." Again, my attention to her drive experience was felt by Paula to be an interference with her progress. Unexpectedly, this led to understanding Paula's reluctance about having a child. In her fantasy, we discovered, a child would restrict her ability to, she said, "move around and do just what I want to do" and would make her resentful. An additional factor was her refusal to be at all like her mother:

> Another fear of having a child is that I might like it and that would make me like my mother. Where would that fit in with what makes my life my own? I've always sensed my mother as a negative role model. The thought of being like her was an electric shock to have me jump ahead. If I look to you as I wanted to be able to look to my mother, am I losing some hold on myself? As a child, I'd have to say to my mother, "Yes, you are right," but inside I'd say, "You are a jerk." It seems that being tied in this way means giving up my right to disagree or be angry.

The experience of having Paula retreat to the good-girl "Yes, you are right" state in response to my focus on hostile, competitive strivings

directed at me was often repeated. Her unspoken anger and resentment at this "thwarting" would be palpable through the "good girl"
armor and gradually became speakable. Ultimately, I became convinced that Paula's requirement that I serve an affirming, idealizable
function was not a defense but a developmental need.

About two and a half years into the treatment Paula reported a
vivid dream. This followed a session in which she had initially
misheard me as discouraging an assertive move and then realized her
distortion:

> I was showering after exercise class. A friend said, "Oh, you have a
> penis!" I looked and I did. It was coming out of my vagina. My friend
> saw I was shocked and said, "Everyone has one," and then she showed
> me hers.

Paula felt slightly embarrassed at the manifest content of the dream.
She had read in the newspaper about penis envy but could not relate
to the idea of actually wanting a penis. As far as anatomy went, she
said she would prefer having her husband's firm derriere. What
struck her about the dream was the feeling of competence and
self-sufficiency associated with the realization of having a penis. This
she said she would very much like to have. I felt the dream was a
representation of Paula's consolidation of a sense of herself as a
competent and assertive woman in the context of my presence as an
affirming feminine oedipal selfobject (Stolorow and Lachmann, 1980)
and, in so many words, told her so.

Paula began to speak openly of the importance of "role models"
and to hint at being curious about me. My pointing this out released
a flood of questions about me and my life. Paula related these
questions to concerns about the acceptability of the emerging aspects
of her self. Meanwhile, she competed for and received another job
promotion. Finding herself with much more work, she said, "It must
be like when you first started practice. You have to not do some of the
usual things for yourself, like taking clothes to the tailor you might
once have repaired yourself." She dreamt that her office and my
office were somehow one and the same. We looked back at the early
dream in which she was denied the help she needed to prepare for
her wedding. We saw how it had expressed her highly defended-
against need for the kind of experience she was now having with me.
In retrospect, the experience was of an oedipal selfobject transference
with prominent idealizing and emerging twinship characteristics.

Paula was now notably more spontaneous with me, others, and
herself. Her fantasy life was more accessible and she began to do

some art work. Also, her sexual responsiveness increased and positive thoughts about having children appeared. She began to express a vague longing to find out about me that ultimately focused on my sexuality. Paula mused:

> I probably wonder if I will get the same reception from you around these things that I got from my mother. Will I be laughed at? I remember telling my mother a dream I had about a man being short and fat, then getting skinny and tall, and getting short and fat again. I've always thought that dream was very sexual. My mother probably did too, because she said it was a stupid dream.

She recalled that her mother's response to her announcement that she was dating someone new was always, "You aren't sleeping with him, are you?" Paula's curiosity about me peaked in her asking me directly and with some urgency if I was or had been married. From her associations it seemed she was trying to find out if I accepted my sexuality and, by extension, hers. In retrospect, the specific oedipal feature of the transference here was Paula's need to be able to idealize and feel twinned with me as a sexually responsive female. With great trepidation, she revealed her speculation that I had been married and was now divorced. She said that if this were true she could "once and for all let go of the ideal of being a nun." I saw this as her being able to fully embrace an idealized feminine image that included sexuality, healthy self-interest, and human limitation. Paula also described a feeling of relief connected to the fantasy that I was divorced, relief that had to do with thinking that I, as opposed to her mother, could survive her being separate from me. Even after considerable analyzing, Paula had a need to know if her fantasy was correct. Ultimately, I acknowledged that she in fact was right; interestingly, this disclosure did seem to solidify the feminine self that Paula had developed in relationship to me.

As the analysis drew to an end, Paula reported experiencing herself in a new way, which she felt she could best describe by the phrase "My life is my own." She was expressive of a wide range of feelings about ending, from proud excitement to sadness. This loss felt novel to her in that it was the first loss she had the "luxury to mourn." Occurring in the shadow of her relationship with her mother, all previous separations had felt like "escapes." As our final session drew near, Paula looked back on the analysis:

> Since I was last here, I've been thinking about missing and mourning. My thoughts went back to the start of therapy: all the images I've had

of you and how they've changed. How I was afraid of depending on you. It was something I'd never been able to do. I will miss analysis, but I will also miss you. And not just an image of you. I did make you into the mother I never had, but I also appreciate what you have actually done for me, like allowing me to look at the things I was afraid of without fear of losing you. That is something I'd never had before.

DISCUSSION

When I examined these cases for the specific self weaknesses and selfobject failures that led to each young woman's difficulty, the following ideas seemed relevant: Marisol did not have a cohesive sense of herself as an adult female. Ornstein (1983b) could have been speaking of Marisol's growing up when she referred to the special neurosogenic significance of the mother's jealousy of her little girl's relationship with her father during the oedipal phase. Ornstein noted that this type of mother is unable to delight in this specific progressive move in the little girl's development: "Such a failure in parental selfobject responsiveness can severely affect a girl's self perception in terms of her femininity and sexual functioning" [p.388]. Her mother's skewed perception deprived Marisol of a way of integrating her phase-appropriate assertiveness and sexuality into the fabric of her self. As a result, she experienced herself as a little girl who would never grow up to have a husband, babies, or a successful career. This was the basis for her hostile, apparently competitive stance toward other women. In her analysis Marisol established, after some work on her "bad girl" defense, an idealizing transference to me as an oedipal mother. She wanted to look at me in a way that would provide direction for her own psychological maturation as a woman. My insistence that such yearning and related behavior were hostile and competitive was experienced as a repetition of her mother's psychotic view of her healthy assertiveness and sexuality. Marisol's mother's most striking failure seems to have been as a mirroring maternal oedipal selfobject. Marisol's turning to me as an idealized oedipal selfobject is consistent with Kohut's (1984) observation that development in psychoanalysis is likely to renew itself around the least damaged pole of the self. Marisol, with her single-minded devotion to helping minority students, had been primarily organized around her ideals prior to her treatment, indicating that she had managed to erect a compensatory structure around this pole of her self. I think that if I had been able to provide her a more consistently empathic analytic experience, the revision and strengthening of this structure would have been a major area of intrapsychic change for Marisol.

Paula, on the other hand, could not idealize a feminine image consistent with her nuclear self. The feminine ideal of the nun that she had been offered by her mother did not fit, yet anything else seemed "second-rate." After a working through of her "good girl" defense, Paula established a selfobject transference to me as an oedipal mother who was primarily mirroring in nature. She responded with enhanced vitality to comments of mine that merely appreciated the healthy significance of her feelings and her renewed development. Paula experienced my interpretations focusing on her competitive feelings about me as indications of my discomfort with her affects and an insistence that she fit my mold. This, of course, was a repetition of her relationship with her mother, whose character and acute depression led her to fail Paula primarily as an idealized oedipal selfobject. As Paula said, "The idea of being like her was like an electric shock that made me jump ahead." Paula's lifelong focus on her achievement and appearance reflected the compensatory structure she had established around the pole of the grandiose self. Although the analysis resulted in Paula's being able to make use of a full range of selfobject experience in relation to me as an oedipal mother, her renewed development also took place, at least initially, around the least damaged pole of the self.

Turning to the role of the twinship selfobject experience, what specific self weaknesses can be seen to derive from failures in this area during the little girl's oedipal phase? Detrick (1985) describes the need for sameness underlying the twinship experience, while Basch (1992) focuses on the importance of the experience of acceptance that comes from being like the other. Paula and Marisol both presented with a sense of badness about their assertiveness and sexuality and felt alienated from other women. While this symptomatology could be explained on the basis of a failure in a mirroring or an idealizing selfobject experience, the absence of a sense of *alikeness* with other females inherent in these complaints implicates the twinship selfobject experience. And how does a little girl feel twinned with her mother? Kohut called upon images of shared activities, like the little boy shaving alongside his father, to capture this subjective state. I think of my daughter, who at age two was inclined to joyfully announce in the most unexpected places, "Daddy and Brother got penises. *Mommy* and *me* got 'bulbas.' " Contrast this prideful state with Marisol and Paula's inability and/or unwillingness to feel twinned with their oedipal mothers. I would also suggest that it is significant, in light of the absence of healthy twinship experience, that the mirroring and idealizing selfobject failures that both young women suffered were in the nature of *impingements*, to borrow Winnicott's term. Marisol's and Paula's mothers were not merely unable to provide a healthy oedipal selfobject presence; their acute psychopathology during their daughters' oedipal phase made their presence noxious. Marisol and Paula were required to actively keep their mothers away from contact with their healthy oedipal selves. From these considerations I propose that the oedipal twinship selfobject transference manifestations seen in these two analyses were in the realm of new psychological experience.

Given Marisol's and Paula's overt rejection of their mothers as twins, what is most curious is that in their "bad girl" and "good girl" defensive modes, Marisol and Paula were near replicas of the failed maternal selfobjects from whom they required protection. Marisol defended against her mother's attacks on her self with an assault of her own. Paula warded off her mother's attempts to mold her by adopting a facade that matched her mother's own "good girl" defensive presentation. The "bad girl" and "good girl" presentations can be seen to serve multiple functions. Newman (1980) and Ornstein (1983b) have emphasized the role of defensive structures in maintaining a connection to a desperately needed mother. Indeed, Marisol's drawing fire by being a "bad girl" did guarantee an ongoing lively involvement with her mother, and Paula's compromise of her self allowed a placid relationship with her superficially idealized mother. Of course, true engagement and the associated risk of retraumatization were simultaneously warded off. The behaviors also provided a way of being a woman in the world, filling in for missing psychic structure. Marisol's determined, angry activism and Paula's compliant charm gave each a sense of who she was and brought some real rewards along with the complications. In addition—and perhaps most importantly—the "bad girl" and the "good girl" presentations represented, I believe, a profound unconscious need to feel an *alikeness* with the oedipal mother.

Ornstein (1983a, b), focusing on the realm of idealization, pro-posed that the formation of a gross identification with the homogenital parent during the oedipal phase is the result of selfobject failure. In my mind, both the "bad girl" and the "good girl" structures qualify as gross identifications. We know that a child will perform to obtain a mirroring selfobject response and will disavow disillusionment to try to maintain an idealizable selfobject. Might not the child shape his or her self to be *like* the same-sex parent in an attempt to provide something akin to a twinship selfobject experience when one is not naturally forthcoming? In other words, can this type of identification be conceptualized as a structure deriving from a twinship selfobject experience gone awry? This structure would be more or less a gross one, depending upon the extent of the gap between the child's genuine propensities and those relevant personal qualities of the parent and upon the degree of desperation for a psychic structure to maintain self functioning. I also suspect that failures in the mirroring and idealizing oedipal selfobject experience put more pressure on the area of twinship development as a site for the formation of defensive or compensatory structure, while simultaneously making the same-sex parent a less appealing figure with whom to feel twinned. This could also help account for the apparent paradox in these two cases in which the two women were so like the mothers they vehemently rejected on a conscious basis.

Related to the issue of the twinship selfobject experience is another that bears discussion: the influence of my being a woman on the course of these analyses. I think that in both cases a twinship selfobject experience, with my being a woman as the foundation, promoted the patient's renewed oedipal development. I felt this most clearly with Paula; my being female and my having much in common with her socially, culturally, and generationally facilitated her relinquishing her defensive "good girl" identification with her mother and enhanced the transmuting internalization of an assertive and sexual addition to her feminine self. Kohut (1977) proposed a developmental sequence in which the mother early on performs as a mirroring selfobject and the father later enters as an idealized selfobject. He noted, however, that the girl may direct both sets of selfobject needs toward the mother. Ornstein (1983a, b) argued that it is the homo-genital parent that provides the crucial developmental experience for the primary task of the oedipal phase, the acquisition of gender-related goals and delineations. I think the possibility that the gender of the analyst plays a significantly limiting or facilitating role in this process as it is reactivated in an analysis must be entertained.

Kohut (1984) suggested that there may be more than one road to an analytic cure. He was tentative in this assertion, as I read him, possibly out of a concern over having it seem that the actual person of the analyst plays a determining role in shaping analytic outcome. More recently, Goldberger and Holmes (1993) concluded, after studying transferences in male patients with female analysts, that the analyst's gender can have evocative and/or limiting effects on transference development. Solomon (1991) also suggests that the reality of the therapist's gender can crucially affect a female patient's selfobject relations. Ornstein (1983a) and Terman have shown that a heterogenital analyst can provide mutative idealizing and mirroring selfobject experiences for patients with oedipal phase problems. However, I wonder if a patient can have a meaningful twinship selfobject experience *related to the oedipal phase task of acquiring highly differentiated gender-specific traits* in the transference with an analyst of the opposite sex. This does not mean that oedipal phase problems could not be cured in an analysis in which the patient and analyst are of opposite sex, only that the process and the shape of that cure would be different. For example, the patient might make use of an important same-sex person outside the analysis for the needed twinship selfobject experience, or renewed development might occur more around idealizing or mirroring selfobject experiences in the transference.

In summary, the two cases presented here confirm the mother's central importance as an oedipal selfobject who provides essential mirroring, idealizing, and twinship selfobject opportunities for her daughter. The clinical material also underscores the oedipal girl's vulnerability in the face of her mother's impaired functioning as an oedipal selfobject. In addition, these cases support Kohut's hypothesis that the twinship selfobject experience is crucial during the oedipal phase. The need to feel alikeness with a same-sex parent to accomplish the developmental task of acquiring more differentiated gender-specific traits provides a rationale for this. Failures in the mirroring and/or idealizing selfobject functioning of the oedipal same-sex parent may put more pressure on the area of twinship while simultaneously making the parent less desirable as a selfobject for this experience. The grosser taking in of a defensive structure, which might be labeled an identification from the perspective of classical theory, would from this vantage point be understood as an attempt to compensate for the deficits in the oedipal self via a distortion of the twinship selfobject experience.

While the crucial role of the parent in providing selfobject experiences for the oedipal child is now well established, we are far from meeting Kohut's challenge of outlining the specific self weaknesses and selfobject failures that lead to specific oedipal pathology, particularly with regard to the twinship selfobject experience. The usefulness of these two cases in clearly and specifically addressing this task is limited by my largely retrospective understanding of the relevance of the self issues for these women. There are many questions for self-psychologically informed analysts to investigate about psychoanalytic cure in patients, like these women, who have more complexly developed psyches. For example, the role of the father in the oedipal development of these women was neglected in my presentation. In this continued pursuit I think we are wise to keep an open mind in considering the role of the unique person of the analyst as an influence in shaping the renewed development of the patient's self.

In particular, the possibility that the analyst's gender may facilitate or limit opportunities for growth in aspects of renewed oedipal phase development via the twinship selfobject experience in the transference deserves further investigation.

REFERENCES

Basch, M. (1992), *Practicing Psychotherapy*. New York: Basic Books.

Detrick, D. (1985), Alterego phenomena and alterego transferences. In: *Progress in Self Psychology, Vol. 1*, ed. A. Goldberg. New York: Guilford Press, pp. 240–256.

Goldberger, M. & Holmes, D. (1993), Transferences in male patients with female analysts: An update. *Psychoanal. Inq.*, 13:173–191.

Kohut, H. (1971), *The Analysis of the Self*. New York: International Universities Press.

_____ (1977), *The Restoration of the Self*. New York: International Universities Press.

_____ (1979), The two analyses of Mr. Z. *Internat. J. Psycho-Anal.*, 60:3–27.

_____ (1984), *How Does Analysis Cure?* ed. A. Goldberg & P. Stepansky. Chicago: University of Chicago Press.

Newman, K. (1980), Defense analysis and self psychology. In: *Advances in Self Psychology*, ed. A. Goldberg. New York: International Universities Press, pp. 263–278.

Ornstein, A. (1983a), An idealizing transference of the oedipal phase. In: *Reflections on Self Psychology*, ed. J. Lichtenberg & S. Kaplan. Hillsdale, NJ: The Analytic Press, pp. 135–148.

_____ (1983b), Fantasy or reality? The unsettled question in pathogenesis and reconstruction in psychoanalysis. In: *The Future of Psychoanalysis*, ed. A. Goldberg. New York: International Universities Press, pp. 381–395.

Solomon, B. (1991), Self psychology may offer new ways to understand how penis envy functions. *Psychodynamic Letter*, 1(11):1:1–4.

Stolorow, R. & Lachmann, F. (1980), *Psychoanalysis of Developmental Arrests*. New York: International Universities Press, pp. 144–170.

Terman, D. (1984–1985), The self and the Oedipus complex. *The Annual of Psychoanalysis*, 12/13:87–103. New York: International Universities Press.

Chapter 10

Sexuality and Aggression in Pathogenesis and in the Clinical Situation

Paul H. Ornstein

Sexuality and aggression, in their varied forms, so deeply and thoroughly permeate our individual and social existence that their clinical and theoretical importance seems to require no further justification. History, religion, art, and literature throughout the ages document their centrality in everyday human affairs. Who could question their basic motivational role in human behavior? Small wonder, therefore, that psychoanalysts of all persuasions, ever since Freud, have recognized the ubiquitous presence of these two complex human proclivities in health as well as in nearly every form of psychopathology. Thus, there has long been a broad consensus about the fact that on a clinical–empirical level sexuality and aggression are inevitably aspects of both emotional health and emotional illness. Questions and controversies have arisen only in connection with determining the origin, development, and nature of human sexuality and aggression and in specifying their role and function in pathogenesis.

What is normal sexuality and what is normal aggression? When does each become pathological? Or, to ask it more pointedly, in reference to the controversies about their role in development and pathogenesis: How do they develop so that they, in turn, affect personality development, and when are they primary and causative in psychopathology? And when are abnormal sexuality and aggression the results of an unfolding psychopathology that has other fundamental or primary causes? Furthermore, what are the relationships between normal and abnormal sexuality and aggression? How can we tell them apart, phenomenologically and dynamico-structurally?

Instead of answering these questions directly, I shall immediately turn to Kohut's perspective on sexuality and aggression.

KOHUT'S PERSPECTIVE ON SEXUALITY AND AGGRESSION

To introduce the comprehensive, major shift that has occurred in the clinical and theoretical approach to sexuality and aggression in Kohut's work, it is not only fitting but actually necessary to begin with a clinical vignette. How else could we concretely underline the fact that Kohut's ideas derive from that distinctive clinical approach that is characterized by the prolonged, empathic immersion of the analyst in his patients' transference experiences? It does, indeed, need to be said at the outset that unless we keep in mind that the empirical data on which these theories rest were, by dint of the method of its gathering, deliberately delineated from biology on one hand and sociology on the other, we would be able to neither grasp properly nor appraise adequately Heinz Kohut's self psychology.

Mrs. A was a widowed professional women in her late thirties who had come into analysis some years before because of a chronic depression, apathy, and profound inability to experience any sustained and sustaining joy or pleasure in her personal or professional life. She had made excellent progress over a number of years, especially in the core areas of her initial difficulties: She wanted to feel more comfortable in her body as a woman, and now she did. She wanted to be able to shed her "masculine, tomboyish image" of herself and feel comfortable in feminine, attractive clothes. Later on she wished to be less frightened of intense bodily sensations and sexual feelings on the couch, and these she had also attained to a degree.

On this particular Friday Mrs. A approached her analytic session with considerable uneasiness and reluctance, the source and meaning of which feelings she did not yet understand. In a muted tone, with barely a hint of excitement, she described an experience that morning of having sat for quite a while with an agitated, severely depressed women. "I was able to be with her," she said, "calmly, without offering meaningless reassurance," as she had never been able to do before. "Do you know what I mean by just being with her?" she asked with a slight tinge of excited teasing, which we both understood to refer to her having told me many times in the past how much she needed and appreciated my just being with her (she often explicitly asked that I not say anything for a while but just listen and let her talk). She went on to say that the second thing she did before coming to her session was to go to a meeting, where she was calmly effective with a good degree of emotional presence. As soon as she finished her story, she immediately recalled a feeling from childhood of vaguely wanting something from her mother and wishing to turn to her, but she was never quite able to turn to her mother and actually ask. She wondered if I remembered her telling me about this in the past. I said I did. She then reported that it was a frighteningly uncomfortable feeling to come to this session "with that same sort of a vague expectation from you." She both wanted to come to her session and didn't want to come. Now there was more of a trace of excitement in her voice but also some fear. I said, "You are excited about your experiences this morning. You were in touch with something in yourself, having been able to be with this depressed women. You have never experienced this before in quite this way. It must have been difficult to be alone with this excitement and also the pride in your calm effectiveness at the meeting."

"Yes," she said tearfully, "I felt so alone, empty, and depressed."

"You needed to share this discovery and excitement, like you wished you could have done as a child with your mother but never did. Now you brought it in here, reluctantly, fearfully, keeping your excitement in check, and wondering how I would receive it."

"No, I was more worried of how I would feel telling you about it." I agreed with her correction. What felt so exciting to her was that she had done what I generally did—and successfully at that. Mrs. A continued to look at her experiences of the morning for a while, including her excitement in talking about it as freely and as animatedly as she was finally able to do. Then she said, "Now that we talked about it, I am even more excited that I got your attention. I knew I could not share this with anyone. Nobody would understand." After a brief pause she said that for the last few minutes physical sensations were part of her excitement. These were diffuse, all over her body. "Are you sure it's all right to talk about this?" she asked, as she had done on many other occasions. "These are sexual feelings. I also feel like eating. Both would get out of hand in this excitement, with the urge to fill the emptiness and to do away with the depression."

Mrs. A now understood the incongruity of her emptiness and depression in the face of such a desirable step. She knew that she should have felt pride in her effectiveness and in having made contact with a capacity in herself that she longed to exercise, knew that she should have been happy that she was able to bring these experiences into the analysis, albeit against great resistance, to display to me and to have me admire. But she felt just the opposite. The emptiness and depression on coming to her session, she now thought, had to do with her childhood memory of never having been able to report on her accomplishments to her mother or display them freely to her. The poignancy of the memory on her way to the session was, she realized on reflection, due to the fact that she was not even sure in the memory what she wanted from her mother, just as she was not sure what she wanted from me in anticipation of her session.

This brief vignette shows how quickly bodily sensations of excitement, which escalated into diffuse sexual and alimentary sensations and feelings, were introduced into the analytic moment. This occurred in a specific context and in a fairly well delineated sequence, thereby opening a window into this patient's sexuality but leaving me at that moment with some ambiguity as to its precise nature. This episode, nevertheless, permitted a crucial recognition: it is always only the sexual "experience," its meaning in context, that is available for our view. We as analysts are, therefore, in search of a psychology of sexuality.

In order to explicate a bit more fully the meaning of this clinical vignette, I should remind you of the fact that we have to limit our inquiry to what we can encompass with empathy, our tool of observation, and, through it, with our appreciation of the nature of the selfobject transferences. Mrs. A's experience, which took the form of a diffuse sexual excitement, could thus be interpreted in one of two ways: (1) as a defensive effort to overcome her inner emptiness and depression, which she dreaded, or (2) as a developmental achievement, however tentative it may have been at this time.

In the first instance we would be dealing with a pathological structure. Certainly, Mrs. A's sexual excitement could be seen as her effort to deal with her emptiness and depression, as she herself put it, in which case it would be more accurately designated as a "sexualized excitement." Here, Mrs. A's sexuality would have to be considered a breakdown product of her enfeeblement- and fragmentation-prone self. Her experience on the couch would then appear as an expression of her overstimulation from the telling of her experiences—that is, from having been able to turn to the analyst as she never could turn to her mother—and from the analyst's acceptance of her excitement and pride at showing off her successes.

In the second instance, however, Mrs. A's sexual feelings would indicate progress in the analysis. Her experiencing of the excitement could be viewed as part of the newly found functions of an increasingly more consolidated self, functions that signal a belated developmental achievement in her analysis. As a result, Mrs. A could now feel more safely sexual or, at least, she could respond to the overstimulation within much more tolerable bounds than before. Indeed, she was not unduly embarrassed or inhibited and could reflect on as well as communicate about her experience.

To put this more generally, the selfobject transferences and their working through help us in distinguishing two groups of sexual experiences: first, those that are efforts to bolster an enfeeblement- or fragmentation-prone self or to prevent a further, more serious, fragmentation (these experiences exhibit a quality of compulsion and drivenness) and, second, those that accompany the growth and expansion of a well-consolidated, cohesive self and constitute its enrichment. There is an important qualitative difference between these two "sexual" experiences. One creates intense discomfort; there is a threat in the excitement that may then be quickly inhibited. The other is experienced with an uplifting, genuine pleasure since this constitutes an enrichment of the cohesive self. This qualitative difference is similar to the distinction that can be made between the experience of self-consciousness, which is accompanied by patchy, irregular blushing, and the experience of inner pride, which is accompanied by a diffuse, undisturbed warm glow.

Let us return to Mrs. A for another moment. She reported how well she had done and what specifically she had done well: she contained someone else's depression and felt effective at another aspect of her work, where she was the center of attention at a meeting and did well. Though fearful of showing her joy over these activities, she was capable of experiencing that joy. Once she had her feelings accepted and thereby affirmed, it was as if she had permitted a new kind of excitement to enter her body, an excitement that made the experience of her own competence more intense and profound rather than threatening or overwhelming. But the sexualization of this process indicated that she could not yet adequately contain the overstimulation caused by the analyst's responsiveness to her excitement about and pride in her accomplishments. She experienced the analyst as receptive to her affects whereas she had never been able to experience her mother that way during her childhood. As a result, she felt an unusual degree of intimacy with the analyst in that session, and this contributed to her feeling overstimulated.

A brief sequence from the next session (which occurred after the weekend interruption) will aid us in resolving the ambiguity we are left with regarding the nature of Mrs. A's sexual experience on the couch. On Monday she reflected further, with evident curiosity and puzzlement, both about the Friday session and about her ensuing calm and reasonably productive weekend. She did not miss me much, she said; it was as if I had been with her in some fashion, even after the session, but not in conscious awareness. Almost as an afterthought and in an effort to contrast this last weekend with many others in the past, she reported that during some of those weekends when she felt restless, upset, alone and depressed, she would eat, read, and watch TV—all at the same time—for hours. And when this did not help her calm down, she would masturbate and have an orgasm and then fall asleep. This pattern of behavior is now a rare occurrence.

Additional data from the second session after the weekend indicate the overall favorable changes in Mrs. A's general capacity for tension regulation, which includes her sexual experiences. Slow accretions of psychic structure, almost imperceptible, from day to day and week to week, have finally led to better containment of her various disruptive affects, with fewer constraints; Mrs. A can experience more, with less overstimulation or fragmentation. The decisive change, however, is not in her sexuality per se but in her more integrated use and experience of it, that is, in the cohesiveness of her self.

I believe the foregoing analytic episode and its cursory explication bring us face to face with certain clinical and theoretical issues, pertinent to our theme, and we shall now turn to their more general and theoretical consideration in Heinz Kohut's work.

Kohut's first decisive contribution to psychoanalytic drive theory, and hence to the issue of sexuality and aggression, went almost unnoticed. As a matter of fact, its full impact has still to be absorbed by the psychoanalytic community. I am referring to his statement, by now widely familiar, that as psychoanalysts we can only speak of drives as the experiences of drivenness. We cannot learn via empathy about their known or assumed biological underpinnings. Whatever the origin and nature of these drives, their most significant element, in Kohut's view, is that they are "at the beginning of psychological life . . . already integrated into larger experiential configurations" (Kohut, 1978, p. 790). These larger and more complex configurations, within which the drives are integrated as their constituents or building blocks, are the primary units of psychological experience. They are to be encompassed in their wholeness through the analyst's empathic observational mode. When these larger configurations are weak in their structure, or crumble in the face of traumatic experiences, we witness the emergence of intensified drivenness as a breakdown product of the self. What we mean by the breakdown product—a term to which many take such intense exception because it "slights the drives"—is similar to the well-recognized "word salad" of schizophrenic patients, an example of the extreme breakdown of cohesive and logical thought processes. Kohut used the analogy of an organic molecule breaking down into its inorganic components to suggest the psychological experience of a fragmentation of the self. By calling certain forms of sexuality and aggression breakdown products of the self, we are also indicating that we place the self in a supraordinate position vis-à-vis "the drives." Thus, the building blocks of the self, such as normal sexuality and self-assertive aggression, attain their particular pathological configurations upon the weakening or crumbling of the structure into which they are built and within which, if this structure is intact, they find their channels for normal expression. Our primary focus on the whole structure thereby apparently "slights" the drives (if that is an acceptable phrase in a scientific discussion), the same way that placing the emphasis on the ego's response (at the behest of the superego) to sexuality and aggression has "slighted" the supremacy of the drives with the paradigm change from id psychology to ego psychology. In the paradigm of ego psychology the responses of the ego seem to have attained greater importance in pathogenesis. The claim was made that it was not so much the drives themselves but the ego's response of intolerance, a weakness in the ego's defensive structures, that contributed to the development of overt neurosis. If this shift was not as jolting as the current one of Kohut's reformulation of the position of the drives in pathogenesis—although some contemporary observers of that era of Freud's paradigm shift experienced it that way— it had to do with the fact that the then-new paradigm of ego psychology did not seem to immediately require a radical revision of its underlying drive theory, libido theory, and theory of infantile sexuality. But this was, as we now know, only a temporary respite since Freud shifted his focus again (now remaining within the newly established paradigm or simply completing it) to the nature intensity of the anxiety as the ultimate determiner of the outbreak of overt psychopathology (Freud, 1926).

Perhaps it still needs to be stressed that it was the systematic application of the empathic observational mode that led Kohut to all of his innovative formulations in every area of psychoanalysis. It is from this vantage point, the view from within the self-experience of the patient, and from a consideration of the bipolar self-structure as supraordinate that sexuality and aggression assume their many different psychological configurations and also come to have differently conceived roles and functions in neurosogenesis as well as in the overt manifestations of psychopathology. Added to the fundamental points made earlier, namely, that for us "drives" are the experiences of drivenness and that they are integrated within the psychological structures of the bipolar self from the outset, is the recognition that our theoretical language properly de-emphasizes the *primary* pathogenic significance of sexuality and aggression when it focuses on the *whole experience.*

But to continue our systematic survey and assessment of Kohut's contributions to the question of the pathogenic role of sexuality and aggression, we should turn to the archaic selfobject transferences and their later extensions, the oedipal selfobject transferences, for further insights. Kohut's carefully and extensively presented clinical material in describing these archaic selfobject transferences and their working through demonstrated the revival during analysis of patients' non-drive-related, hitherto thwarted mirroring and idealizing needs and identified the resulting deficits in the self-structure as the fundamental etiologic and pathogenic factors in their psychopathology. At the same time, it became abundantly clear that the traditionally postulated primacy of the drives and the ego's defenses against them were in these transferences misleading assumptions. Here was a significant and incontrovertible clinical refutation of the ubiquitous centrality of the drives as well as of the Oedipus complex as *primary* pathogenic agents in these transferences.

It was a mark of Kohut's careful empirical approach that he did not immediately claim that his discoveries of needs, wishes, fantasies, and demands other than those that could be traced to the two basic drives could fundamentally alter our ideas about human motivational structures. Those of us who recognized this wider implication in *The Analysis of the Self* (Kohut, 1971) and saw in these first contributions already the beginning development of a new paradigm (e.g., Basch 1973, Gedo, 1975; Ornstein, 1974, 1978) were impressed with several components of that work that are immediately relevant to our topic. We should now examine some of these.

Not until Kohut was able to extend his approach to the oedipal selfobject transferences in *The Restoration of the Self* (1977) did he introduce the more encompassing, fundamental changes regarding the basic motivational structures in normal development and in psychopathology. His reconstruction of the basic infantile and childhood developmental needs in relation to the two poles of the bipolar self drastically changed the traditional view of psychosexual development. Infantile sexuality and the ego's responses to it no longer seemed to be primary ubiquitous motivational factors in health or disease. The emphasis is again on the word *primary.* The proper overarching term is simply *self development,* or *personality development,* within which the development of human sexuality and aggression has to be traced in relation to the primary self-structures.

After having dealt with the neuroses, Kohut did indeed offer us a broader motivational theory within which his concepts of normal and pathological sexuality and aggression are embedded. The human infant, with its innate capacity to elicit from its selfobject milieu what it needs for its emotional survival and growth, is "motivated" to attain the cohesiveness of its nuclear self with a basic life plan or program built into it. If a sufficiently stable cohesiveness is achieved, the central motivating factor will be the effort to put that intrinsic program at the disposal of ambitions, in keeping with internalized values. The successful living out of this program constitutes the cardinal factor in mental health. The vicissitudes of sexuality and aggression have to be understood in terms of their either making a contribution to and thereby implementing and enriching that nuclear program or interfering with and thereby inhibiting the unfolding of the basic design of the nuclear self.

After Kohut had identified in the clinical setting of the selfobject transferences the many details for the mobilization and working through of the motivating factors, he was also able to spell out many details of normal and pathological development in the traditional manner, that is, on the basis of reconstructions from the transference. He was fully aware of the need for their continued verification in the clinical setting as well as from independent observations of mother–infant pairs outside of the analytic situation.

As you recall, Freud completed his theory of sexuality and aggression by regarding the Oedipus complex as the culmination of infantile sexuality. Kohut saw evidence in his own clinical findings not only for his own view of the Oedipus complex but also for his ideas on the primacy and centrality of mirroring and idealizing needs for all of normal development, their unreliable or deficient availability being responsible for all forms of psychopathology. The need for mirroring and idealization of the oedipal boy or girl in order to consolidate the development of gender-specific functions appeared to Kohut to be a continuation of the same needs of the earlier period in life when gratification was necessary for the consolidation of nuclear self-assertive ambitions as well as internalized nuclear values and ideals. This consolidation appeared to be, indeed, the prerequisite for making proper use of those gender-specific and phase-appropriate emerging needs for mirroring and for idealizable parental imagos, that is, for bringing sexuality as well as the capacity for assertiveness into free functional availability within the bipolar self.

Kohut's conclusion that the oedipal experiences are fundamentally joyful and not pathogenic, and that the pathological Oedipus complex is already a secondary formation, was the empirical as well as the logical correlate of what he discovered in the archaic and in the oedipal selfobject transferences. In other words, the absence of the primary psychological nutrients of development took the place of polymorphous perverse infantile sexuality (or incestuous oedipal sexuality) and aggression as the key neurosogenic agent. The possible innate biological factors that may contribute to the development of neuroses were never discounted by Kohut, but he knew that with the psychoanalytic method he could not contribute to identifying their specific nature and how exactly they made their contribution to development. Just as innate skills and talents—for which biological anlagen are also assumed—become mobilized in the service of self-assertive ambitions, in keeping with internalized values and ideals, so does normal sexuality become mobilized at the behest of a healthy, cohesive bipolar self. Likewise, pathological manifestations of sexuality are mobilized at the behest of a deficient or fragmenting self-structure in either one or both of its poles.

Rather than being either de-emphasized or denied as an important part of human functioning—as is often asserted—sexuality is actually given its proper place and due importance in self psychology. By not mixing up the breakdown products of sexuality with healthy sexuality, as is inevitably the case in considering its precursors as polymorphously perverse, Kohut's concepts have made the psychology of sexuality in health and illness clearer than have the primarily biologically oriented explanations of human sexuality. In the latter, sexuality was considered to be part of our animal nature, in need of taming, subduing, or neutralizing, rather than a feature that was evolving and becoming increasingly better integrated into the total fabric of the self and thereby enhancing its functioning. This description applies to the psychology and psychopathology of aggression as well. By not confusing the manifestations of rage and destructiveness (the breakdown products of aggression) with healthy aggression (self-assertiveness), Kohut has also opened up this area of human experience for a fresh psychological appraisal of its role and function in health as well as in psychopathology.

This last statement requires a more extensive elaboration. What precisely is this window that Kohut has opened more directly into the psychology of healthy as well as pathological sexuality, healthy as well as pathological aggression? As is well known in the psychoanalytic literature, the concepts of "sexualization" and "aggressivization" have played a prominent role in psychoanalysis from its very inception.[1]

In Kohut's work the concepts of sexualization and aggressivization, as well as their progressive neutralization, always played a prominent role. These concepts were already present in his earlier work, although they were used in a metaphorical and not concretely biological sense. That is, Kohut accepted the standard language of metapsychology and used it to express his empathically perceived psychological insights.

In the context of the archaic selfobject transferences Kohut repeatedly observed the sexualization of various regressive self-structures, within the grandiose self as well as within the idealized parent imago. Kohut demonstrated this in many of his clinical examples.[2]

At one point, this is what Kohut (1977) found in connection with the phenomenon of sexualization as reflecting pseudo-vitality:

> Behind [it] lie low self-esteem and depression . . . a deep sense of uncared-for worthlessness and rejection, an incessant hunger for a response, a yearning for reassurance . . . an attempt to counteract, through self-stimulation, a feeling of inner deadness and depression . . . through erotic and grandiose fantasies [p. 5].

Since the basic neutralizing or tension-regulating structures of the psyche are acquired through transmuting internalizations during early mirroring and especially during early idealizations, defects in these structures lead to a general structural deficiency whose functional correlate is the sexualized relationship to selfobjects. Appearing in the transference, these sexualizations provide the opportunity to study the structural deficits that are their correlates. It is in this clinical context that we can study the manner in which structural accretions during the analytic process occur and in this context that we may distinguish between sexualization in which the sexuality is a breakdown product and healthy sexuality and its correlated self-assertiveness, that is, healthy, pleasure-seeking and pleasure-giving sexuality and unencumbered self-assertiveness.

---

[1]We can now return to these earlier attempts and reexamine the many beautiful case illustrations they contain, using the window Kohut opened with his focus on sexualizations in the transference to study their psychologically relevant (debiologized) vicissitudes in the self–selfobject matrix, and thereby demonstrate the increased explanatory power of the new conceptualizations.

[2]Especially in those of Mr. A, Mr. E, Ms. F, Mr. M, and Mr. U. All contributions in the Case Book (Goldberg, 1978) also amply illustrate sexualization and/or aggressivizations in the transference.

When the developmental phases of early mirroring and idealizations are felicitously traversed and the child reaches the oedipal phase with a reasonably cohesive self, the availability or relative unavailability of oedipal mirroring responses or idealizable imagos will determine how freely available or incestuously encumbered sexuality will be. Thus, here too the conflicts involved in inhibiting or otherwise distorting sexual responsiveness will be secondary to the structural weakness, which is the primary cause in pathogenesis.

The decisive technical implications of these clinical-theoretical innovations deserve a more extensive survey and explication than can be offered here, along with additional clinical illustrations. For obvious reasons only the initial clinical vignette and its brief explication could be included in this chapter. However, a few additional remarks, contrasting the implications of a drive-theory-based approach with those based on a self theory, should be added to expand on my view that Freud's final drive theory has cast a long shadow on clinical practice, even if most analysts claim to adhere only to a drastically modified version of it (see especially Brenner, 1982).

The primacy of drives (however diluted or altered a particular drive theory might be in comparison to Freud's) still commands a primary focus on drive–defense constellations rather than on the underlying structural deficits in the bipolar self. The technical stance dictated by all other approaches contrasts sharply with the one developed by Kohut (cf. Gill, 1985). First, the clinical atmosphere is very different when the analyst's attention has to be directed toward the remobilized and unacceptable incestuous strivings that were already taboo in childhood. These will, therefore, certainly have to be viewed as anachronistic in the present, that is, as chronologically out of place in terms of the patient's current reality and are considered to be the manifestations of a revived oedipal transference neurosis. Thus, even the most tactful and accepting interpretations carry with them a tone of disapproval. By contrast, when the focus is on those wishes and needs that were thwarted in infancy and childhood—when they should have been phase-appropriately gratified—their remobilization is welcomed and accepted as legitimate in the analyst's interpretive responses. If structure building and the reestablishment of empathic contact with selfobjects are at the core of the curative process, as Kohut claims they are, then drive–defense interpretations will often thwart the feeling of being understood. Hence, they will also thwart the felicitous underpinning for subsequent transmuting internalizations.

To sum up the essential points in Kohut's work covered thus far: The contrast with previous psychoanalytic contributions to drive theory and its technical implications is here quite striking, but they need to be spelled out briefly. The supraordinate position of the bipolar self directs our primary focus to the state of the self, to its structural and functional weaknesses, deficiencies, and defensive and compensatory structures on one hand, and to its cohesiveness, vigor, and vitality on the other. The ubiquitous sexualization of any mild or severe defects in the self–selfobject unit and the vicissitudes of these sexualizations in the course of the analysis are, in fact, our window into human sexuality in health and illness, just as aggressivization under the same circumstances is our window into human destructive aggression.

The breakdown products of the self have to be distinguished from healthy sexuality and aggression, which are the unmistakable expressions of a structurally and functionally intact self. The principle of focusing on the state of the self and the vicissitudes of its fragmentation and cohesion dictates the analyst's responsiveness in the transference.

CONCLUDING REMARKS

In this chapter I have focused on Kohut's clinical and theoretical contributions to the role of sexuality and aggression in pathogenesis. I have reviewed how he defined sexuality and aggression, how he saw their role and function in pathogenesis, how he conceived of the phenomena of sexualization and aggressivization, and how he used them. I have also described Kohut's solution to many lingering clinical and theoretical problems revealing that Kohut and self psychology have not underplayed—as some critics have claimed—the role of sexuality and aggression in health and illness.

To this last point I wish to add some additional remarks: I have on other occasions (Ornstein, 1983) given some scattered responses to critiques that claim that self psychology neglects or de-emphasizes sexuality and aggression or, even worse, that it could not bear to behold the raw id in any of its manifestations and therefore proceeded to sanitize psychoanalysis. Kohut himself raised this question when he asked, "Is it not an escapist move, a cowardly attempt to clean up analysis, to deny man's drive-nature, to deny that man is a badly and incompletely civilized animal?" (Kohut, 1977). On balance, after having reviewed the literature and scrutinized Kohut's own contributions, we can say that, yes, from the vantage point of most— though by no means all!—earlier theories we do indeed de-emphasize sexuality and aggression, regarding their *primary* role in pathogenesis. But we definitely do not neglect or de-emphasize the enormous importance and power of sexuality and aggression in human experience. It is impossible to overlook the ubiquitous presence of sexuality and aggression as components of manifest psychopathology. It is equally impossible to overlook their ubiquitous presence as expressions of health, vigor, and vitality and their capacity to generate pleasure through peak experiences. Nor is it possible to overlook the fact that the sexual apparatus of human beings is a channel for the satisfaction of a variety of other needs and wants, under both normal and, especially, disordered circumstances. The difficulty of separating the normal from the pathological remains a problem, but a consideration of the structural deficiency or completeness of the total self and of its functions is still our best available guide. In addition, it is careful listening that subjectively distinguishes the experience of drivenness from the experience of pleasure and the sense of fulfillment and joy. Sociocultural and political influences of any era have their imprint on our notions of health and illness. Kohut saw that clearly. But he also claimed, in the same sense as did C. Daly King (as quoted by Kohut [1984]), that "the normal is to be defined as that which functions in accordance with its [structural] design" [p. 187]—a view that minimizes the importance of cultural bias in arriving at our assessment of what is normal and what is not.

But what of the claim that self psychology not only neglects and de-emphasizes sexuality and aggression but in a cowardly and retrogressive act attempts to "clean up" analysis and deny man's true drive nature, his inescapable biology, and his being a deficiently civilized animal? This particular accusation is perhaps—and I am trying to find the mildest possible characterization—the most ridiculous nonsense.

This question would not deserve a special response were it not for the fact that we ourselves have been searching for an answer to the legitimate and recurrent concerns at the core of it. Are we, in fact, inadvertently underplaying the obvious power of these passions that poets, novelists, and playwrights have portrayed since the beginning of recorded history? Thus, apparently, intuitive knowledge and overall sentiment—claimed as conviction on the basis of personal and clinical experiences—holds that sexuality and aggression are qualitatively unique passions. This view has long had a deep anchoring in the Western mind. We must run through these questions and concerns briefly in order to know what culturally and personally ingrained convictions fuel and direct our scientific attitudes. We often feel that sexuality and aggression are somehow more highly charged and have a different quality to them than do other human motives for action. Sexuality seems to have such an immense directing power or motivational force. Calling its healthy version simply "pleasure seeking" and its pathological version a "breakdown product" is too mild or too bland for a description of its intensity and its many twisted forms. As an extension of this, we also wonder at times whether inner tension regulation through sensual experiences and the response of our culture to these does not, indeed, place these "passions" into a different category from all other "passions." After all, are they not generally seen as the "prime movers of things"; that is, are they not the ultimate and most powerful motivators of human activity, from the most valued to the most dreaded? Does not treating them in these pathological forms as breakdown products credit them with much less than their full power, complexity, and place in human affairs would warrant? Do we not fail to account for and in fact lose something of their essence if we call them breakdown products? And are we not also giving thereby our critics further ammunition? Even when we differentiate between primary and secondary phenomena, we are essentially saying that the sexuality and aggression we call secondary are merely the by-products of the primary phenomena. It sounds to our critics, then, like we are saying that sexuality and aggression are simply static, but they are obviously more than that— or so the challenge goes.[3] It appears to those who pose these searching questions that self psychology has not captured the unique quality of normal or pathological sexuality and aggression as yet. The same critics usually insist that sexual and aggressive phenomena do stand out qualitatively even when they are integrated into the whole personality and that they have a notable unique intensity and peremptoriness even as pathological breakdown products. How do we respond to some of these claims from the vantage point of our theory?

I have listed these questions in some detail since they require further clinically documented responses. In this format I have to be brief. We should not confuse normative and pathological forms of sexuality and aggression. The normal human passions do not belong under the rubric of pathogenesis; they are not in themselves illness-creating per se. Of course—and Kohut was unmistakably clear on this—normal sexuality and aggression are not just static. The concept

---

[3]It is rarely recognized by our critics that we differentiate more sharply than they do between normal sexuality and normal aggression (self-assertive ambition) and their pathological manifestations as breakdown products. This differentiation decisively contradicts the critics' claim that self psychology considers normal sexuality and normal aggression as merely "static." If the designation "static" applies at all, it does so only to the pathological breakdown products of the drives, never to their normal equivalents—as discussed further below.

of breakdown products is not about normal, integrated sexuality or aggression. Breakdown products refer to particular psychological conditions in which we have only the disordered forms, the twisted forms, of sexuality and aggression in view. We are so used to regarding archaic sexuality and aggression on a continuum with their supposedly normal equivalents, as Freud suggested, that we generally do not differentiate, as we should, between the normal and the pathological. Thus, when we speak of breakdown products, it is not a question of minimizing or denying the power of human passions but a question of what elements of pathogenesis and psychopathology are at work that lead to the appearance of these breakdown products. Adult sexuality may become secondarily involved in neurotic disturbances. Freud's own tenet was that intrusions of the memory of infantile sexual experiences or fantasies into the ego in adulthood created the overt psychopathology. From that base of secondary involvement, sexuality and aggression are frequent coparticipants with other causative factors in creating the manifest psychopathology.

Many questions have been raised that remain unanswered or only partially answered in this chapter. One question that is blatantly missing is this: How do love and hate relate to sexuality and aggression? This is too complex a question even to raise in this context and will have to be dealt with separately on another occasion.

By means of the transference, the analytic microscope enlarges, as it has to, human experience. This view is different—in spite of all the similarities in content—from the perspective of poetry, fiction, and drama in its scientific regard for the phenomena of sexuality and aggression. Reading Kohut's clinical illustrations we witness not only the breakdown products but, along with them, all the drama and passion of human existence, preserved, valued, and illuminated. Anyone who sees in self psychology denial or cowardly retreat from the intensity of the passions or from the "ugliness"—hardly a value-neutral, scientific term—of its breakdown products will have to look again, more carefully this time, at the clinical data and the claims of self psychology for further dispassionate exploration.

REFERENCES

Basch, M. F. (1973), Psychoanalysis and theory formation. *The Annual of Psychoanalysis,* 1:39–52. New York: International Universities Press.

Brenner, C. (1982), *The Mind in Conflict.* New York: International Universities Press.

Freud, S. (1926), Inhibitions, symptoms and anxiety. *Standard Edition,* 20:75–175. London: Hogarth Press, 1959.

Gedo, J. E. (1975), To Heinz Kohut: On his 60th birthday. *The Annual of Psychoanalysis,* 3:313–322. New York: International Universities Press.

Gill, M. M. (1985), Prespectives on countertransference. Presented at The Austen Riggs Center, Stockbridge, MA, September 1.

Goldberg, A., ed. (1978), *The Psychology of the Self*. New York: International Universities Press.

King, C. D. (1945), The meaning of normal. *Yale J. Bio. Med.* 17(no. 3):493–501.

Kohut, H. (1971), *The Analysis of the Self*. New York: International Universities Press.

_____ (1977), *The Restoration of the Self*. New York: International Universities Press.

_____ (1978), A note on female sexuality. In: *The Search for the Self, Vol. 2*, ed. P. H. Ornstein. New York: International Universities Press, pp. 783–792.

_____ (1984), *How Does Analysis Cure?* ed. A. Goldberg & P. Stepansky. Chicago: The University of Chicago Press.

Ornstein, P. H. (1974), On narcissism. *The Annual of Psychoanalysis*, 2:129–147. New York: International Universities Press.

_____ (1978), Introduction: The evolution of Heinz Kohut's psychoanalytic psychology of the self. In: *The Search for the Self, Vol. 1*, ed. P. H. Ornstein. New York: International Universities Press, pp. 1–106.

_____ (1983), Discussion of papers by Drs. Goldberg, Stolorow, and Wallerstein. In: *Reflections on Self Psychology*, ed. J. D. Lichtenberg & S. Kaplan. Hillsdale, NJ: The Analytic Press, pp. 339–384.

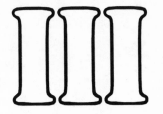

Aggression
and Rage

Chapter 11

Rage Without Content

Richard C. Marohn

Psychoanalytic thinkers have struggled with the concept of aggression almost from the beginning. Freud's earliest dual instinct theory included not the aggressive drive but libido and the self-preservative or ego instincts. As Terman (1975) observed, what Freud later called aggression is similar to today's formulation of narcissistic rage in that hate derives from the struggle to preserve the self (ego) and is a derivative reaction by the ego instincts of self-preservation.

Today a Kleinian may say that what Klein saw was not a destructive orality but the urgency of an infant not responded to, an infant striving to extract something from its mother. Or a traditionalist may say that he does not consider the aggressive drive to be destructive in its aim but assertive, and that destructiveness occurs when assertiveness is thwarted. Both my Kleinian and my traditionalist colleagues consider these views consistent with their specific school of psychoanalytic thinking, a surprise to the self psychologist who thinks that other psychoanalysts all believe the aggressive drive to be a destructive drive.

In her closing remarks to the 27th International Psycho-Analytical Congress in 1971 in Vienna, Anna Freud (1972) took note of the disagreement:

> Aggression can associate itself with aims and purposes of extraneous kinds, lending them their force. . . . Aggression also comes to the aid, either constructively or destructively, of purposes such as, for instance,

vengeance, war, honour, mercy, mastery, etc. . . . . the intrinsic aim of innate, primary aggression . . . [is an] unsolved question [pp. 165, 170].

Contemporary infant research (Lichtenberg, 1983; Stern, 1985) does not support the drive concept, certainly not the destructive drive formulation. Stechler (1987; Stechler and Halton, 1987) sees assertion as *proactive*, the experience of the active, outreaching, and engaging baby who establishes contact with the world and acts upon it with interest, excitement, and joy. Aggression, arising from the self-protective system, is a *reactive* response to threats that trigger inherent or learned self-protective mechanisms, including an attack mode designed to destroy or drive off the threat. Often, the developing child confuses *assertion* and *aggression* because of faulty parental responses, since one contaminates the other. Yet the perspective of a destructive aggressive drive is fundamental to much contemporary work with sicker patients, especially as formulated by Kernberg (1975) and his colleagues.

THE PERSPECTIVES OF SELF PSYCHOLOGY

Early in his writings Heinz Kohut (1957) was strongly influenced by psychoeconomics and the metapsychological point of view:

The earliest psychological organization (pre-ego, pre-object, and, of course, preverbal) is characterized by increases and decreases of inner tensions. The psyche can neither register its needs (that is experience them as wishes) nor provide for their relief; the tensions remain, without psychological elaboration, on the physical level. The rage caused by the mounting "unpleasure" can be understood as a form of automatic tension relief which is also not psychologically elaborated by fantasies [p. 244].

In those writings patients such as those with hypochondriasis were said to be "characterized by absence or paucity of psychological elaboration of their tension states, that is, by the absence of neurotic or psychotic symptom formation" (Kohut, 1957, p. 250). This is the "unstructured psyche," which Gedo and Goldberg (1973) later described as their first stage of development and which relates to their first level of psychopathology. Here, the mental apparatus confronts overstimulation, and as structure is built, tension regulation develops. Pacification is the appropriate treatment; there is no dynamic to interpret.

Kohut (1971) returned frequently to psychoeconomic explanations —

in reformulating acrophobia, for example, or in comprehending the traumatic state in an overstimulated analytic patient. When he later presented his ideas on narcissistic rage, he saw the rage reaction as a psychoeconomic imbalance involving the omnipotence of the grandiose self, just as shame is a psychoeconomic imbalance of exhibitionism. When the environment or the selfobject fails to respond, "smoothly deployed forces" are disrupted and there is simultaneous or successive discharge and inhibitions: "The disorganized mixture of massive discharge (tension decrease) and blockage (tension increase) in the area of unneutralized aggression, arising after the noncompliance of the archaic selfobject . . . is the metapsychological substratum of the manifestations and the experience of narcissistic rage" (Kohut, 1972, pp. 655–656). As Paul Ornstein (1978) notes:

> Kohut always stressed the uniquely psychoanalytic quality of the psychoeconomic theory . . . [His] sensitivity to increase or decrease of inner tension, to the manifold distribution of cathexes, permitted him to conceptualize psychic events, especially in early life, without adultomorphic formulations, without resorting to the postulation of archaic fantasies in the "prepsychologic" period of infancy. This classical Freudian stance, coupled with the recognition of the limitations of introspection and empathy in the reconstruction of the beginnings of psychic life—yet applying both introspection and empathy consistently and persistently to the limit—contributed considerably to the heuristic value of Kohut's early work. . . . The psychoeconomic point of view in Kohut's work . . . [is] one of the most important methodologic precursors of his work on narcissism [pp. 8–9].

Freud's (1917) concept of the actual neurosis is predicated on just such an imbalance, namely, a weakened self unable to cope with rising tension but without psychological elaboration.

The immature self is inevitably vulnerable to such disruption, and though this stirs the developing self to firm cohesion (Terman, 1975), the ultimate reliability of the self rests with the degree of structuralization that the parental selfobject environment can facilitate. Just as narcissistic injury and some propensity for narcissistic rage are inevitable in development, so too are they inevitable in treatment as transferences unfold. How disruptive these treatment experiences are is a measure of the health of structures and the propensity for psychoeconomic imbalance. As Kohut (1984) notes in his last work, with "the transference clicking into place . . . the analytic situation has *become* the traumatic past and the analyst has *become* the traumatizing selfobject of early life" (p. 178). We realize that even at the end Kohut had not abandoned the economic perspective. He noted, for example, how the classically reserved psychoanalyst protected certain patients from being overstimulated again or how the self psychologist's type of interpretation can protect the patient from entering "manic excitement" (p. 189).

How inevitable is a psychoeconomic imbalance in the treatment of relatively healthy individuals? How often is an early imbalance, like a phobia, telescoped into later dynamic psychopathology and later remembered with genetic content? Since self psychology has progressed from the study of the newly recognized narcissistic transferences and attempted to become a more general psychology with the description of the bipolar self and the self–selfobject paradigm, new and exciting formulations have emerged. Psychoeconomics remains with us, but we do not emphasize it. Clinically, we see angry, rageful, and/or destructive feelings, affects, behaviors, and, sometimes, thoughts and fantasies. Content-laden material with rich dynamics lies at one end of the spectrum. Vague forces with no specific dynamics, primitive in nature and suggestive of an economic imbalance, a random energy discharge, and a state of near chaos, are at the other pole. A specific dynamic can overtax the system and create this chaotic state, but the state itself does not contain specific dynamisms. Any point along the entire range of this spectrum can be understood from a self psychology perspective and approached with advantage.

What is significantly different today is that all pathology is now assessed in the context of the self–selfobject relationship. We note how the selfobject creates or regulates the traumatic overstimulation.

RAGE WITHOUT CONTENT

In thinking about narcissistic rage, we must remind ourselves that not all injury leads to narcissistic rage and that not all fragmentation leads to rage, but sometimes to panic, frantic behavior, depression, or emptiness. There are instances when violent, rageful, or destructive behavior may not be associated with any clearly delineated destructive thoughts, wishes, or fantasies. In these instances the behaviors seem to have no content associated with them, no psychodynamic meanings. Although these episodes may follow an experience that has great psychodynamic significance to the subject and that ends in fragmentation, the ragelike behavior itself represents merely the disintegrated condition or, sometimes, an effort to reorganize the self by restoring its primacy. As such, it may be that the person is striking out randomly at the environment, which has so fatefully failed the self. In Kohut's (1951) words, the borderline patient seeks "reassurance" and to restore or maintain "a precarious balance of self-esteem"

(p. 163). This is a patient whose dysregulation needs pacification, who needs to be held and contained psychologically just as one would hold an overwrought and overstimulated child having a temper tantrum, which is the frantic motor activity of an unregulated psyche needing pacification and restraint. The developmentally more mature person is held by the empathic bond established by explanation and interpretation.

The fragmented state encountered in a variety of pathologies demonstrates what Kohut (1978) meant by the drives being "fragmentation products":

> Drives are secondary phenomena. They are disintegration products following the breakup of the complex psychological configurations in consequence of (empathy) failures in the selfobject matrix. Subsequent to serious and prolonged or repetitive failures from the side of the selfobjects, assertiveness becomes exhibitionism; enthusiasm becomes voyeurism; and joy changes into depression and lethargy. Zonal eroticism (oral, anal, phallic-genital) is pursued in an isolated fashion instead of being experienced as the various pleasure goals of a joyfully assertive total self. It aims either at consolation and soothing or has as its purpose the attempt to regain the lost sense of the aliveness that characterizes the active, healthy self [p.236].

Disjointed drive derivatives are the products of fragmentation when the self loses its unity and coherence and experiences "single, isolated bodily and mental functions" (Ornstein, 1978, p. 100). As Kohut (1981) said in his last and posthumously presented paper,

> Under normal circumstances we do not encounter drives via introspection and empathy. We always experience the not-further-reducible psychological unit of a loving self, a lusting self, an assertive self, a hostile-destructive self. When drives achieve experiential primacy, we are dealing with disintegration products . . . the fragmenting self watching helplessly as it is being replaced by a feverishly intensified rage experience, by the ascendancy of a destructive and/or self-destructive orgy and thus again of the drive over the self [p.553].

One does not treat narcissistic rage but addresses the empathic break that has stimulated it. Primitive psychoeconomic discharge occurs when there is an intrapsychic imbalance, a state for which the selfobject therapist must take some responsibility: he did not anticipate the problem, he overstimulated the patient, he did not protect the patient, and so on. We do no not speak here of blaming the therapist for his mistakes, but we know that he participates in the disruption, including disruptions that occur when there is an over-whelming transference response (like the one experienced by Kohut's [1971] patient who fragmented after a correct interpretation).

How does a therapist empathize with people who are prone to this kind of disintegration? With what aspect of the patient do we empathize? There are several facets to the empathic process. One can become acquainted with the dynamic and genetic issues that may tip the balance, issues either in the patient's "outside" life or, more significantly, in the transference. One can recognize rage that is not informed by logic or reason but is the result of disequilibrium, rage that is contentless, without dynamic meaning, not informed by fantasy. To stand firm in the face of this fragmentation and to try to sustain the patient by recognizing the process that has just occurred is the therapeutic task.

The word *drive* aptly captures the uncontrolled quality of these experiences, and it may be that Freud, seeing such phenomena clinically, formulated the *actual neuroses* and inferred the drive. Kohut affirmed Freud's position that introspection does not uncover psychological content in the actual neuroses or in the prestructural psyche. The analyst observes "tension instead of wish, . . . tension decrease instead of wish-fulfillment, and . . . condensations and compromise formation instead of problem solving" (Kohut, 1959, p. 215). The inability to empathize with such primitive mental states leads one to perceive the situation as a social-psychological or biological problem rather than as an intrapsychic disturbance. Viewing primitively organized persons from the perspective of biology or flawed interpersonal relating misses their propensity for fragmentation. "Persistent introspection in the narcissistic disorders and in the borderline states thus leads to the recognition of an unstructured psyche struggling to maintain contact with an archaic object or to keep up the tenuous separation from it" (Kohut, 1959, p. 218). Even before he spoke of the forms and transformations of narcissism, Kohut encouraged us to try to empathize with the primitive unstructured psyche, characterized by fragmentation, lack of structure, rising tension, dysregulation, and vulnerability to over-stimulation.

The spectrum of narcissistic rage extends from the *primitive* at one pole to the *structured* at the other. As Terman (1975) has written:

> The more boundless violent forms of aggression usually occur in the disruption of earlier phases of self-cohesion (e.g., mergers) or at the points of transition between phases of self-development. . . . The nature of the structure determines the properties of aggression. Before

self-cohesion, aggression can be thought of as a pattern of diffuse discharge [pp. 253–254].

With self-cohesion, aggression or assertiveness becomes more defined and helps to elaborate the self more clearly, often in the context of an "adversarial" selfobject (see Wolf, 1988). What contributes to the movement from pre-cohesion to cohesion developmentally is not within the scope of this chapter, nor is a consideration of how cohesion can be achieved in the therapy of a persistently fragmented individual.

CLINICAL MATERIAL

The recognition of the important role dysregulation plays in the pathology of primitive mental states first came to me when I, as a psychiatry resident, treated a man with a persistent phobia of stuffed animals. His terror had begun as a specific fear of a stuffed bird and had its genetic roots in his attachment to mother and competitive fears of father. However, it later generalized to all stuffed animals and bordered on agoraphobia, with considerable social disability. I tried to interpret specific dynamic meanings of the phobic objects—simultaneously scouring the psychoanalytic literature to understand better the pregenital origins of the oedipal phobia. My supervisor, now a recognized self psychologist, pointed out that the primary issues for this person were the nature of his relationships with others, serious difficulty with self-esteem regulation, problems dealing with intense affect, and his "borderline" pathology. I recognized that although the patient had memories of intense oedipal competition, he also experienced his mother as enraged at him, out of control, and unable to soothe him.

When I later encountered impulsive and violent adolescent boys and girls in a hospital research and treatment program (Marohn et al., 1980), I could see their "driven" quality and recognized that their difficulties did not seem superego-related in nature, though many had been designated "juvenile delinquents." I was pleased, but puzzled, when a tough gang member who had become violent on the living unit relaxed after we removed him from the school program, which was housed in another part of the building, and provided him tutoring on the unit. We thought he had been "overtaxed" by pulling himself together to leave the living unit and attend school. Although I could think in terms of drives, how well or how poorly he controlled or regulated himself was not explained by the psychoanalytic theories I had learned. While Fritz Redl's intuitive and empathic interventions

(Redl and Wineman, 1957) gave us practical methods for helping behaviorally disordered adolescents modulate the intensity of their inner experiences, his recommendations did not seem to fit the theories. Studying a riot on our unit (see Marohn et al., 1973), and recognizing that many patients who assaulted staff or other patients were not angry but disorganized and overstimulated . . . often by affectionate longings . . . led me to appreciate the problems our inpatients had with traumatic overstimulation, escalation of tension, and violent behavior (Marohn, 1974).

For example, Nancy was 13 when she was admitted to the hospital. Before admission she had been violent at home, at school, and at other treatment facilities. She stole frequently, truanted, and ran away and had had multiple group placements and psychiatric hospitalizations. After admission she assaulted staff without any apparent precipitant. It was only after several months that we could begin attaching dynamic meaning to her violence. For a while there was considerable pressure to think of Nancy as having some kind of biological or hormonal imbalance because it seemed that her disruptive and assaultive behavior was not related to any apparent precipitant. However, we held to our philosophy that all behavior has meaning and can be understood psychologically and that if the structure of the unit and of the daily program was maintained, the meaning of Nancy's behavior would become clear. Eventually, Nancy's rage was brought into the psychotherapy rather than displaced onto staff members. The eventually formulated psychodynamic meanings of Nancy's violence are not germane to our considerations here; what is important is that before she could speak with either the ward staff or with her psychotherapist about her assaults, Nancy needed to move psychologically from a more primitive stage of organization, from a primarily psychoeconomic configuration, to a more highly developed, structuralized level, at which she could describe and explain the experiences that stimulated her. Nancy's early affect experiences were ill defined, and all she felt before, during, and after a physical assault was numbness, like the somatic reaction of a primitively organized psyche. It was only later that she could rage at and threaten to kill her therapist. Her early violent and rageful behavior was the manifestation of a disruption and fragmentation, with no associated mental content, though it was stimulated by primitive narcissistic transference issues. As her therapy progressed and facilitated psychic structuralization, Nancy's violent behavior began to look more and more like a narcissistic rage with specific psychodynamics.

Psychoeconomically related rageful responses like Nancy's are not limited to hospitalized adolescent inpatients but can be seen in office patients as well, including people in psychoanalysis. Bruce, a 30-year-old physician, was confronted early in his psychoanalysis with his wife's decision to leave him. He had already demonstrated marked difficulty with tension regulation and narcissistic vulnerability, and as he tried in vain to convince his wife to stay, while fantasizing about new women as replacements, he was flooded with five dreams that he reported in one session. In one dream he was counseling a young couple about a divorce, obviously an effort to gain mastery over his impending loss. Three of the dreams involved cooking: food enclosed in a casserole, cooking for the replacement woman, and cooking without a stove for a colleague at the office. This suggested that as he was losing important selfobject sustenance, he was facing fragmentation and the emergence of strong orality, a need so hot he could cook without a stove. He needed another selfobject to contain him and stay with him. The analyst wondered aloud what was "cooking." In the next session the patient reported a childhood memory involving markedly unempathetic treatment by both his parents in the cold of winter, suggesting his response to the analyst's effort to uncover the dynamic that was "cooking" rather than attend to his need for assistance in regulating himself.

Norbert, another physician-analysand about the same age, was much more definite about what made him angry. After he taught his first class to a group of clerkship students, he was elated with how well he had done and how well he had been received. As he drove home on the expressway, he felt as if he were flying in an airplane. When he arrived home, not only had his wife failed to prepare the favorite meal she had promised to celebrate the occasion but she was not even there! He was enraged and had fantasies about retaliating against her. Norbert's rage was fantasy-related and elaborated and could be worked with in specific transference configurations, while Bruce's experience was one of living on the brink of overstimulation, with his rage, as his self-state dream suggests, nearly boiling over.

Sandra, a paralegal in her middle twenties, had great difficulty relaxing over the course of her lengthy analysis. She had been traumatized by significant losses, and although she could readily verbalize her disappointment and dissatisfaction with family, friends, coworkers, and analyst, she seemed frozen in anger. She lived in a psychological world devoid of soothing selfobjects and struggled to ward off an empty and lonely fragmentation. After lying down on the couch for the first time, she too expressed concern about a pot boiling over; she dreamt that some punks had tied up her boyfriend and threatened to rape her, thus expressing her concern about being restrained and unable to feel or express herself as well as her fear that she would be invaded by intense affects. Problems with affect regulation and experience continued to trouble Sandra throughout her analysis. She felt that my interpretations were correct, but she could not get in touch with the feelings associated with the material under discussion. As she expressed in another early dream, she was watching a party given in her honor, but she was an outsider and could not join in. In other dreams she had the analyst turn away from her to avoid being overstimulated herself. Angrily, she complained that psychoanalysis did not help her defrost.

Carol, a 25-year-old physical therapist, had not only been victimized by impulsive people but frequently engaged in rash behavior herself. During her psychoanalysis of several years she and I used the opportunity to discuss many issues and a variety of psychodynamic meanings for her behavior, but it was the gradual accretion of an internal regulating system, which contact with the selfobject-analyst provided, that made the difference. Her rage attacks at her boyfriend and her parents and her tearful confrontations with me, an analyst who could not regulate her outside the office and who let her risk danger to herself, suggested an intense idealizing transference and attendant disillusion and narcissistic rage. Often, Carol's strong affects and impetuous behavior could not be explained in psychodynamic terms but resulted from psychoeconomic disequilibrium. In her 50th session, for example, she dreamt that she and another woman had walked into a restaurant:

> I don't know who she was. It was a dimly lit restaurant, posh. There were no people around; it was empty. The maitre d' walks us through it all to a classy table, not a table for two but a round table for eight. People had been there before us, and nobody had cleaned off the table. Then, all kinds of people I know sit down and start eating, others standing behind us. Two guys were behind me, and I was trying to eat; one was someone I had met at a party. They kept reaching over me and getting food off my plate. I start getting on them, and I woke up.

Certainly, the dream contained specific references to her mother and to me, but, most remarkably, it depicted the chaos and disorganization in her psychic life. Her hope was that I would clean up the mess. The genetics were that she felt abandoned by her mother, who would leave the house when the patient and her siblings argued.

About one hundred sessions later, after a two-week break, Carol presented me with the following poem:

14 double-edged daggers
cutting thru the ridges of my brain
gushing putrid streams
and red-black clots
of what I've called my lifebath
now released and welling up inside my skull.
Wanting out
Wanting most of all
to trickle down your face
its acid eating ridges
plowing gulleys
into that hard implacable granite
probing for a mineral pool or cavern underground—
musty but alive and giving evidence of time and change.
But if my ruby-acid is too weak
or your granite too impenetrable
then I'll simply wait for sleep
to come softly and gently
whispering "nothing"
blowing cool white air
into the vacuum I have made for it
until it fills my mind with healing space
sealing off the gashes of Indifference.

My two-week absence ("14") cut her deeply. The agony she experienced as she disintegrated ("gushing") and reexperienced the blood-letting of her past injuries prompted her to want revenge. Knowing that she could not destroy me ("implacable granite," the same granite indifference that caused me to leave her), she anticipated that, with reunion, she would be calmed and would sleep. Yet during most of her analysis, she lived on the brink of fragmentation, "a bottle that breaks." When she struggled to control her rage, she needed to sit up and face me, feeling contained by eye contact. Often, she would be overstimulated by correct interpretations, would disorganize, and would miss subsequent sessions. At other times she would sob uncontrollably and be unable to leave the session until she could calm herself.

CONCLUSION

Many clinicians and theorists have challenged the premise of a destructive aggressive drive. Self psychology has clarified much of the confusion within psychoanalysis by proposing and clarifying the concept and experience of *narcissistic rage*. Most of us have found this to be a conceptually useful and therapeutically efficacious formulation.

The initial psychoeconomic explorations of narcissistic rage gave way to a greater emphasis on genetic and psychodynamic explanations. This chapter is an effort to remind ourselves of the clinical value of a psychoeconomic perspective: it helps us recognize and understand episodes of overstimulation and fragmentation and traumatic states, as well as the inhibitions, defenses, and resistances employed to maintain or regain self-cohesion and self-equilibrium.

Many episodes of narcissistic rage are characterized by specific dynamic issues and characterize how the self experiences the selfobject. Other violent, ragelike behavior denotes no psychodynamic content but results from an overwhelmed psychic apparatus in need of containment and control. Although the person seems angry and may feel angry at being overwhelmed and not managed, anger is not the issue; dysregulation is. Such fragmentation may occur in the hospital or in the analytic office. People may be enraged because of specific transference issues, or they may be enraged because the therapist has permitted the disintegration to happen; or they may appear enraged when they are actually fragmented and dazed, or they may appear distant and enraged but are immobilized and incapacitated in an attempt to preserve cohesion.

Therapists try to understand the psychodynamic and genetic experiences that underlie these episodes. They try to empathize as well with the patient's predicament of often (or always) being on the verge of collapse, even in the presence of an attuned selfobject, sometimes precisely because that selfobject is in contact.

If the therapist can maintain the proper empathic stance and recognize the patient's plight, "cool white air" will again fill the "mind with healing space" and composure will return.

REFERENCES

Freud, A. (1972), Comments on aggression. *Internat. J. Psycho-Anal.*, 53:163–171.

Freud, S. (1917), The Common neurotic state (Lecture 24) in Introductory lectures on psycho-analysis. *Standard Edition*, 16:378–391. London: Hogarth Press, 1963.

Gedo, J. & Goldberg, A. (1973), *Models of the Mind*. Chicago: University of Chicago Press.

Kernberg, O. (1975), *Borderline Conditions and Pathological Narcissism*. New York: Aronson.

Kohut, H. (1951), Discussion of " The Function of the Analyst in the Therapeutic Process" by Samuel D. Lipton. In: *The Search for the Self, Vol. 1*, ed. P. Ornstein. New York: International Universities Press, 1978, pp. 159–166.

_____ (1957), Observations on the psychological functions of music. In: *The Search for the Self, Vol. 1*, ed. P. Ornstein. New York: International Universities Press, 1978, pp. 233–253.

_____ (1959), Introspection, empathy and psychoanalysis: An examination of the relationship between mode of observation and theory. In: *The Search for the Self, Vol. 1*, ed. P. Ornstein. New York: International Universities Press, 1978, pp. 205–232.

_____ (1971), *The Analysis of the Self*. New York: International Universities Press.

_____ (1972), Thoughts on narcissism and narcissistic rage. In: *The Search for the Self, Vol. 2*, ed. P. Ornstein. New York: International Universities Press, 1978, pp. 615–658.

_____ (1978), Self psychology and the sciences of man. In: *The Search for the Self, Vol. 3*, ed. P. Ornstein. New York: International Universities Press, 1990, pp. 235–260.

_____ (1981), Introspection, empathy, and the semicircle of mental health. In: *The Search for the Self, Vol. 4*, ed. P. Ornstein. New York: International Universities Press, 1991, pp. 537–260.

_____ (1984), *How Does Analysis Cure?* ed. A. Goldberg & P. Stepansky. Chicago: University of Chicago Press.

Lichtenberg, J. D. (1983), *Psychoanalysis and Infant Research*. Hillsdale, NJ: The Analytic Press.

Marohn, R. C. (1974), Trauma and the delinquent. *Adolesc. Psychiat.*, 3:354–361.

_____ Dalle-Molle, D., McCarter, E. & Linn, D. (1980), *Juvenile Delinquents: Psychodynamic Assessment and Hospital Treatment*. New York: Brunner/Mazel.

_____ _____ Offer, D. & Ostrov, E. (1973), A hospital riot: Its determinants and implications for treatment. *Amer. J. Psychiat.*, 130:631–636.

Ornstein, P. (1978) Introduction: The evolution of Heinz Kohut's psychoanalytic psychology of the self. In: *The Search for the Self, Vol. 1*, ed. P. Ornstein. New York: International Universities Press, pp. 1–106.

Redl, F. & Wineman, D. (1957), *The Aggressive Child*. Glencoe, IL: The Free Press.

Stechler, G. (1987), Clinical applications of a psychoanalytic systems model of assertion and aggression. *Psychoanal. Inq.*, 7:348–363.

_____ & Halton, A. (1987), The emergence of assertion and aggression during infancy: A psychoanalytic systems approach. *J. Amer. Psychoanal. Assn.*, 35:821–838.

Stern, D. N. (1985), *The Interpersonal World of the Infant*. New York: Basic Books.

Terman, D. (1975), Aggression and narcissistic rage: A clinical elaboration. *The Annual of Psychoanalysis*, 3:239–255. New York: International Universities Press.

Wolf, E. (1988), *Treating the Self: Elements of Clinical Self Psychology*. New York: Guilford Press.

Chapter 12

Chronic Rage from Underground: Reflections on Its Structure and Treatment

Paul H. Ornstein

In his *Notes from Underground*[1] Dostoyevski (1864) presents us with an unparalleled portrayal of his protagonist's chronic rage. This rage resides mostly within, a private inner experience that nevertheless dominates all behavior from its internal hiding place. Only occasionally does the rage burst forth into open, violent, vindictive, and revengeful attacks on those whose real or imagined slights create immense suffering for the protagonist. This suffering (as silent to the external observer as the rage it provokes) is marked by a subjectively painful sense of humiliation and degradation; by pervasive hypochondriacal preoccupations; by a constant elaboration of the most detailed plans for revenge to right even the slightest, but greatly magnified, wrong; and, most significantly, by a whole series of behaviors that we would undoubtedly judge from the outside as self-defeating but that Dostoyevski illuminates from the inside as desperate attempts to regain lost self-regard. All these reactions are embedded in the context of a pervasive sense of superiority and self-importance, which exists side by side with a sense of utter worthlessness and unbearable shame.

Dostoyevski lets the fictitious author of *Notes* reveal his agonies in the first person, thereby lending these compulsively honest, often monotonously repetitious, yet courageous and cogent self-revelations

---

[1] The literal translation of the original Russian title is, more accurately, "Notes from a Hole in the Floor," i.e., from a mousehole.

a particular urgency and dramatic intensity. This succeeds in drawing the reader inside the whole experience, inside every detail of it. The immediacy of the communication in the first person is so compelling that we cannot emerge from the reading of these notes (or from listening to them on tape, as I have recently done) unscathed. A whole gamut of reactions is mobilized in the process, as if we were listening to a patient's free associations. And we can completely extricate ourselves neither from the "underground man's" revelations nor from our own affect-laden reactions to them. We admire him for being able to see so clearly into every nook and cranny of his inner world, but we get frustrated and annoyed that all this power of observation, all this cogent knowledge, is unable to move him out of his self-defeating behavior. We get bored with the repetitiousness of his reacting to such minuscule slights with such huge investments of energy in planning his revenge; we see that it brings him no relief, whether he is able to go through with his revengeful act or not. If he does act, he agonizes over having done it; and if he does not, he ends up in endless recriminations for his cowardliness. There is no escape for him from self-loathing and self-torment. His constant inner dialogue with those who already harmed him in the past and with those who inevitably will in the future takes up every moment of his waking hours and animates his inextinguishable memories of a lifetime of insults and injuries.

Notes from Underground reads as if Dostoyevski were familiar with "Thoughts on Narcissism and Narcissistic Rage" (Kohut, 1972). In fact, Dostoyevski has provided us with an independent data base of observations and interpretations that not only buttresses our own but actually fills in many of the details not yet fully articulated in our literature. These "notes" present a remarkably vivid, pertinent microscopic study of the personality structure and experiences of those who suffer from chronic rage.

But my goal here is not an exhaustive analysis of Dostoyevski's *Notes from Underground*, tempting as it would be to offer a comprehensive exploration of it in all its details. I have referred to it here only to set the stage for my brief remarks on some theoretical as well as clinical issues related to the broad topic of aggression and rage.

I shall first reflect briefly on Kohut's fundamental contributions to our understanding and treatment of aggression and narcissistic rage and then introduce a particularly difficult clinical problem in the analysis of a patient of mine, Mr. K, who has been feeling dominated by his chronic, silent rage and revengefulness and has long been presenting me with his own "notes from underground," to which it has often been difficult for me to find a sustained, optimum analytic response.

REFLECTIONS ON KOHUT'S FUNDAMENTAL CONTRIBUTIONS ON AGGRESSION AND RAGE

Kohut's (1972) "Thoughts on Narcissism and Narcissistic Rage" has long been considered one of his most brilliant contributions (see Ornstein and Ornstein, 1993). It is a veritable tour de force that further strengthened the core of his clinical and theoretical innovations, presented in *The Analysis of the Self* just one year earlier (Kohut, 1971). I have often regretted that he did not extend it to a monograph-length study with more detailed, lengthier clinical illustrations. But even in this relatively brief essay Kohut advanced a number of clinical and theoretical formulations that are to this very day the cornerstones of our approach to aggression and rage—even if some of them (since they were advanced prior to 1977) have to be reformulated or otherwise updated within the framework of an evolving psychology of the self. I need not review here what Kohut said in 1972, but I wish to review some of his key propositions in order to highlight why they are of such fundamental significance and to indicate in what areas they need further empirical validation as well as conceptual clarification.

It is remarkable that although he did not assemble his experiences and ideas about narcissistic rage into a monograph, Kohut did deal rather systematically with this topic: He offered an encompassing classification; he postulated the etiology and pathogenesis of narcissistic rage and of a whole spectrum of related phenomena; and, finally, he outlined the principles of treatment and portrayed the gradual transformation of narcissistic rage into mature aggression. I shall comment in passing on each of these three main areas.

Classification

Kohut constructed a spectrum of rage experiences, starting with fleeting annoyance and anger at one end and culminating in the furor of the catatonic and the grudges of the paranoiac at the other. The spectrum includes additional forms of rage, such as the well-known "catastrophic reaction" of the brain-damaged and its many attenuated variations, as well as the child's reaction to painful injuries, and Kohut left it to further empirical research to delineate still other forms.

Kohut viewed narcissistic rage as just one specific band in this whole spectrum, but because he considered this the best-known among all related phenomena, he designated the entire spectrum as narcissistic rage. This has created some ambiguity and has led to the frequent question, Is all aggression narcissistic rage? Yes, from our current perspective I would say that all destructive aggression is at its roots narcissistic rage—whatever its outward manifestation, however mild or severe, acute or chronic. Kohut (1972) himself wrote that "underlying all these emotional states [within the spectrum] is the uncompromising insistence on the perfection of the idealized selfobject and on the limitless power and knowledge of the grandiose self" (p. 643). This "dynamic essence" of narcissistic rage is common to all experiences within the broad spectrum of rage phenomena, from the mildest and most fleeting to the most persistent and destructive.

Note that Kohut did not construct a spectrum from mature aggression at one end to the most destructive rage at the other, arranging these phenomena on a continuum, the usual analytic approach in portraying drive-related phenomena being to place the normal at one end of a spectrum and the pathological at the other. Instead, in 1972 Kohut properly contrasted narcissistic rage with mature aggression and thereby indicated their separate origins and development. Once he replaced the concept of mature (or nondestructive) aggression with self-assertiveness (or self-assertive ambition), he further sharpened the view that the latter was primary and the former was secondary or reactive and that the two were clearly not within the same developmental line.

Thus, we can reaffirm that it is appropriate to speak of the various forms of rage as all belonging under the umbrella of narcissistic rage and contrast these with self-assertiveness. To label one specific band in the spectrum as well as the whole spectrum itself as narcissistic rage has the advantage of indicating the commonality or fundamental characteristic of all phenomena included in the spectrum. It would be desirable, however, to find an equally evocative but more fitting designation to finally leave behind the now-ambiguous and undesirable term *narcissistic*.[2]

---

[2]In a more comprehensive discussion of our nosology I would draw the analogy between Freud's 1937 assessment of the entire spectrum of psychopathology, from the neuroses at one end through the various personality disorders in the middle to the psychoses at the other end, using the parameter of qualitatively different structural changes in the ego. Freud described the ego in psychoses as characterized by a structural defect, in personality disorders by a structural deformity, and in the neuroses—where the ego was hitherto considered intact—by a structural modification. Each of these ego alterations was then specified. Kohut did the same in 1977 when he

Etiology and Pathogenesis

It is in relation to the etiology and pathogenesis of narcissistic rage and its experiential content that Kohut made his most innovative contributions. While many analysts before him had given up the notion of aggression as a drive and considered it as arising second-arily due to frustration, Kohut specified both the matrix from which the rage arose and the structural and dynamic conditions under which this occurred. He pinpointed various kinds of traumatic injuries to the grandiose self and traumatic obstacles to merger with the idealized parent imago and thus located the propensity for rage within this highly vulnerable, archaic, narcissistic matrix of the personality. In this connection he elaborated in some detail on the experiential content of the various forms of narcissistic rage.

The 1972 essay fits in with and also buttresses the conceptual edifice that Kohut (1971) built in *The Analysis of the Self*. The key point he made is this: It is not the rage as an intensification and unbridled expression of the aggressive drive that is the essence of the pathol-ogy; the essence of the pathology is the underlying structural deficiency of the self – its vulnerability and periodic, transient collapse in response to certain types of injury. The implication is clear: We do not achieve a direct transformation of narcissistic rage into healthy self-assertiveness. To the degree that we can restore the structural integrity of the self it will gradually become capable of asserting itself and pursuing its ambition. To the degree that it still suffers from enfeeblement or periodic fragmentation it will continue to show a propensity for rage reactions as a consequence of fragmentation and/or efforts at restitution. In other words, self-assertiveness is a function of the healthy self whereas rage is a function of a vulnerable, structurally deficient self.

---

assessed the entire spectrum of psychopathology using the parameter of qualitatively different structural changes in the self. He described the self in the psychoses as fragmented (never having attained cohesiveness); in the personality disorders as enfeebled and/or fragmentation-prone (but having at one time been cohesive); and, finally, in the neuroses as cohesive (with sufficient stability) but capable – under the impact of traumata during the oedipal phase – of becoming secondarily enfeebled or fragmented. The main point is that each component of the spectrum of psychopa-thology can profitably be viewed from this perspective as a self disorder at bottom, albeit with qualitative differences in both phenomenology and structure.

In a more thorough reassessment of our nosology the impact of Kohut's 1978 postulate that we need selfobjects from birth to death, i.e., that development proceeds from archaic to mature selfobjects, would also have to be considered. Would then the assumption that the mature selfobject replaces the "object" in our theoretical discourse (Ornstein, 1991) further affect our nosology of rage?

Treatment Principles

Psychoanalysts frequently assert that there is only one way to understand psychopathology, namely, analytically – and they have in mind their own preferred psychoanalytic paradigm for this purpose – but that there are many ways to treat the patient. While this may well be a widespread attitude, I see it as a special advantage of Kohut's formulations that his nosology (including etiology and pathogenesis), as well as his dynamic and structural considerations, leads directly to the treatment principles he espoused. There is in his work a closely intertwined connection between theory and practice. Thus, it logically follows from his view of rage that it is the underlying self disorder per se that occupies center stage within the psychoanalytic or psychotherapeutic process via the particular selfobject transference. The interpretive emphasis in the working through is on the disturbances that produce the rage and/or on how the rage is used to prevent further disintegration or to attempt to restore the integrity of the self.[3]

Certain forms of chronic rage, walled off from being experienced by the patient and from reaching direct expression in the transference, present particular difficulties in the treatment process. It is to such a difficulty that I shall now turn with the aid of a brief clinical example.

I hope to illustrate aspects of the nature of the particular self disorder in which the patient's chronic rage was embedded. Along with that I wish to show that the usual effort of focusing on the repair of the various kinds of disruptions of the mirror transference (rather than seeking direct access to the rage), when successful, regularly diminished the outward manifestations of the hidden rage to a good degree. The patient would behave in a calmer, more integrated fashion but would still bitterly complain about not feeling anything or not really participating in his own inner experiences, and he would again, at the next disruption, feel nothing of his rage. It was only after the discovery of an attitude in myself – a somewhat camouflaged reluctance or reserve vis-à-vis the patient's concrete mirroring needs

---

[3]Critics have claimed that self psychologists do not deal with narcissistic rage interpretively but, instead, bypass it. These critics are superficially accurate in that we pay no direct interpretive attention to tracing the source of the rage to the aggressive drive at various developmental levels (oral, anal, phallic, and oedipal) – if that is what is meant by its analytic interpretation. That our interpretations focus on the surrounding psychopathology and its amelioration – with salutary consequences for decreasing the propensity for rage – has thus far not altered this particular criticism. Nor have the critics acknowledged that this is primarily an empirical question.

and demands—that locked in his inability to feel his rage or to participate in any of his own experiences that further progress could be made. The patient sensed this reservation no matter how much I acknowledged the legitimacy of his archaic needs and demands. This discovery and the changes I was able to make in my approach as a result were followed by a slow transformation of the patient's archaic expectations for concrete, overt responses for mirroring into an expectation that I should know precisely and accept without reservation all of his feelings, needs, and demands (and give evidence of this acceptance through my emotional presence with him!). It was only then that a prolonged stalemate began to be resolved.

MR. K'S PERVASIVE, CHRONIC UNDERGROUND[4] RAGE

In Mr. K's prolonged and arduous analysis his profound and persistent hunger for mirroring appeared to be the central theme. For quite some time, however, this remained hidden and unavailable to our joint analytic scrutiny. No matter what the varied contents of his free associations were, our joint effort at their elucidation was frequently greeted by one of the following remarks, uttered with painful resignation: "That didn't work for me" or "That failed for me completely." Since our understanding appeared to hit the mark just moments before, I was often quite puzzled. "In what way did it not work?" I asked. Mr. K had no immediate response. It took a while to discover that the failure related to the fact that Mr. K secretly expected some sign of explicit appreciation of his considerable interpretive skills, his scrupulous honesty in not holding back anything, or the precision and fearlessness with which he could describe inner experience, even of the most disturbing kind. It was these that he wished to show off; the actual content was of lesser significance. What we finally understood in this phase of the analysis was that Mr. K cared little about what he alone or we jointly discovered—although he sharply objected to every inaccuracy regarding his subjective experiences that I may have introduced into our analytic conversation. What mattered to him was whether or not he could feel that I truly appreciated what he brought to the session. If he felt that I was not with him in his (often considerably subdued or hidden) excitement but maintained an analytic neutrality, as he viewed it, the failure was disturbing to him and its consequences would last for days or weeks.

---

[4]*Underground* symbolically refers here to the hidden, sequestered, or walled-off "depth of his soul," as Mr. K frequently put it. It is where his rage resides and where he cannot get to it. He does not feel the rage; he cannot experience it or connect to it, but he knows it is there.

He would become withdrawn, apathetic, and without energy. He would then speak in a colorless monotone for a while, without his usual vivid imagery and richly expressive metaphors. This would tone me down too, and Mr. K would then rightly point to my "apathy," no matter how slight—and often not even recognized by me until his comment on it or until it dawned on me that he was holding up a mirror to me with his own behavior to express how he experienced me. Nothing was more effective in reestablishing good communication or in repairing the breach in the mirror transference than when I could show him what in my attitude, tone of voice, or behavior he experienced as hurtful to him and would then say that he was portraying this feeling of having been assaulted in his own behavior toward me. This not only made good sense to him, but he also experienced it as an accepting stance on my part. He did not feel criticized for behaving the way he did or feel he was being asked to modify his own behavior—which is how his parents always responded ("You shouldn't feel this way!"). Thus, repair could be established and Mr. K's inner rage would temporarily subside. I say "inner rage" again because he could not *feel* the rage. He only knew that he acted on it because his behavior revealed it to him.

An example will illustrate what I mean. Mr. K started one early morning session with an apathetic demeanor and a long silence. It was difficult to get going and we could make no headway until I realized that his nonparticipation might have been triggered by something that transpired between us. On my way to the waiting room a few minutes earlier I had suddenly realized, with some concern, that I had forgotten to prepare for an important meeting later that day. Preoccupied briefly with this thought, I did not have a receptive smile for Mr. K on encountering him. When I inquired at first in general terms as to what might have triggered his withdrawal, we got nowhere. When I suggested that his gloomy demeanor perhaps reflected how he experienced me on entering the waiting room, he immediately confirmed my assumption. He added that whenever he felt that he was not eagerly met but only "routinely" invited into the office, he rebelled against being there: "If you are not present [emotionally], I won't be either. I will not come out of my rabbit hole into a vacuum, it is dangerous for me." He then elaborated at great length on the poisonous atmosphere at home during his infancy and childhood, and it became clearer how the analytic situation at times inadvertently replicated for him his early environment.

It was henceforth somewhat easier for both of us to discern and deal with disruptions and repair. After we recovered from such an episode, however, the cycle would soon begin again. I admired Mr. K's tenacity and his, in many subtle ways, unextinguished hopefulness in the face of repeated "failures," and I hoped that he would ultimately sense my full appreciation of him and what he was accomplishing in gaining a better sense of the nature of his inner experiences. What I still found myself reluctant to do was to offer him an unrestrained, explicit admiration—at times it seemed he wanted that escalated into outright jubilation—for his, admittedly, great analytic feats of remarkable insightfulness, especially in relation to his ingenious interpretation of his dreams. I was reacting to the fact that there was no carryover from one such apparently successful session to the next. It was as if in each session trust had to be built up again from the beginning.

Only much later did it become clear to me that since I truly admired Mr. K in many ways, I had expected him to discover this without my having to prove it to him at every turn. But before I knew this as explicitly as I am relating it now, my expectation that he should discover it had become a countertransference obstacle in the analytic process. As was usually the case, Mr. K helped me discover it, which ameliorated it somewhat. His frequent bouts of emotional withdrawal—his "defiant nonpresence in the room," as he put it—tipped me off. I could see his withholding and reluctance, expressions of his unforgiving, chronic rage, as a magnified reproduction of what he accurately perceived as some reservation or reluctance on my part to give him the explicit admiration he craved. He once characterized my withholding explicit approval and appreciation for some brilliant work he had done in the session as the same "arrogance [his] father would show under similar circumstances." The word arrogance—as you might imagine—prevented me for a time from seeing its relevance, that is until I could calmly reflect on the fact that I held a certain view as to what was a proper analytic response and to the degree that I held that view, I could not listen to him from his vantage point without reservation. I then no longer bristled at his description of my behavior as arrogance. (If Breuer had refused to follow Anna O's request that he listen to everything she had to say in a particular way, she might rightly have called him arrogant and given up treatment. Where is the limit to the extent to which we have to follow the patient's need [request or demand] for a certain kind of responsiveness in order to enable the analytic process to move forward—and without which it would stagnate? Who can tell? And why is it so difficult to find it?)

Whenever the issue of my "withholding" could be included in the analytic conversation, there were, at least temporarily, some salutary effects. At other times Mr. K insisted that withdrawal and nonpresence constituted a baseline state for him and that this could change only after we established "rapport" (an emotional presence on my part that then—and only then—allowed him to be present) in the session. Only under these conditions could he climb out of his "rabbit hole." Otherwise, he would have to remain emotionally absent.

During some stretches of this period, Mr. K would sense my "presence" only when he felt enough of an appreciation and affirmation from me through my tone of voice (to which he was very sensitive), the amount I talked (the more I did, the more valued and valuable he felt), and the number of "genuine" questions I asked (the greater the number of questions, the more he could feel my participation in his struggle; otherwise, he felt alone with it). The accuracy or correctness of my understanding mattered little, and that rankled me at times, even if only mildly. Mr. K could acknowledge my having hit the nail on the head—"but only intellectually," he would add; something was always missing. Only the absence of appreciation and affirmation was registered and put on the ledger, rarely to be forgotten. Mr. K experienced these episodes as devastating. He could not imagine that my repeated "stupidity" or "callousness" was not a deliberate attempt to foil his efforts, put him in his place, humiliate him, a belief that chronically fed his rage.

What sustained me in the interim, nevertheless, was the fact that while these ruptures were frequent, painful, and lasting, the efforts at repair always yielded significant memories from the past as well as some additional understanding of what was going on in his experiences with me, namely, how I affected him and how he needed to protect himself from feeling "foiled, defeated, and humiliated."

To give you just one telling example from this period: Mr. K would frequently pepper his free associations (whatever the content, to which I was listening attentively) with some hurried, offhanded, "tucked away" remark about a physical sensation he was just having—such as "My anus is tense now" or "There is a cramp in my rear end"—and would then, without stopping, go on with whatever he was talking about. When I would later on recap what he said and try to make sense of it, he would have two strenuous objections. I almost said "violent objections," but this was precisely the problem; he could not feel his rage at me, just as on the many occasions when he spoke of his inordinate rage at his mother and father (for their emotional distance and other more specific hurtful behaviors) he was unable to make contact with the rage on an experiential level by feeling it and owning it. He only "knew" that he was enraged. His first objection was that I was trying to make sense of what he said instead of just registering it and letting him know that I heard it (this is reminiscent of Kohut's [1971, pp. 283–293] Ms. F). He wanted me to first ask him what sense *he* made of it; otherwise, he felt "annihilated" by my comments and felt that I was appropriating his thoughts for my purposes, leaving him with nothing. His second objection was that I did not pick up and reflect his reference to his anal sensations. He felt that this was a deliberate disregard of him and that it meant that I was as repulsed by his anal references as his mother had been in wiping the feces off him in his infancy and childhood, a response that contributed, he believed, to his feeling like a "repulsive little shit" ever since. Furthermore, Mr. K insisted that those few references to his body and its functions were the only real "feeling-communications," that the rest was all unreal (from his left brain) and of little consequence in this analytic endeavor. It was not knowledge that he lacked but an ability to put thoughts and feelings together, or, as he put it, "to experience fully and own what was going on inside of [him]." It was late in this phase of the analysis that I translated his many references to his anal sensations as his relentless efforts at getting connected to his archaic mother. My earlier frequent misses thwarted this development of finally understanding the meaning of the patient's side-remarks, whereas my subsequent alertness to them enhanced progress.

Through numerous such incidents we learned that Mr. K was putting himself forward for acceptance and approval in this tentative and cautious way, and that my "nonresponse" to his side remarks about his bodily sensations were therefore understandably devastating to him. It was as if I did not permit feelings to enter our relationship; I was putting obstacles in the way of his establishing "rapport" with me and was thereby keeping him at a distance and preventing him from bringing the two-year-old walled-off child in him together with the adult.

It was evident from the beginning of the analysis that Mr. K's numerous "dysfunctions" (as he called them)—his inability to attend to trivial household chores, finish important tasks he began to work on, pay his bills on time, and so forth—were almost lifelong behavioral expressions of his rage and revengefulness at his parents, particularly his mother. They were also his defiance vis-à-vis his coercive father and his expressed profound need to extract from his parents, in fantasy, what they never gave him and what he felt he could not go on without. This attitude and behavior led him to an elaborate fantasy, his "symbiotic scenario," in which he had to obtain from the outside what he never received from his parents: a feeling of being valued (and thereby gaining self-regard and a sense of personal

dignity and worthwhileness). These became central themes in the
transference, and Mr. K's rage became focused around his frustrations in obtaining them in the analytic situation.

I shall now move quickly across a prolonged time span. I recognized that it was not enough to acknowledge the legitimacy of Mr. K's
archaic needs in words, no matter how much I believed in the
sincerity of my own acceptance of them. The words of acknowledgment had to reflect genuine receptivity to the emergence of these needs
in the transference, whatever form they took. This was not always easy
to convey. Mr. K had to feel the genuineness of my receptivity, the
absence of any reluctance or reservation, in order to experience
himself as genuine and to be able to connect to his inner feelings—but
not yet to his rage. His expectations in this new phase were clearly
articulated by him at the tail end of a prolonged effort to repair a
painful disruption. He wanted to feel free to lambast me and express
his rage (even if only in words without feeling), and he wanted me
"to accompany [him] into the depth of [his] abyss, without criticism
and intolerance for [his] fury." He was confident that if he could feel
that I was with him without reservation and without reluctance, he
could make contact with whatever he would find there.

Mr. K found an apt metaphor to help me accompany him on this
journey into his "underground": he wanted to pull up to the screen
of the analysis all that he saw there and have me witness it, accept it,
and thereby help him detoxify it. He did not want me to *do* anything
about it except to perfectly reflect his inner experiences. Such a
reflection, he believed, would make them real for him, with a good
chance that he would then be able to own them with feeling and then,
hopefully, let go of them. After what we had been through before,
this was an easier task to follow, I thought. And for a while it was. But
the demand for perfect attunement still leads to painful disruptive
episodes. Occasionally, Mr. K reflects on the fact that he is now able
to feel "somewhat better connected" to me and hence also to his own
inner self.

CONCLUDING REMARKS

Among the many lessons I have learned from my work with Mr. K
and have illustrated in this chapter, several stand out as of fundamental importance. Although Mr. K undoubtedly suffered from
lifelong "dysfunctions" (see also Ornstein, 1987, p. 91), he began his
second analysis with me with a certain intensity of hope that he could
overcome them. In spite of the fact that he built around himself a

"defensive wall of apparent tranquility . . . maintained with the aid of social isolation, detachment, and fantasied superiority" (Kohut, 1972, p. 646), he began on the couch as if this wall did not exist. Only after the first major disruption of his quickly developing mirror transference did it seem to have been brought visibly into play. Mr. K's fear of becoming retraumatized kept him behind his wall, with repeated, subtle (indeed, to me often barely recognizable) forays outside his wall to extract the appreciation and validation he felt I was deliberately withholding. When I would inadvertently miss these efforts—rather than notice, explicitly welcome, and admire them— Mr. K felt justified in retreating again.

It would be an easy way out to say simply that at that point in the analysis Mr. K's transference "clicked in" and we were dealing with the inevitable. While this is true, this does not permit us the proper "reparative" focus. It is more important for the treatment process to center on those elements of the current precipitants for the disruptions that are truly unwelcome intrusions into the treatment process, some of which can and should be remedied by the analyst. These intrusions may be classified as countertransference phenomena, inadequate understanding of the nature of the patient's subjective experience, or incorrect application of existing theory and treatment principles. The term *failure* in describing analytic interventions that lead to severe disruptions has become very unpopular—to the detriment of progress in the theory of treatment and in refining the analyst's proper responsiveness.

The question of how to deal with persistent demands for the concrete satisfaction of various archaic mirroring needs—the question, in other words, of whether the self-psychologically informed analyst should actually mirror his patients or not—is a frequent one, and the available answers are not always clear-cut. Mr. K provided me with some additional guidelines, worthy of further empirical study. A less reserved response to his initial demands for mirroring (of the sort that Kohut acceded to with Ms. F?) might well have prevented the escalation of these demands to the point of a transference–countertransference stalemate. A tonally expressed emotional receptivity on my part—which I thought was there from the beginning but which he experienced as missing—might well have led us much earlier to the point where Mr. K could accept me as a validating witness to his experiences rather than as someone concretely fitting in with his archaic "symbiotic scenario," a function with which I obviously had some difficulty.

The manifestations of Mr. K's chronic rage, as would be expected, fluctuated very much in accordance with whether he felt my "receptive and willing presence" or not. They were clearly secondary to disruptive experiences in the transference and were both consequences of these disruptions as well as relentless retaliations for them. Simultaneously, they were also efforts to get reconnected to me and to attempt to extract penance: "I need a dignity payment from you, because you defeated me and humiliated me," he said. At least in words, if not yet in feeling, at the point where my narrative ends Mr. K is able to express his fury unsparingly. Nothing appears to ameliorate his rage, however, more consistently than "establishing rapport," his phrase for getting emotionally reconnected to me.

POSTSCRIPT

In comparing the protagonist of Dostoyevski's novel and Mr. K, there is one striking observation that immediately attracts the attention of the clinician: both are highly expressive in words, images, and metaphors, and both have an extraordinary degree and quality of insight—without this being a leverage for change.

The man from underground is deeply locked into a chronic, repetitive cycle of behavior and experiences that constantly validate his negative self-assessment, a situation that only reinforces his rage and revengefulness. He strives to improve his situation and relationships, but he cannot elicit the desired responses from his environment that would, it may seem to the reader, make internal change possible. He is on the verge of reaching out to others on a few occasions, but these end disastrously. The man's narrative ends abruptly with this sentence: "I've had enough of writing these *Notes from Underground*." Dostoyevski appends the following remarks: "Actually the notes of this lover of paradoxes do not end here. He couldn't resist and went on writing. But we are of the opinion that one might just as well stop here" (p. 203), indicating that there has been no movement thus far and there will be none.

Mr. K, on the other hand, struggles with establishing a different kind of relationship from his previous ones in the treatment situation. He rightly expects that the therapist's responsiveness will make a difference. If that responsiveness catalyzes Mr. K's ability to connect to his inner feelings, to undo his internal polarization (as he describes it), and if his feelings from underground then emerge into an analytic milieu of safety and are greeted with acceptance rather than being recoiled from (even if ever so mildly), a process of change may be initiated that predominant emphasis on insight cannot achieve.

REFERENCES

Dostoyevski, F. (1864), *Notes from Underground* (new translation with afterword by Andrew MacAndrew). New York: Penguin Books, 1961.

Freud, S. (1937), Analysis terminable and interminable. *Standard Edition*, 23:216–253. London: Hogarth Press, 1964.

Kohut, H. (1971), *The Analysis of the Self*. New York: International Universities Press.

_____ (1972), Thoughts on narcissism and narcissistic rage. In: *The Search for the Self*, Vol. 2, ed. P. H. Ornstein. New York: International Universities Press, 1978, pp. 615–658.

_____ (1977), *The Restoration of the Self*. New York: International Universities Press.

_____ (1978), Reflections on advances in self psychology. In: *Advances in Self Psychology*, ed. A. Goldberg. New York: International Universities Press, 1980, pp. 473–554.

Ornstein, P. H. (1987), On self-state dreams in the psychoanalytic treatment process. In: *The Interpretation of Dreams in Clinical Work*, ed. A. Rothstein. Madison, CT: International Universities Press, pp. 87–104.

_____ (1991), Why self psychology is not an object relations theory: Clinical and theoretical considerations. In: *The Evolution of Self Psychology. Progress in Self Psychology*, Vol. 7, ed. A. Goldberg. Hillsdale, NJ: The Analytic Press, pp. 17–29.

_____ & Ornstein, A. (1993), Assertiveness, anger, rage, and destructive aggression: A perspective from the treatment process. In: *Rage, Power, and Aggression*, ed. R. A. Glick & S. P. Roose. New Haven, CT: Yale University Press.

Chapter 13

Commentary on Marohn's "Rage Without Content" and Ornstein's "Chronic Rage from Underground"

Mark J. Gehrie

Marohn begins by reminding us of the problems in the conceptualizations of aggression that have vexed psychoanalysts since Freud. He reminds us that Kohut borrowed much from classical drive theory in his own conceptualization of aggression, in particular, the economic aspect of the concept and the idea that pleasure and unpleasure relate to discharge and inhibition, respectively. In one of his most famous and evocative works, "Thoughts on Narcissism and Narcissistic Rage," Kohut (1972) described narcissistic rage as a psychoeconomic imbalance arising from "the noncompliance of the archaic selfobject" (p. 396). Marohn cites the continuity of this idea with Freud's concept of actual neurosis, although Freud did not link this imbalance with the particular failures of early caretakers.

Marohn's argument has two prominent threads: First, as did Kohut, Marohn relates the phenomenon of aggressive expression to disruption of the self, where the state of the self is dependent upon the quality of the selfobject environment. The parental selfobjects are understood as responsible, developmentally speaking, for the optimal structuralization of the child's psyche via their attentiveness to fundamental selfobject needs of the child. Failures in such caretaking are evidenced in rageful (or depressive or sexualized or whatever) breakthroughs, or "disintegration products," related to the drives (Kohut, 1977). The second thread is about cure: In treatment these "inevitable" experiences—that is, the "empathic breaks"—are what gets treated, not the expression of the rage itself. In other words, a

159

psychoeconomic imbalance is treated by addressing the presumed source of that imbalance: a disturbance in the balancing effect of the self–selfobject matrix. Optimal selfobject responses are understood as both maintaining the (internal) environment (in the developing child) for structuralization and providing a background for the management of self disruptions so that they do not become traumatic. Analogously, that kind of empathically balanced environment during an analysis is understood as providing a similar kind of developmental opportunity, via transmuting internalizations, as well as protection from traumatic repetitions during empathic breaks. Failures in this process, Marohn says, are seen clinically as "angry, rageful, and/or destructive feelings, affects, behaviors . . . [on a spectrum from] content-laden material with rich dynamics to, at the other extreme, the contentless with no specific dynamics, only vague forces, primitive in nature and suggestive of economic imbalance, a random energy discharge, and a state of near-chaos." He then adds that "points along the entire range of this spectrum can be understood from a self-psychology perspective . . . all pathology . . . is now assessed in the context of the self–selfobject relationship."

Marohn's concerns about early disruptions in the development of the self that lead to psychoeconomic imbalance and to states such as "contentless rage" direct our attention to a central and difficult issue in the theory of self psychology. While acknowledging that "not all injury leads to narcissistic rage" and also that some behaviors associated with psychoeconomic imbalances have "no content or psychodynamic meanings," Marohn maintains that it is *always* the self–selfobject dimension that is at the crux of the matter, regardless. In other words, he asserts (and, to be fair, so do a number of others), first, that the relevant level of damage is *always* this interpersonal aspect, that a psychoeconomic imbalance is always a product of the relationship with the therapist, and, second, that its treatment *always* involves the empathic repair of the "break" that led to the imbalance. Even in instances of what he calls "contentless rage" we must presume that at its root lies an empathic break in the relationship with the therapist. This view is maintained despite his own emphasis on the enormous developmental variation in the genesis of narcissistic rage—for example, from "primitive" to "structured"—and his citation of several clinical examples that suggest a broad range in meanings and significance of rageful experience.

How can so much developmental diversity be addressed from a single unitary view of the cause of the problem and yield to a single treatment modality? (see Gedo and Goldberg, 1973; Gedo, 1988, 1989). Taken at face value, this position exposes us to the same criticism that we have levied against classical analysts, whom we have accused of forcing all experience into the procrustean bed of oedipal conflicts. While we pay lip service to selfobject functioning along a developmental spectrum, from primitive to mature, our repertoire of understanding has remained rooted in the original transference configurations described by Kohut, which may not represent a complete picture of the elongated spectrum of disturbances in development that we now wish to pursue (Modell, 1986; Gedo, 1988). And in particular I refer to those very early states of disequilibrium, such as those that may account for what Dr. Marohn refers to as "contentless states," that may not have at their root a disturbance in the self–selfobject matrix. Might they not be profitably viewed, for example, as archaic transference states that are repeated in the analysis not because of an empathic break but, rather, because such states are expressions of a preexisting chronic condition of life the organization of which is primarily presymbolic? Under such circumstances it is not a question of "who did what" to create a difficulty but, rather, an experience such as being overwhelmed, for example, which is not necessarily always a function of selfobject failure in the present. The fact that such states might be kept at bay by extraordinary responses of the therapist is not evidence that the core level is being addressed (Gedo, 1988). Obviously, any data can be pushed to fit a paradigm, and it could be insisted that even "contentless overwhelmedness" must relate to a failure in early selfobject tension-regulating functions, for example. But is this consistent with the prescription that it must be the self–selfobject dimension in the treatment that automatically evokes this level of experience? Might there be some value to the concept of states such as these very early developmental disturbances being understood as formed in a primordial selfobject context and now an integral adaptive fixture of the psyche that a different kind of approach (i.e., not by addressing self–selfobject relations more likely to represent a later phase) is indicated if the core of the pathology is to be truly accessed? Rather, this kind of core pathology might first require dealing with the intervening layers of adaptation seen as effects of this adaptive fixture. If we must try to empathize with "the primitive, unstructured psyche," with the fragmentation, overstimulation, and so forth, that Dr. Marohn refers to, what does this mean? I suggest that it may not mean that all such phenomena should be lumped together with more structured experiences of self disorder and treated similarly. When in more structured states we know that our failures have precipitated a regression, we attempt to repair this damage by acknowledging our role in that process. However, to force this paradigm on much more primitive states of disorder, which may not have been caused by our failures and which may not represent regressions from a more integrated position, is tantamount to insisting that a single concept of disorder (with a single technique to treat it) is behind all the phenomena that we see (Gedo, 1988; Modell, 1989; Gehrie, in press).

Marohn is correct, I think, when he suggests that aggressive breakthroughs in a treatment situation may represent some failure in the selfobject bond, but, as I have said, I don't think that this need always be the case. Aggression is more than an indicator of psycho-economic imbalance, and defining it as such doesn't help us understand why today the expression of such an imbalance may be aggression and tomorrow (or with someone else) it may be sexual or something else. If we consider that aggression is a potential that always exists and that its expression may accompany a variety of self states, not just disorder, then perhaps some light may be shed on the problem of empathy that Marohn raises at the same time.

Suppose, for example, that in a given instance we are able to show that a patient suffering from traumatic and very early failures in caretaking was forced to identify with this primitive selfobject, in which case the tie was, objectively speaking, fundamentally negative. And suppose that this negative attachment supplied certain essential nutrients for life and led to a psychic organization of a particular quality. A well-to-do patient of mine from an upper-middle-class white family spends some volunteer time tutoring a black child from a background of poverty and deprivation. My patient often overhears telephone conversations at her Lake Shore Drive apartment between her young student and his mother, for he calls home to tell his mother about all the good stuff he's getting from his tutor: food, small gifts, excursions to various museums, and so on. The boy's mother reliably rages at and loudly threatens her son on these occasions, berating him for not bringing some of this wealth home to give to her or for not using the opportunity to get some gifts for her. Even at a polite distance my patient could overhear the mother yelling over the phone, and this scenario would be repeated at each visit. My shell-shocked patient once asked the boy after he hung up from one of these conversations how he could stand being yelled at like that all the time. He replied, "She's my mother," and returned to his lesson with an impassive expression. This mother is who this boy has, and his way of surviving with her could already have become an adaptive fixture contained within his self structure and not directly accessible via our usual approach.

Although this example is obviously incomplete, it sets the stage for considering that early and often fundamental ties with selfobjects may be negative and that this negativity must come to form an essential piece of the adaptive apparatus of the developing child. This would not be the result of a fragmented or fragmenting self but, rather, of a self organized around an adaptive strategy that permitted survival under otherwise unbearable circumstances (Gedo, 1981, 1988). Certainly, this point is not relevant to all or even many of the cases that we see, but in those instances to which Dr. Marohn refers as "unstructured primitive mental states" it may be that empathy requires a recognition of the role of the aggressive enactment in the patient's adaptive organization and that treatment of such patients may involve an engagement of that enactment on other levels. But more of that in another paper (Gehrie, in press).

Ornstein begins by reviewing Kohut's paper on narcissistic rage and highlights a critical question: Is all aggression narcissistic rage? Although Dr. Ornstein answers this in the affirmative, it is not clear to me that this is precisely what Kohut meant in the section that was cited. Kohut (1972) wrote:

> Strictly speaking, the term narcissistic rage refers to only one specific band in [a] wide spectrum of experiences . . . however, I shall use the term "a potiori" and refer to all the points in the spectrum as narcissistic rage, since with this designation we are referring to the most charac-teristic or best known of a series of experiences which. . . with all their differences, are essentially related to each other [p. 379].

Kohut goes on to inquire about the common elements in all these experiences. But to follow up on his other point we should also ask, What is different about them? If, as Ornstein says, the pathology is *always* the "underlying structural deficiency of the self—its vulnera-bility to and periodic, transient collapse in response to certain types of injury," then it follows that the interpretive emphasis should be "on the disturbances that produce the rage." But it is precisely this point that is at issue in the clinical example he gives and that I think is involved in the difficulties that presented themselves.

Ornstein is to be complimented on the sensitivity of his clinical description and, most particularly, on his devotion to his task. There seems to be not a fiber of his being that is not engaged in the continuous effort to understand and process perplexing experience. He presents this case as an instance of "underground rage" in which the usual approach "of focusing on the repair of the various kinds of disruptions of the mirror transference . . . regularly diminished the outward manifestations of the hidden rage to a good degree." No problem there, except that there doesn't appear to have been much improvement over the long term, and the cycle would keep repeating itself regardless of the extent to which Ornstein "acknowledged the legitimacy of [Mr. K's] archaic needs." Mr. K clearly needed more than empathy, in the usual sense, to deal with his injury, and what we hear is that he required "explicit appreciation . . . unrestrained, explicit admiration . . . [even] outright jubilation" in response to his demonstrated talents. To be sure, this was beyond the bounds of management in the mirror transference, in the ordinary sense.

Ornstein chose to focus on his own countertransference response to this situation and to his personal struggle to overcome his reluctance to offer such responses. Certainly, this is an admirable and essential self-analytic position that we all aspire to, that is, attempting to examine just how our own character may be interfering with the process. However, it may be that in instances like this one this is not the problem and that Ornstein's countertransference response was a sign, on the contrary, of something essential in himself: a gut-level recognition that to provide what this patient seemed to require—namely, an unrestrained form of mirroring in response to all levels of his archaic neediness—was to address a level of the patient's experience that was more a *product* of the core disturbance than it was the core issue itself, which has remained hidden behind the enactment in the transference. Ornstein's more perfect attunement, while temporarily assuaging Mr. K's archaic needs, had no reliably curative effect on its own. Indeed, the cycle seems to still be repeating itself despite Ornstein's campaign of self-improvement as a source of mirroring. It is not, I suggest, Ornstein's ability to finally overcome his countertransference limits in order to more clearly express his "true" admiration for his patient that is the essential issue in this case. Or even that Mr. K's inability to feel his rage is related to Ornstein's setting the stage so perfectly as to finally nurture its emergence.

Although I don't wish to second-guess Ornstein's assessment of his patient, I was struck by the power struggle involved in eliciting the desired response that appeared to be such a prominent dynamic in their relationship. In any case, we must keep in mind that the point behind the understanding that Dr. Ornstein is at such pains to provide is for Mr. K to realize the nature of his enactment in the negative transference. In no way is this the "easy way out." When primitive enactments are so global and seem inaccessible by ordinary means, then perhaps we must consider that access to such states may require a more flexible technique that accommodates the effects of the primitive adaptive strategy rather than presuming that our standard technique is being imperfectly applied.

Anyway, to get back to aggression, it seems likely to me that Mr. K's rages were more than a result of Ornstein's presumed empathic failures. (If they had been a result of such failure, Ornstein's perfectly acceptable empathy would have had the desired result.) I think we have to look at Mr. K's early history, particularly the nature of the "poisonous atmosphere" that he described, for more clues about the underlying nature of the pathology, the role that aggression plays in it, and the structure of his adaptive solution. Unfortunately, I do not have these data.

Finally, I must once more suggest that when a theoretical framework fails us under certain circumstances, it is not in the interest of science to insist that the only possible explanation is that it was imperfectly applied (Goldberg, 1988, 1990). We must, if we are to continue to grow, accept the possibility that our system may not *always* match the data, even if it does a good job much of the time. I think it remains prudent to maintain the position that aggression, whether it be experienced as narcissistic rage or healthy assertiveness, must be understood by us as a human potential that, along with other broad sources of biologically based experience, plays many kinds of organizing and expressive roles in our minds, roles that have yet to be well understood.

REFERENCES

Gedo, J. E. (1981), *Advances in Clinical Psychoanalysis*. New York: International Universities Press.
_____ (1988), *The Mind in Disorder*. Hillsdale, NJ: The Analytic Press.
_____ (1989), Self psychology: A post-Kohutian view. In: *Self Psychology: Comparisons and Contrasts*, ed. D. Detrick and & S. Detrick. Hillsdale, NJ: The Analytic Press, pp. 415–428.
_____ & Goldberg, A. (1973), *Models of the Mind*. Chicago: University of Chicago Press.
Gehrie, M. J. (in press), Psychoanalytic technique and the development of the capacity to reflect. *J. Amer. Psychoanal. Assn.*
Goldberg, A. (1988), *A Fresh Look at Psychoanalysis*. Hillsdale, NJ: The Analytic Press.
_____ (1990), *The Prisonhouse of Psychoanalysis*. Hillsdale, NJ: The Analytic Press.
Kohut, H. (1972), Thoughts on narcissism and narcissistic rage. *The Psychoanalytic Study of the Child*, 27:360–400. New York: Quadrangle Books.
_____ (1977), *The Restoration of the Self*. New York: International Universities Press.
Modell, A. (1986), The missing elements in Kohut's cure. *Psychoanal. Inq.*, 6:367–386.
_____ (1989), The psychoanalytic setting as a container of multiple levels of reality: A perspective on the theory of psychoanalytic treatment. *Psychoanal. Inq.*, 9:67–87.

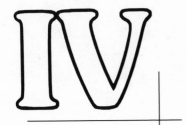

Clinical

Chapter 14

Mourning Theory
Reconsidered

R. Dennis Shelby

The inspiration for the beginning reformulation of mourning theory presented in this chapter came from two sources. The first was a research endeavor designed to reconstruct the experiences of gay men whose long-term partners contracted and died from acquired immunodeficiency syndrome (Shelby, 1992). The second was the considerable reformulation of clinical theory: the psychology of the self and long-overdue efforts to reexamine analytic theory in light of cognitive and linguistic theories.

The study design consisted of a series of open-ended interviews with well partners, ill partners, and surviving partners in long-term relationships impacted by AIDS. Individuals and couples were interviewed over a 9- to-12-month period. The interviews were then coded and analyzed according to the grounded theory method of Glaser and Strauss (1967) and Glaser (1975). This relatively open-ended interview approach, in which the study participants were asked to tell me what was going on in their lives versus answering my questions about their experience, yielded data not previously elucidated in the analytic literature on mourning: The first topic is the integral role other people play in facilitating the survivors' mourning process; the second concerns the impact on the mourning process of a surviving partner when he too is infected with the same agent that resulted in his partner's death.

Clinical theory has evolved considerably since the work of Pollock (1961) in which mourning was conceptualized as a realignment and

169

modification of the self-representation and object representation. Self psychology has gained an ever-increasing influence; analytic theorists such as Basch, Goldberg, and Palombo, in addition to their many contributions, have begun to reconsider analytic theory in light of cognitive and linguistic theories. Stern, drawing on infant research studies, has also challenged many of our long-held assumptions about the human mind and its development.

The results of the study and advances in clinical theory indicated that a beginning reformulation of our theory of mourning is in order, if not long overdue. The data also demand that attempts be made to give a theoretical accounting for the observed differences in the mourning experiences of seropositive and seronegative men. Though discussed in the context of a population of gay men whose lives have been irrevocably changed by the HIV virus, the theoretical formulations are applicable to mourning theory in general and offer a framework for understanding not only the experience of mourning per se but phenomena both environmental and intrapsychic that can interfere with the process.

To develop the framework I will discuss the development of psychoanalytic mourning theory, including the problems with the theory in general and for the understanding of gay men in particular; offer a more elaborated self-psychological model; and present two cases of surviving partners who were experiencing a complicated mourning process. One case involves a man who was seronegative for the HIV virus, the other a man who was seropositive. Hopefully, the cases and the discussion will illustrate the process of mourning and the complications in the mourning process often observed in seropositive surviving partners.

THE DEVELOPMENT OF MOURNING THEORY

The basic formulation regarding the nature of the mourning process that has guided our theoretical and clinical understanding for more than 70 years can be found in Freud's (1912–1913) work "Totem and Taboo": "Mourning has a quite specific task to perform: its function is to detach the survivor's memories and hopes from the dead. When this has been achieved the pain grows less, and with it the remorse and self reproach" (pp. 65–66). The two interrelated and enduring elements are the following: (1) Mourning concerns two central figures, the mourner and the deceased, or, more specifically, their memories, hopes, and affects. That is, mourning essentially concerns the meaning of the particular relationship and its loss. (2) Mourning is a process that, in an undistorted form, consists of a reorganization of the ego of the mourner. Essentially, the loss of a central person and the accompanying psychological manifestations of loss gradually move from a central, painful, and often overwhelming aspect of the survivor's experience to a less central affectively charged position. When this reorganization has been achieved, the survivor is able to again feel a part of the world of the living and has the psychological resources to actively participate in new love attachments.

With the publication of "Mourning and Melancholia" Freud (1917) laid out a theory of relationships, including their loss and subsequent role in the structuralization of the mind. The process consists of a libidinal cathexis to another person. With the loss of the person, the libidinal energy must be withdrawn. The ego initially protests and resists as this represents the abandonment of a libidinal position. In successful mourning the object is eventually preserved in the form of an identification and libidinal energy is available for new attachments. In pathological mourning, or melancholia, the object is not decathected owing to unresolvable ambivalence; rather, the libido is withdrawn into the ego and the ambivalence toward the lost object becomes an aspect of the ego's structure.

Pollock (1961), using the framework of analytic ego psychology, describes the mourning process as a gradual realignment of the self-representation and the object representation, which are intrapsychic counterpoints to the individual's experience of the world. Object representations consist of the images and experiences with individuals to whom the person has formed an attachment, while self-representations consist of images and experiences the person has of himself. Over the course of the life cycle, reality calls for modifications in both self and object representations. In the case of mourning, the process consists of integrating the reality of the loss. The object representation is decathected, giving rise to the pain associated with the loss of an attachment. As part of the process, the mourner experiences a gradually shifting series of identifications with the deceased. Eventually the self-representation is modified and "reshaped," partially in the image of the dead individual. Two potential pathological outcomes to the process are (1) an excessive identification with the lost individual, in which the object representation becomes incorporated into the self-representation, and (2) an inability to tolerate the process of mourning with the result that the object representation remains intact and the fantasy evolves that the person never died. Crucial to the mourning process is the ability to work through ambivalent feelings toward the deceased. As the ambivalence toward the deceased is resolved, the object representation is transformed into a set of memories, cathexis is withdrawn, and the individual is available for new attachments.

The emphasis on the ability to work through ambivalent feelings toward the deceased indicates the extent to which traditional analytic theory is based on the concept of drives, with their organization or psychic structures being the primary determinants of behavior; consequently drives are key determinants in the ability of the individual to mourn. The ability to resolve ambivalence is contingent on the resolution of the oedipal phase and the consequent laying down of the repression barrier. A reflection of the importance of ambivalence resolution is seen in the debate concerning what age and level of intrapsychic structure a child must theoretically obtain in order to be able to mourn (see Shane and Shane, 1990, and Palombo, 1981, for more thorough reviews of this literature). This connection between ambivalence resolution and resolution of the oedipal phase is the very problem that makes traditional analytic theories problematic in understanding the mourning process of gay men; in the traditional analytic framework, homosexual men and women have not reached the oedipal level of drive organization (Lewes, 1988). Consequently, children and homosexuals are considered to be infantile in terms of psychic structure and hence, theoretically, unable to mourn. The theoretical consequences of an unmourned loss in an individual incapable of mourning are considerable. Shane and Shane (1990) observe:

. . . it has been felt that without the capacity to adequately mourn an overwhelming loss, the child's development is significantly impeded. It is postulated that because the child cannot mourn—that is, give up (decathect) the attachment to an investment in the representation of the lost person—or cannot preserve the relationship in the form of an identification, the search goes on forever for the parent whose death is unconsciously denied, and the person remains, in an important sense, the child at that phase or age when the loss was sustained. Thus, the fantasy that the parent still lives and can be found again precludes the possibility for true replacement, not just in childhood, but throughout life [pp. 115–116].

CLINICAL THEORY AND HOMOSEXUALITY

The relationship between mourning, ambivalence, and homosexuality is but one of the many theoretical problems one encounters when addressing psychological phenomena in a homosexual population. Friedman (1988) states: "Concepts about male homosexuality, of undeniable importance in their own right, are also an organic part of the larger issues in the history of psychoanalytic ideas" (p. 269). Given this centrality, a brief discussion of homosexuality is in order.

Clinicians who strive to practice from a depth psychology model with gay men or lesbian women face a central theoretical problem. Until fairly recently, all of our depth, or analytic, psychological models were rooted in libidinal drive theory. The self psychology framework helps us avoid the multiple theoretical problems one encounters with libidinal and ego-analytic theories, which ultimately rely heavily on the cornerstone of Oedipus and the heterosexual functioning that successful resolution represents (see Lewes, 1988, and Friedman, 1988, for more thorough discussions of the multiple theoretical problems). Isay (1989) has attempted to describe clinical intervention with gay men within a drive-theory-based theoretical framework. However, his selective inattention to key aspects of the theory—especially the resolution of the oedipal conflict and the formation of the superego, the laying down of the repression barrier, and the difference between homosexuality and neurosis—essentially leaves him operating from an atheoretical position.

The basic issue comes down to the role of sexuality in the development or organization of the mind. Does the development of sexual or libidinal drives shape the mind, or does the self's organization and coherence influence the experience of sexuality and the ability to form relationships that are mutually enhancing? Clearly, the general direction in which analytic theory is currently moving indicates that the latter provides a broader explanation of the phenomena than the former.

In clinical work with gay men "the issue is not what caused the patients' homosexuality, it is the meaning that being homosexual has for the particular person" (Shelby, 1989). In the course of development homosexual children live in the context of a selfobject environment (both parental and the larger environment) that is culturally phobic, if not outright hostile, toward homosexuality and its sexual expression. Consequently, the developing self often experiences numerous selfobject failures and outright narcissistic assaults.

The shared sense of sexuality or masculine competence is an important element in the mirroring and alter ego components of the father–son dialogue and often dramatically affects the idealizing sphere as well. Temperamental differences that are often read and responded to along gender lines, as well as the basic lack of a shared sexual orientation, often result in distortions in the relationship with the same-sex parent. Subsequently, the homosexual child does not experience selfobject functions that pertain to the realm of gender in an uncomplicated manner, and the self organization begins to include the experience of being different and incompetent. If the child's temperamental and/or orientational differences are experienced by the parent as a narcissistic injury, the child may be subjected to narcissistic assaults. The implication of this perspective is that there is a normative developmental process observed in homosexual children and that the pathogenic process often centers around the lack of environmental sustaining and modulating of the child's evolving self in the areas of gender and sexual orientation.

A series of meanings often becomes structured around these frequently painful experiences, and a gap often develops in the father–son dialogue that is difficult to mediate. These early experiences become the organizers through which messages from the larger homophobic environment are understood and become the basis for the self-experience that Maylon (1982) has referred to as "internalized homophobia." In the course of the mourning process these experiences and meanings are often reawakened. If the environmental response is nonsupportive or attacking, they may take on a central significance.

MOURNING AND SELF PSYCHOLOGY

Palombo (1981, 1982) points out that "in the self-psychological model, the loss [of a significant relationship due to death] is viewed as the loss of a selfobject relationship, which brings about an imbalance in self-esteem." In many cases the imbalance in self-esteem is more accurately described as a massive disorganization of the self and a shattering of self-esteem. Relationships vary in the degree to which individuals rely on one another for specific selfobject experiences; hence, each relationship varies in terms of the meaning of the loss and, consequently, in the psychological impact on the mourner.

Shane and Shane (1990) extend formulations of mourning theory within a self psychology framework. Though they focus on children, they assert that it is not the degree of psychic structure that enables the child to mourn but, rather, the presence and ability of the surviving parent or other adult to tolerate, mirror, sustain, and share the range of the child's affects regarding the lost parent, essentially the ability of that adult to provide "compensatory self-structure . . . to repair the weakened aspects of the self, but facilitate continued or renewed development" (p. 199).

In the face of the massive loss of selfobject functions of the decreased parent, the surviving parent (when not overly compromised by his or her own grief) serves as a selfobject that facilitates the mourning process. When this supportive environment is available, the child is able "to face the impact of the loss without feeling the risk of being overwhelmed, annihilated, or fragmented. . . . The pain of the loss can be borne and the necessary capacity to think, talk, and reflect about it can be sustained if the child is helped to mourn" (pp. 118, 119). The Shanes postulate that for many children the surviving parent's inability to perform these functions results in a double loss for the child and accounts for the considerable pathology observed later in life. The loss of the parent is complicated when the surviving parent is so compromised by his or her own grief as to be unable to provide the sustaining selfobject environment to support the child's mourning process. Hence, in the face of an overwhelming loss the child is once again abandoned.

It is reasonable to assert that adults as well as children require selfobject experiences to facilitate the varying degrees of self-reorganization that mourning involves. While Shane and Shane (1990) indicate that the presence of a required "optimal selfobject environment [is] more available to the adult" (p. 119), they do not elaborate on the nature of the role of the selfobject matrix in adult mourning. The results of the study on which this chapter is based illustrate the central role that selfobject encounters with those individuals who exhibit their understanding and tolerance of the mourners' affects, concerns, and general psychological state play in facilitating the reorganization of the self that mourning involves.

At this point in time an elaborated theory of mourning in a self-psychological framework has not been posited. The basic elements exist in the literature: Kohut's (1977) assertion that there is "no mature love in which the love object is not also a selfobject, or, to put this depth psychological formulation into a psychosocial context, there is no love relationship without mutual self-esteem enhancing, mirroring and idealization" (p. 141); Palombo's 1981 statement that "the loss must also be viewed as the loss of a selfobject relationship which brings about an imbalance in self-esteem"; and the Shanes' 1990 statement that there exists a "required optimal selfobject environment" for the mourning process. The results of the present study and recent advances in clinical theory enable us to make a beginning in the formulation of a theory of mourning within a self-psychological framework.

In recent years many theorists have worked toward integrating linguistic and/or cognitive theories into psychoanalytic theory. As Krystal (1990) points out, analytic theory since the time of Freud has tended to develop in a context of its own, generally ignoring advances in cognitive and linguistic theories. This reexamination of psychoanalysis in the context of theories of other parameters so basic to human experience—cognition, language, and development—has resulted in a necessary revision of the philosophical underpinnings of clinical theory, including issues such as how the mind develops and is organized and, perhaps most importantly, the nature of the therapeutic process itself (e.g, Stern, 1985; Saari, 1986; Basch, 1988; Goldberg, 1990; Palombo, 1991).

Palombo (1991) presents an integration of numerous theorists into a cohesive theory of the nature of meaning, of the processes by which it is organized into the structure we refer to as the self, and of the process we call psychotherapy. The central stance concerns the innate aspect of being human, namely, that from birth onward humans strive to organize or give meaning to their experience. "Meanings are initially constituted by the sense a person makes of his or her lived experiences as filtered through his or her own peculiar environment. These meanings are residues from these experiences that are retained by the person but they go beyond the facts of the experience itself. They initially are the definitions a person uses to organize and integrate experiences" (p. 181). Central to the organization of meanings is the role of others in the environment: "They [Meanings] evolve out of the early affective states which in infancy occur in interaction with a caregiver who attempts to both give significance to the affective states, to modify them, and to share in them (p. 181). Meanings then, whether personal or shared, are embedded within a matrix of affectivity and cognition" (p. 182). The interplay between affect and the role of other individuals in the formation of meaning is a key component: "The integration of affect serves to organize experience. Affects constitute a signaling system which when joined with cognitive faculties and a caregiver's responses result in a residue of comprehension of the experience by the child" (p. 182). This is the process by which the self-narrative, the individual's account of his own experience, is formed. Palombo defines narrative as "the means to which we organize and integrate our experiences. They make our experiences coherent by integrating them into each other" (personal communication, May 12, 1992).

Language plays a central role in the development and organization of the mind. For Palombo (1991), "language . . . is a medium through which meanings become encoded and are capable of being recalled and of being communicated to others" (p. 183). Thus, language is the central tool by which we encode personal meaning and participate in the larger world. Palombo states that language mediates "experience." In a similar vein, Goldberg (1990) states: " Language as a link to other people produces a different kind of orientation that says that the signifiers allow for a developmental process to take place, which process allows for the completion of a configuration, in this case a configuration called the self, one that was not completed during development" (p. 111).

The nature of the mind or the self is defined by Palombo (1991) as a "hierarchy of meanings"; thus "psychic structure may be defined as a set of symbols that remain stable over time" (p. 178). "Eventually the hierarchies of the meaning systems acquire a coherence that defines the personality. This coherence is experienced as a sense of cohesion . . . the sum of these coherent systems may be said to constitute a person narrative" (p. 184). While there is a considerable degree of stability to the self's organization, elements are subject to change and reorganization: "Experiences and events may not retain their original meanings but are constantly re-interpreted" (p. 184).

While the basis of these theories is the development of meaning in the context of childhood development, they include models that can be thought of as part of a dynamic process that extends throughout the life span. As human beings living in the context of the larger world, we are exposed to events and experiences that tax our psychic resources, reactivate old meanings, and challenge us to form new meanings and engage in relationships that often serve a central role in the process.

Thus, while psychic structure is reasonably stable over time, elements of our personal narratives are subject to change and revision. In defining the therapeutic process Palombo quotes Saari (1986) as saying that it "involves the organizing of old meanings into newly constructed consciousness. What is curative is not so much the recovery of deeply rooted repressed material, but the reordering of structures that underlie personal meaning and the symbolic capacities of the individual so the new meanings can be differentiated, con-structed or abstracted" (p. 27).

THE PROCESS OF MOURNING AND THE ROLE OF THE SELFOBJECT MATRIX

Drawing on current clinical thinking, I am proposing the following definition of mourning: a process that involves a reorganization of central aspects of the self, of major affect states, and, consequently, of the meaning of the loss into a narrative that can be integrated into the overall structure of the self. Mourning begins with a state of acute disorganization of the self, with a resultant lack of coherence and disequilibrium in self-esteem, brought about by the loss of a relation-ship in an individuals' life. Central to the disorganization and self-esteem difficulties are the massive loss of selfobject functions that the survivor experienced within the context of the relationship, the loss of the shared experience or dialogue that occurs within a relationship, and any specific meaning that the loss entails (in the case of an AIDS-related death, the potential that the survivor may also die of the same disease).

Mourning as a process involves a gradual and often painful reorganization of the affects secondary to the loss and an integration of the meaning of the loss into the self. The degree of disorganization and intensity of the affects involved depends on the centrality of the relationship and the degree to which the individual relied on the deceased person to complete his own experience of self. Initially, the self is in a deficient state; the person has lost a sense of coherence because it is impossible to integrate the meaning of the loss of a central person in his life, the selfobject dimensions of the relationship, and the intense affects associated with the loss. Initially in the mourning process the emphasis is on the missing of the lost individual and the desire for the experience of the relationship. Cherishing the belongings of the deceased, holding personal "conversations" with the deceased, and visiting the gravesite offer the mourner a sense of continuing the relationship with the lost individual.

This is a crucial distinction: The mourner is not missing, yearning, or searching for a lost figure, "object," or representation thereof; rather, what is absent is his particular unique experience of that individual and the shared experience, the dialogue, that an intimate relationship entails. Goldberg (1990), using cognitive and linguistic theories, presents a thorough and convincing argument for essentially dispensing with the concept and theory of representations. He argues that analytic theories of representations are not consistent with the findings of cognitive and linguistic science, namely, that the mind is not structured or "mapped" by a series of object representations. There are no "objects" in our minds, only the subject— ourselves. For Goldberg, "the Kohutian analyst is not concerned with the hidden representation of the object as with the representation of the deficient self" (p. 110).

If mourning does not center on the preservation of the object in the form of identifications or realignment of self and object representations, then just what does the process entail? The process is the reorganization of affects and the construction of a new or modified narrative: an account of the meaning of the death that can then be integrated into the self organization. The person who has become increasingly accustomed to an intimate, ongoing dialogue, the bedrock of shared experience with another, must now integrate the experience of being alone. In this disorganized and vulnerable state, affects are intense and volatile and self-esteem is diminished and unstable; consequently, the environment feels very unsafe and unfamiliar. The work of mourning concerns the gradual reorganization of the affect states and integration into the experience of the self. As the affects become less intense, a narrative can be formed; the mourner makes meaning out of his loss. Language and the narrative gradually supplant shifting affect states. As this is achieved, the narrative can be integrated into the overall self organization. The experience of the loss comes to be viewed as a complicated and painful event in a larger life experience.

The central figures are not so much the mourner and the deceased as the mourner and the selfobject environment. By responding to the mourner's affect states and the meaning or centrality of the loss, the environment assists in the organization of affect and, consequently, in the construction and integration of the narrative. Stolorow, Brandchaft, and Atwood (1987) state that "selfobject functions pertain fundamentally to the integration of affect into the evolving organization of self experience" (p. 86). Hence, selfobject encounters help modulate and regulate the intensity of affects, which enables the individual to integrate the meaning of his experiences. Socarides and Stolorow (1984/1985) assert that "what is crucial to the child's (or patient's) growing capacity to integrate his sadness and his painful disappointments in himself and others is the reliable presence of a calming, containing, empathic selfobject, irrespective of the 'amount' or intensity of the affects involved" (p. 113). Ultimately, the result of the mourner's encounters with the responsive selfobject environment is the transformation of the experience from one of massive selfobject loss, with its attendant fragmentation states and loss of coherence, into a very sad and painful life event, one that has been lived through and overcome, the process often stimulating renewed growth.

Affects are soothed and organized, and the narrative is formed through the mourner's personal and public activities and selfobject relationships. The mourner's cherishing of, and interactions with, symbols of the relationship and his shared experience with the deceased complete the configuration that represents the deficient self in a personal manner. The empathic response of the selfobject environment to the mourner's missing of the individual, the associated affects, and the general psychological state complete the configuration in a shared experience with living people.

Public encounters serve to orient the self toward the world of the living and rekindle the hope that the self can become enriched through participating in ongoing shared experiences with the living, rather than by attempting to find meaning and solace by recreating the shared experience with the deceased. Ultimately, these experiences often result in the formation of idealizing relationships with living people, which can spur further growth, enabling the person to take on new challenges in his career and form relationships that reflect a higher level of self organization.

I am proposing that the mourning process consists of three distinct but interrelated elements: The first is the cherishing of the deceased's possessions and of photographs and memories of the relationship, "conversations" with the deceased, and rituals such as visits to the gravesite and acknowledging anniversaries. All these acts reflect not an identification with the deceased but, rather, attempts to complete the familiar configuration of the relationship, which ultimately serves to soothe and modulate affect. The second element concerns the response of the selfobject environment to affects associated with the loss. Mourners often turn to others whom they experience as sharing the meaning of the loss—relatives or close friends of the deceased—during times of acute loneliness, which holidays and anniversaries tend to represent. Mourners consider the sharing of mutual affects regarding the loss as deeply meaningful and helpful, and a greater degree of coherence is often evident. This represents the completion of the configuration of the deficient self in a public way with living people. The third element of the mourning process is the gradual formation and integration of the narrative of the loss in the mourner's overall life experience.

CASE ILLUSTRATIONS

An important finding of Shelby's study (Shelby, 1992) concerned the differences in the mourning process of seropositive and seronegative surviving partners. Essentially, seropositive partners tended to be in a more protracted mourning process and were not able to reengage with the world in the same manner as seronegative survivors. As I turn to clinical application of the framework, I will present two cases: The first is of a man who was seronegative, the second a man who was seropositive. Both men had encountered difficulty in their mourning process, and both were significantly depressed upon entering treatment. However, there were significant differences between the two cases; hopefully, these important differences will come through as I recount aspects of the clinical process. The cases are presented in a way that emphasizes the process of mourning and intervention aimed at reestablishing the process. The area of preexisting self pathology and its role in complicated mourning is another topic entirely.

Case I: The Seronegative Survivor

Mr. B was a 35-year-old professional man who sought treatment at the insistence of his physician. His partner had died approximately five months earlier. He had gone to his physician with a long list of somatic complaints and preoccupations, including lack of energy, chest pains, and headaches. His physician had worked him up and could find nothing amiss. His assessment was that Mr. B was severely depressed, and he prescribed Prozac on the condition that Mr. B seek psychotherapy. Mr. B was rather chagrined by this assessment but dutifully followed through with the firm recommendation. Further questioning revealed that Mr. B was sleeping 14 to 16 hours a day; he would come home from work at lunchtime and sleep and would go to bed shortly after he returned home in the evening.

Mr. B was very reluctant to enter treatment. Although his affect was excruciatingly depressed, he was very resistant, maintaining that he was only interested in short-term intervention and had come at the insistence of his physician. I had worked with his partner and, periodically, with his partner's family for over two years during a long, complicated illness. Mr. B sought me out, he said, because I knew his partner and, therefore, he would not have to explain everything to me the way he would to someone else.

Mr. B related that immediately following his partner's death the family began harassing him by demanding things that went against the spirit and specifications of the will. They had also begun a lawsuit challenging the document even though they had been handsomely provided for. As Mr. B had been given power of attorney, they demanded a thorough accounting of the money spent during his partner's illness, outrightly accusing him of embezzlement. The first two months after his partner's death were spent attempting to account for every penny spent, an exhausting and complicated task since Mr. B. often contributed his own money to pay the expenses even though his partner had ample resources. Although he came up with an accounting, the family went ahead with their lawsuits. Several of his partner's cousins, whom Mr. B. had become quite close to, stopped returning his calls, which enraged and devastated him. He felt all alone, with sharks circling about him.

As we explored this, Mr. B came to realize that his desperate attempts to account for the finances were also an attempt to convince his partner's mother that he was not a bad person. Which, of course, was futile. He related that he had come to question himself, at times believing he was the awful, vile embezzler of a helpless, dying man's estate that his partner's mother said he was.

As I listened to Mr. B I sensed no mourning process and heard mention of none of the activities, concerns, and rituals that mourners often engage in; instead, I heard depression and a questioning of his own integrity. Mr. B also reflected on this, pointing out that he did not find himself missing his partner or feeling grief stricken. At times he felt the lawsuits were not worth the hassle of fighting them; he was not actively cooperating with his lawyers and had begun to consider just turning over his partner's entire estate to his parents. Shortly after he realized that he was engaged in a desperate, futile effort to prove his integrity to his partner's mother, he became less resistant and more engaged with me and began to actively work with his attorney.

During the next session Mr. B obliquely hinted at regrets in his associations. I asked him what regrets he had. He began to cry. He related that he had fallen in love with his partner all over again during the last few months of the illness and that he was devastated that his partner had died during the night, by himself in his sleep, when neither he nor the family were present. Mr. B also admitted that this was the first time he had cried since his partner's death.

Following that session I began to hear evidence of a mourning process. Mr. B flew to one of the places where his partner's ashes had been dispersed. He began to seek out contact with his partner's best friend, someone also deeply affected by the loss, and they would spend a great deal of time reminiscing. He also began to reminisce with me and to try and sort out several old and often painful conflicts between himself and his partner. Mr. B also became determined to do his best in defending himself and the will—the will, especially, because it was what his partner had wanted. Needless to say, his depression was lifting considerably. Although he had been dreading his partner's approaching birthday, he went alone on that day to a restaurant the two of them had gone to practically every Sunday they were together. Mr. B related that this visit was "sad and bittersweet, but it felt good, it felt right." He then began planning a panel for the AIDS Quilt and invited a group of his partner's close friends to participate in making it and to make their own contributions to the memorial.

Though the lawsuits continued to be quite taxing and a nuisance, Mr. B did not become overwhelmed by them as readily as before. Concurrently, his sleeping pattern returned to normal, and he became more actively engaged socially and at work, even earning a promotion. Approximately six months after beginning treatment he went off Prozac, his affect held, and he continued his process of mourning and engagement. Nevertheless, he also became preoccupied with his antibody status and became convinced that he was seropositive. Though he had consistently tested negative prior to his partner's death and had had no sexual contact since, he became convinced that he too was positive. He eventually was tested and was again negative.

Discussion of Case I

The case of Mr. B illustrates a number of important aspects of working with people who are having difficulty in the mourning process. The first concerns the delicate balance between depression and mourning. When the mourning process is thwarted in adults, one often sees depression. Mourning does involve a great deal of sad affect, but if a process of integrating the experience is occurring one also hears of efforts to soothe the affect through rituals and by engaging with others who are also deeply affected by the loss. In theoretical terms, efforts to complete the now-missing configuration of the dialogue are made. When the process essentially stops, depression and/or anxiety often comes to dominate. If a person is too depressed he cannot sustain or soothe the sad affect and is overcome by it. Clearly, Mr. B was in the midst of a major depressive episode by the time he came to me. When this is the case, the use of antidepressant medication, in conjunction with individual therapy, is often necessary to essentially reestablish the process of mourning and to return the patient to a more reasonable level of functioning.

Mr. B's selfobject environment was not supportive of him and his efforts to mourn. The challenging of a will interjects chaos, uncertainty, and, often, a profound sense of betrayal when the mourner is in such a highly vulnerable state. Family members were attacking and abandoning Mr. B, rather than engaging with him in a mutual process of mourning their loss. Relatives with whom Mr. B might have shared his grief cut off contact with him. In his disappointment he failed to engage with people who were available for mutual reminiscing and the sharing of affect regarding the loss.

The clinician's role becomes one of helping the patient reestablish the mourning process. In this case it was necessary to first help Mr. B sort out his suspicions regarding himself so that he could then relate to me and the memory of his partner without the fear of his being found out to actually be an evil person. Survivors often experience ruminations of guilt. Many times this feeling of guilt can be traced to the survivor's perceived or actual empathic breaks with the deceased. However, if the ruminations are too intense or are seemingly confirmed by an angry family, the survivor may come to believe them as facts. He may become reluctant to relate them to others for fear they will be found to be true, a reluctance that deprives him of the possibility of an environment that can respond to and modulate his painful self-doubts.

As the treatment relationship evolves, the therapist should express his interest in the mourned relationship and its history and validate the rituals that the survivor engages in. The personal "conversations" with the deceased often provide important data for understanding the selfobject dimensions of the relationship, dimensions that can be used by the clinician in helping the patient understand the many aspects of the meaning of the loss. The therapist's interest in the relationship and his encouragement of the mourner to relate its history, including the good times and the bad, enhances the process of reflection and reminiscing while establishing the clinician as an active participant in the mourning process.

Like many men who have lost partners to AIDS, Mr. B became preoccupied with his antibody status, convincing himself he was positive, despite previous testing. This behavior was consistent with the study's findings in that participants tended to become preoccupied with their antibody status (regardless of prior test results) during the middle phase of mourning, when they were beginning to feel more alive and more engaged with the world. When survivors test negative, one often sees renewed efforts at self-redefinition as a single person and in engagement with the world; when they test positive (or already know they are positive), one often sees the mourning process slow down, if not stop.

Case II: The Seropositive Survivor

One often finds a complicated and protracted mourning process in seropositive surviving partners. In keeping with the theoretical framework I propose, the problem becomes the continued shared experience with the deceased partner that seropositivity represents. These men are infected with the same virus that killed their partner, the implication being that they will follow in their partner's footsteps. Even as these men attempt to integrate the death of their partner from AIDS, they are faced with their own infection and their own potential death. At this point the mourning process often slows down, if not stops, and depression and anxiety come to dominate their experience. Dynamically, one often observes the combination of a strong continued idealization of the deceased partner and an "identification"of the survivor's infection with the partner's death. Though they may be medically stable, these men's experience of self may nevertheless become organized around impending death. Consequently their self-esteem is diminshed and their affects are unstable. Although they feel painfully isolated, these men have considerable trouble feeling engaged with the world and being part of it.

Mr. T was a 41-year-old white male whose partner of ten years had died approximately one and a half years earlier. He had known that he was seropositive a number of years before his partner's death. His chief complaint upon entering treatment was expressed as follows: "Something is wrong. I am not excited about anything. I have this new job with great opportunities. I should be excited, but I am not." The clinical interview revealed several other problems: a significant level of depression and periodic acute anxiety. Although his T-cells were in the 500 range and had been for several years, Mr. T was convinced he was dying, and his self was organized around the assumption of impending death. He had developed a reputation in his seropositive support group as a rebel, actively challenging the leader's " recipes" for seropositive people to remain that way and not contract AIDS. He would often angrily point out that even though his lover had been a vegetarian, had taken massive quantities of vita- mins, had not done drugs, and had gone to the gym daily for many years before he became ill, he died anyway.

Mr. T's partner had died in San Francisco. After the death Mr. T dispersed their belongings and moved to Chicago—a city where he had lived previously and in which several family members resided— to live with his sister and to take "time to heal." After several months he took a job that was well beneath his capabilities to "get back into practice." After several months he took the more challenging position that he held when he entered treatment.

Mr. T reported that both his family and his partner's had been very supportive and that he felt his need to mourn had been respected and validated by them. However, in the community he felt like a pariah. Several old acquaintances had become anxious and then had with- drawn when he related that his partner had died of AIDS. When Mr. T attempted to go out and meet new people, he quickly became anxious and gave up his plans, fearing that he would eventually have to tell people about his partner and his own seropositive status. This was in sharp contrast to his previous experience of himself ·as outgoing and highly social.

In general, Mr. T felt that no one understood or cared to under- stand, though he was not quite sure what he wanted people to understand. He felt that moving to Chicago had been a mistake; he longed for San Francisco, where he felt being a surviving partner and being seropositive was more readily accepted as the norm rather than the exception. Perhaps there, he thought, people would not treat him differently. Though he assumed he was dying (he knew his lab counts via a research study), he was not being followed by a physician. He resisted my attempts to get him engaged in a medical assessment, stating that when the time came for him to have a physician, he would find one. Though he had developed a number of friends in the seropositive support organization, he was beginning to alienate them. In fact, it was at their urging that he came for psychotherapy.

As treatment progressed, Mr. T related more of his personal experience to me. He continued to carry on elaborate conversations with his deceased partner, and a strong element of idealization of the partner was evident. He felt very embarrassed to relate the extent of these conversations, fearing that he would be labeled as crazy. Severe self-esteem problems were evident: he felt diminished and unable to function as well as he had previously in job or social settings. For example, he panicked at the idea of purchasing new clothes, feeling that everything looked terrible on him; he was profoundly anxious at the idea of looking in the mirror with salespeople nearby. (This is especially interesting in that his partner had died of Kaposi's sarcoma and was horribly disfigured.) It became increasingly clear that Mr. T felt desperately out of control and that his anxiety over feeling out of control was as disabling as his clinical symptoms.

After several weekly meetings Mr. T requested and began twice-weekly sessions. He quickly formed an idealizing transference. Initially, some erotized elements were evident but not to the extent that they threatened to disrupt the treatment alliance. The erotized elements quickly diminished over the next few weeks and were replaced by a more solid idealization of the therapist.

Very quickly, I pointed out that a great deal of what Mr. T was experiencing was due to his being a seropositive surviving partner and that at this point in time after his partner's death he should be getting excited again and probably would be if he were not carrying the same virus that killed his partner. Although I validated and attempted to normalize the continued dialogue or conversations with his partner, I was also interested in what he talked about with his partner. I encouraged him to relate the story of their relationship and of his partner's illness and death. Initially, in a very real way I felt that there were three people in the consulting room: myself, Mr. T, and his partner.

Mr. T proved to be a vivid dreamer, and his dreams often beautifully and succinctly summed up the current themes in his treatment. Over the first two months of our work, he related the following three dreams:

Jim [his partner] and I were on an island in a river. Jim was sick and lying on a cot. The river was raging, it was storming, there was chaos all around us. I was worried about keeping him dry and was busy making sure he did not get wet. Though there was chaos all around us, I felt calm inside.

I was going somewhere on a train. All of sudden I was outside of the train. I felt fine until I thought that I should hold on to something, since the train was moving so fast. I panicked when I realized there was only a little rail to hold on to that I could barely get my fingers around.

I was getting on a plane to go to Florida. I sat down in the cramped and shabby tourist section. The stewardess approached and said there had been a mistake, that I was to sit in first-class. She pointed to an escalator that was going up. I rode up and was in a first-class section that had plush seats and huge windows. I became anxious and thought, "I do not belong here; I am going back to tourist were I belong."

The first dream was understood to summarize the common experience of men caring for their ill partners: though their world may be falling apart around them as the partner becomes increasingly ill, the well partner is still sustained by the relationship. He has an important job to do: caring for his ill partner. The sense of duty and the sustaining power of the relationship help the partner to feel grounded and to avoid feeling as vulnerable or buffeted by chaos as he feels in the wake of a disruption in the relationship (or as he will feel on the death of his partner). The second dream was understood as symbolizing the panic that Mr. T came to experience as he realized the world was still moving on, perhaps even toward his own illness, and how little grounded he felt, let alone secure that there would be a relationship that could sustain him the way he sustained his partner. The third dream was understood as relating to Mr. T's own damaged and diminished self-esteem, which ultimately was preventing him from engaging in relationships that could help him feel grounded and secure and, consequently, was enhancing his feeling of not belonging. (The dreams could also be understood as reflecting the deepening transference; the explanations are not mutually exclusive.)

Over the next five months of treatment Mr. T's depression lifted considerably and his anxiety diminished. The dialogue with his partner diminished over the first several months of treatment, and he became more interested in other people. He became increasingly comfortable with himself and was less abrasive in his support group. He pursued other interests; took another, more challenging, job; hosted a holiday party (this was especially significant in that he and his partner were avid entertainers, and each event was very much an effort in teamwork); and eventually began a dating relationship.

The continuing idealization of the deceased partner is often a central component in the complicated mourning process of seropositive partners. This must be handled appropriately and empathically: otherwise, one risks traumatizing, if not enraging, the patient. The idealization cannot be interpreted away; rather, it must be allowed to gradually deflate. One could argue that the patient is gaining a sense of comfort through the idealization at a time when the self may not be able to take comfort in other relationships. As the surviving partner forms a relationship with the clinician—one that will deepen the more the clinician is able to be empathically in tune with his experience of mourning—the transference will deepen and solidify. As this happens, one will also observe that the idealization of the deceased partner gradually wanes.

As in this case, erotized elements may emerge in the transference. If this is not distressing to the patient and does not threaten to disrupt the treatment, no interpretation is in order; the erotized elements will also wane as the transference deepens. If the patient is showing signs of distress, then a discussion that points out that the erotization is a sign of his feeling understood, comfortable, and excited about the possibility that perhaps he is capable of forming new attachments may be called for.

Another aspect of work with these men involves the therapist pointing out to them the distorting influence of seropositivity. While this may potentially be an intellectual intrusion into the dialogue between the patient and the therapist, it offers an important structure with which to help the patient organize his experience. The patient is already feeling depressed, anxious, isolated, and, perhaps most painful of all, weird and different, apart from the rest of the world. The patient often explains his ongoing experience to himself in these terms. Offering the patient the explanation that part of what he is experiencing is due not to his personal pathology but to the distorting effects of something beyond his control helps him organize the experience as something considerably more benign, cuts into the negative experience of self that often comes to dominate the self organization, and offers him the opportunity to relate his fears, connected to the loss of his partner, about his own health and life.

Pointing out the distorting effects of seropositivity also provides the opportunity for the patient to experience with the clinician any angry affect surrounding his experience. Several men expressed considerable anger (once given permission to do so) as they related their feeling of being cheated, of being in a situation that is "unfair." I tend to respond that, yes, they have been cheated, AIDS has taken a great deal away from them, and they have every right to be angry over their situation. This can be especially helpful in that often these seropositive men adopt a "walking on eggshells" approach, fearing that the experience of any angry affect (save perhaps a projected anger toward institutions or unhelpful individuals) may disrupt their equilibrium and bring their world crashing down; essentially, they fear that they will become ill.

Mr. T's selfobject environment was very supportive and responded to his status as a mourner, recognizing his need to gradually regroup and helping him make a new start. However, these responses were primarily to the more readily understandable and recognizable human experience of loss. Unless we know about the complicating and distorting effects of seropositivity on the mourning process we cannot adequately respond to these individuals. My experience is that they are at once surprised and highly relieved when this complicating aspect of their attempt to mourn is addressed.

SUMMARY

This chapter is a cursory overview of a very complicated yet crucial aspect of the human experience in general and the AIDS crisis in particular. Though discussed in the context of men whose losses occurred in the context of gay relationships and the current epidemic, the beginning reformulation of mourning theory and the process of mourning is applicable to the general population. Clearly, mourning involves more than the mourner and the deceased: the selfobject matrix plays a crucial role in modulating the mourner's affect, subsequently assisting in the formation of the narrative and its integration into the overall structure of the self. The empathic responses of the selfobject environment also serve to orient the mourner back to the world of the living. The mourner's capacity to tolerate the affective dimension of mourning and the environmental response to the mourner's affect and situation in general are factors that may impede or facilitate the process. Another implication of this perspective is that the clinician is more than a facilitator of the mourning process; we are, instead, integral participants.

REFERENCES

Basch, M. (1988), *Understanding Psychotherapy*. New York: Basic Books.
Freud,S. (1912–1913), Totem and taboo. *Standard Edition*, 13:1–164. London: Hogarth Press, 1957.
———— (1917), Mourning and melancholia. *Standard Edition*, 14:243–258. London: Hogarth Press, 1957.
Friedman, R. (1988), *Male Homosexuality: A Contemporary Analytic Perspective*. New Haven, CT: Yale University Press.
Glaser, B. (1975), *Theoretical Sensitivity*. Mill Valley, CA: The Free Press.
———— & Strauss, A. (1967), *The Discovery of Grounded Theory*. Chicago: Aldine.
Goldberg, A. (1990), *The Prisonhouse of Psychoanalysis*. Hillsdale, NJ: The Analytic Press.
Isay, R. (1989), *Being Homosexual*. New York: Farrar, Straus & Giroux.
Kohut, H. (1977), *The Restoration of the Self*. New York: International Universities Press.
Krystal, H. (1990), An information processing view of object-relations. *Psychoanal Inq.*, 10:221–251.
Lewes, K. (1988), *The Psychoanalytic Theory of Male Homosexuality*. New York: Simon & Schuster.
Maylon, A. K. (1982), Psychotherapeutic implications of internalized homophobia in gay men. In: *Homosexuality and Psychotherapy*, ed. J. Gonsiorek. New York: Haworth Press, pp. 59–70.
Palombo, J. (1981), Parent loss and childhood bereavement. *Clinical Social Work Journal*, 9 (1):3–33.
———— (1982), The psychology of the self and the termination of treatment. *Clinical Social Work Journal*, 10 (1):46–62.
———— (1991), Bridging the chasm between developmental theory and clinical theory: Part II. The bridge. *The Annual of Psychoanalysis*, 19:152–194. Hillsdale, NJ: The Analytic Press.
Pollock, G. (1961), Mourning and adaptation. *Internat. J. Psycho-Anal.*, 42:341–361.
Saari, C. (1986), *Clinical Social Work Treatment*. New York: Gardner Press.
Shane, M. & Shane, E. (1990), Object loss and selfobject loss: A consideration of self psychology's contribution to understanding mourning and the failure to mourn. *The Annual of Psychoanalysis*, 18:115–131. Hillsdale, NJ: The Analytic Press.
Shelby, R. D. (1989), Internalized homophobia as narcissistic injury. Unpublished paper.
———— (1992), *If a Partner Has AIDS*. Binghamton, NY: Haworth Press.
Socarides, D. & Stolorow, R. (1984/1985), Affects and selfobjects. *The Annual of Psychoanalysis*, 12,13:105–120. New York: International Universities Press.
Stern, D. (1985), *The Interpersonal World of the Infant*. New York: Basic Books.
Stolorow, R, Brandchaft, B. & Atwood, G. (1987), *Psychoanalytic Treatment: An Intersubjective Approach*. Hillsdale, NJ: The Analytic Press.

Chapter 15

The Search
for the Hidden Self:
A Fresh Look at Alter
Ego Transferences

Doris Brothers

When asked "What is a friend?" Zeno, the Greek philosopher (ca 362–ca 264 B.C.), is reported to have given the somewhat cryptic reply "Another I" (or, in Latin, *alter ego*). Just what did Zeno mean? Did he consider a friend to be a duplicate, a twin, of oneself? Or, as I prefer to believe, did he mean a friend is an alternate or somewhat different version of oneself? I find support for my understanding in *The American Heritage Dictionary's* (1980) definition of *alter ego* as, first, "another side of oneself, a second self" and, second, as "an intimate friend, a constant companion." The word *twin*, on the other hand, is defined as "one of two identical or similar persons, animals, or things." Clearly, the two words are not synonymous.

Heinz Kohut (1971, 1977, 1984) used the words *twin* and *alter ego* interchangeably; at times, he used one word to amplify the meaning of the other. For example, he often put the word *alter ego* in parentheses when referring to twinship transferences, one of his major clinical discoveries. He explained in a personal communication to Detrick, "The relationship to a twin is that of an alterego" (Detrick, 1986, p. 300).

Detrick (1985, 1986), however, proposed a "sharp distinction" between alter ego and twinship phenomena, urging that the term *twinship* be reserved for "an experience of sameness or likeness [that] serves the central function of the acquisition of skills and tools" and the term *alter ego* be used for "experiences of sameness or likeness that anchor the individual in a group process" (Detrick, 1986, p. 300).

191

This chapter represents a fresh attempt to separate the two concepts. It is my contention that although Kohut often used the two terms as if they were synonymous, his clinical illustrations reveal two very different kinds of selfobject experiences. One of these selfobject experiences corresponds to the aforementioned definition of *twin* while the other corresponds more closely to the definition of *alter ego* as another aspect of oneself—or, more specifically, as an aspect of oneself that has been disavowed. What is more, with the blurring of the differences in meaning of these two phenomena, a valuable category of selfobject experience has been overlooked.

I am in complete agreement with Detrick that twinship phenomena are well defined as "the need to experience the presence of essential alikeness" (Kohut, 1984, p. 194). Kohut (1984) poignantly illustrated this sort of twinship transference in his clinical vignette of the woman who on being apprised of Kohut's plan for a summer vacation reported a childhood fantasy of "the genie in the bottle." The genie, as the patient reluctantly confessed to Kohut, was "a little girl, a twin, "someone who was, Kohut pointed out, "just like herself and yet not herself" (p. 195). Kohut came to realize that the announcement of his planned vacation had disrupted a sustaining selfobject connection based on the woman's experience of him as essentially like herself.

I have more difficulty with Detrick's assertion that the need to experience sameness or likeness as a means of anchoring the individual in a group process warrants the designation of an alter ego phenomenon. As I see it, this is simply a variant of twinship experience. Instead, I propose that alter ego phenomena within the treatment situation be reconceptualized as *the need to experience the presence of essential sameness or alikeness with disavowed or hidden aspects of self.*

MR. C'S ALTER EGO TRANSFERENCE

The case of Mr. C, summarized by Kohut (1971) in *The Analysis of the Self,* powerfully illustrates an alter ego transference in which the analyst was perceived as embodying disavowed aspects of the patient's self-experience. The patient, a moderately successful professional in his mid-forties, consulted Kohut after numerous attempts at treatment had failed to cure a mild case of premature ejaculation and a lack of emotional involvement during intercourse. Mr. C also complained of a variety of vague symptoms that often attend disorders of self-experience, including "a pervasive feeling that he was not fully alive . . . and a brooding worrisomeness about his physical and mental functions." Kohut described Mr. C's treatment as follows:

Concerning each new theme in the patient's analysis, his associations would regularly, and for prolonged periods, refer at first *not to himself but to the analyst*: yet this working-through phase, which manifestly dealt with the analyst, always produced significant psychological changes in the patient. . . . Even in the later phases of his analysis when he already anticipated that he would end up talking about his own psyche, he continued to proceed in the characteristic sequence: he would first, and for prolonged periods, see in me the (usually anxiety-provoking) affect, wish, ambition, or fantasy with which he was dealing, and even then it was only after he had worked through the currently activated complex in this way would turn to it with reference to himself [p. 194; italics added].

Thus, despite the coexistence of contradictory evidence about Kohut, Mr. C for a time maintained a perception of Kohut as "a person devoid of ambitions, as emotionally shallow, pathologically even-tempered, withdrawn and inactive" (p. 194). Only after a prolonged working-through process involving his perception of Kohut's personality as being "torn by conflict," which was followed by some external events signifying that he had made progress in areas corresponding to the disavowed aspects of himself, did Mr. C gradually experience the conflict fully in himself. At this point his experience of Kohut was no longer clouded by his perceptions of himself. Kohut notes that the conflicts with which Mr. C struggled were usually connected with "poignantly remembered childhood events and childhood emotions" (p. 195).

ALTER EGO TRANSFERENCES, PROJECTION, AND PROJECTIVE IDENTIFICATION

Kohut observed that if during periods in which Mr. C attributed to him disavowed aspects of himself he would state or imply that Mr. C was "projecting," Mr. C would withdraw emotionally and complain that he had been misunderstood. Although Kohut does not explain the reasons for Mr. C's rejection of these interpretations, they are well worth considering. There are many confusing similarities between projection, projective identification—a concept that, as Sandler (1987) points out, is not always fully differentiated from projection—and alter ego transferences. A brief comparison of these concepts may prove helpful.

According to Anna Freud (1966), in projection "ideational representatives of dangerous instinctual impulses [are] displaced into the outside world" as a means of protecting oneself against various kinds of anxiety (p. 122). Kernberg (1987) sees projection as having four

components: "(a) repression of an unacceptable intrapsychic experience, (b) projection of that experience onto an object, (c) lack of
empathy with what is projected, and (d) distancing or estrangement
from the object as an effective completion of the defensive effort"
(p. 94).

According to these definitions, Mr. C was not using projection as
a defense. That is, he was not attempting to distance himself from an
object onto whom he had projected an unacceptable intrapsychic
experience. Rather, Mr. C appears to have been striving to connect
with previously disavowed aspects of himself that he experienced as
belonging to another person. His selfobject fantasy of himself in
relation to Kohut as an alter ego who embodied hidden parts of
himself enabled Mr. C to experience a sense of self-cohesion that
previously had been unattainable. Moreover, the working through of
this transference fantasy led to the integration of these disavowed
aspects of himself. If projection is understood as a need to rid oneself
of unacceptable impulses, wishes, and emotions, alter ego transferences signify a longing for closeness with someone functioning as a
selfobject who embodies these hidden aspects of the self. Such
closeness provides an experience of self-cohesion otherwise impossible to achieve.

As Kernberg (1987) observes, the term *projective identification,* first
introduced by Melanie Klein, has been used to mean too many different things by too many different people under too many differing
circumstances" (p. 93) (see also Sandler, 1987). Kernberg distinguishes projective identification from projection in the following
ways: Projection is used primarily by patients with neurotic
personality organizations whereas projective identification is used
by patients with borderline and psychotic personality organization;
projection involves repression whereas projective identification
depends on splitting or "primitive dissociation"; unlike projection,
projective identification involves the maintenance of empathy with
what is projected and, most importantly, "Induction in the object of
a corresponding intrapsychic experience." Sandler (1987) points out
that the notion that the object is induced to have a corresponding
intrapsychic experience is a relatively recent elaboration of the
concept.

My understanding of the clinical examples of projective identification presented by Kernberg (1987) is that what most distinguishes
projective identification from alter ego transferences are differences in
the way these transference manifestations are regarded, differences
that are largely determined by countertransference reactions stemming from the therapist's theoretical biases. Consider Kernberg's

(1987) clinical example of a female patient whom he diagnosed as having "a narcissistic personality disorder with overt borderline functioning" (p. 104). After an inpatient hospitalization for "severe suicidal tendencies" at the institution where Kernberg serves as director, the woman beseeched him to treat her privately. Soon after beginning treatment with Kernberg, however, the patient expressed doubts about continuing. In a condescending manner she put down Kernberg's provincial way of dressing and his lack of the "quiet yet firm sense of self-assurance" that she admired in men. She also made derogatory remarks about the small town in which he lived and had his office.

Kernberg reports having a severe reaction to his patient's criticisms, which included experiencing "a sense of futility and dejection," believing he was having "difficulties in thinking precisely and deeply," and feeling "physically awkward." After becoming aware that he and the town in which he lived represented the patient's devalued self-image projected onto him, Kernberg interpreted this to the patient:

> I now said that her image of me as intellectually slow, awkward, and unnattractive, "stuck" in an ugly town, was the image of herself when she felt criticized and attacked by her mother . . . and that her attitude toward me had the quiet superiority, the surface friendliness, and yet subtle devaluation that she experienced so painfully as coming from her mother [p. 107]

Although, according to Kernberg, the woman said she felt better after this interpretation, he notes that "she now reverted to a dependent relationship with me, practically without transition, while projecting the haughty, derogatory aspects of herself as identified with her mother" onto a man she was dating. It would seem that the patient quickly abandoned her efforts to establish an alter ego transference with Kernberg but may have tried to experience her male friend as an alter ego embodying the aspects of herself she needed to disavow in order to establish a relationship with Kernberg.

What shall we make of Kernberg's countertransference reactions, which he refers to as a "complementary identification?" In the face of the patient's devaluing statements about him, Kernberg appears to have experienced a severe loss of trust in himself as a skillful therapist and as an attractive man. From the perspective of self psychology, we might conjecture that the patient failed to live up to her promise as a mirroring selfobject. When Kernberg realized that she had attributed to him qualities she disavowed in herself, he assumed that the patient had unconsciously induced in him what she had found unacceptable in herself. In other words, Kernberg blamed the patient for causing him to believe that her criticisms of him were warranted. Thus, the notion that the analyst is induced by the patient to experience projected intrapsychic experiences appears to be a way of understanding strong countertransference reactions resulting from the analyst's disappointment in the patient as a selfobject.

In keeping with his theoretical inclination to view this as an example of projective identification and given his belief that "Interpretation of projection identification in borderline conditions temporarily *increases* reality testing and ego strength" (1987, p. 96), Kernberg interpreted the transference to the patient. Unfortunately, in so doing he derailed her efforts to experience him as an alter ego selfobject. I therefore propose that what is commonly referred to as projective identification, and thought to be a "primitive defense" common among psychotic and borderline patients, may often represent efforts by patients to establish alter ego transferences.

DISSOCIATION, TRAUMA, AND THE SEARCH FOR THE HIDDEN SELF

Alter ego transferences are likely to occur among patients who disavow aspects of themselves. Who are these patients? Basch (1981, 1983) argues that disavowal entails dissociative splits in vital realms of self-experience, splits that arise in the context of narcissistic trauma. This conceptualization is congruent with the "shattered fantasy" theory of trauma (Ulman and Brothers, 1988), in which trauma is viewed as a dissociative phenomenon resulting from the shattering and faulty restoration of fantasies of self in relation to selfobject that organize self-experience.

Mr. C does appear to have suffered numerous developmental traumas involving his "narcissistically enmeshing mother" (1971) (p. 249), whom Kohut described as "a latent schizophrenic" (p. 257). For example, it seems likely that Mr. C was traumatized by his mother's abrupt withdrawal from him at the age of six when she was pregnant with his brother. During this period, according to Kohut, Mr. C developed fantasies concerning an imaginary playmate. In the clinical and child development literature, imaginary playmates have been described in ways that suggest that they function both as fantasized twins and fantasized alter egos (see, for example, Manosevitz, Prentice, and Wilson, 1973; Harvey, 1975; Fraiberg, 1987). At times they seem to provide companionship for the lonely child and at other times they seem to carry out in fantasy all the naughty, rude, or otherwise unacceptable behaviors the child wishes to display but must repudiate for fear of alienating parental selfobjects.

It may well be that as a child Mr. C availed himself of both imaginary playmate functions. Kohut conjectures that Mr. C envisioned his still-unborn brother as a twin who would be a companion. His imaginary playmate, on the other hand, may well have functioned as an alter ego embodying disavowed aspects of himself, an early version of his transference to Kohut.

Mr. C's need for Kohut as an alter ego selfobject appears to derive primarily from his having disavowed archaic grandiose fantasies; these were " bizarre fantasies of greatness and power in which he had indulged for prolonged periods and [which were accompanied by] the apprehension that he might not be able to return from them to the world of reality" (Kohut, 1971, pp. 195–196). It seems likely that after having encouraged his grandiose illusions, Mr. C's mother traumatically betrayed his trust in her as a mirroring selfobject by suddenly abandoning him psychologically at the time of her pregnancy. Deprived of the empathic responsiveness that would have promoted the gradual transformation of his grandiose fantasies into more mature forms, Mr. C appears to have dissociatively split off his passionate claims to greatness for fear of succumbing to psychosis. Having initially located his struggles to integrate disavowed aspects of himself in Kohut, Mr. C was able, after the alter ego transference had been worked through, to attain a sense of cohesive selfhood.

Another excellent example of the longing for alter ego selfobjects is to be found in Anna Freud's (1966, pp. 123–128) clinical vignette of the analysis of a young governess. The patient reported her childhood preoccupation with two longings: to have beautiful clothes and to have a number of children. Shabbily dressed, unmarried, and childless when she entered treatment, the woman was enormously interested in the love life, the clothing, and the children of other women. Having disavowed her own ambitions and wishes for admiration, she apparently sought the company of vain women and chose a career as a caretaker of their children in order to achieve a measure of closeness with alter ego selfobjects who embodied these disavowed aspects of herself.

Anna Freud explains the woman's situation as reflective of a "renunciation of instinct" and the subsequent formation of "an exceptionally severe superego" that stopped her from seeking gratification of her own wishes. According to Freud, the case illustrates the defense of "altruistic surrender," a "normal" use of projection by means of which people "form valuable positive attachments and consolidate relations with one another." If we attempt to translate

Freud's explanation into terms more congruent with self-psychological thinking, we might hypothesize that the governess, like Mr. C,
could not trust childhood caretakers to function as mirroring selfobjects and therefore disavowed her untransformed grandiose fantasies. Her connection to women who possessed all that she disavowed
in herself appears to have offered her the opportunity to temporarily
experience a sense of cohesive selfhood.

In what follows I present a portion of my self-psychological
treatment of a young woman who had been severely traumatized by
physical abuse and neglect in childhood in the hope that it will further
illuminate the nature of alter ego transferences and their restorative
role in cases of psychic trauma.

THE CASE OF LENA

"I can't stand the way you always agree with me. You remind me of
those wimpy shrinks in the movies. A therapist should have more
guts." Although her treatment had begun only a few weeks earlier,
Lena, a 30-year-old nurse, seemed to have no qualms about bom-
barding me with criticism. Her verbal attacks were usually aimed at
two sets of flaws she perceived in my personality; one set included
my weakness, passivity, and cowardice while the other included my
"chutzpah," exploitiveness, and self-indulgence. For example, after I
once failed to accommodate her request for a change of appointment,
she sneered, "You get everything your way, don't you? You're so
damned sure it's coming to you."

One might imagine that being the target of Lena's relentless verbal
assaults would have been hard to bear. Surprisingly, however, I was
rarely wounded by her vituperations. On the contrary, I actually
looked forward to sessions with her. Perhaps it was the childlike
delight she appeared to take in finding fault with me or the warmth
of her smile as she entered my office or her reluctance to leave at the
end of sessions that informed me of her growing sense of pleasure in
our relationship. Moreover, her criticisms rarely addressed the failings I find most regrettable in myself.

After a while I realized that Lena experienced herself as possessing
qualities that were the diametric opposites of the qualities she found
so deplorable in me. She presented herself as strong, tough, and able
to stand up to the arrogant doctors with whom she worked; at the
same time, she considered herself highly principled, devoutly reli-
gious, and selflessly devoted to the care of others.

Curiously, despite her protestations that she was a woman to
reckon with, Lena looked like a little girl. Slim and petite, she used no

makeup. Her long straight hair was either tied in pigtails or held down Alice-style with a velvet band. With her "uniform" of jeans and sweatshirts, her speech peppered with the latest slang, and the careless, uninhibited way she moved, I frequently had to remind myself that I was in the presence of a grown woman.

Lena's enthusiastic, almost gleeful haranguing of me during sessions contrasted with the darker, more depressed tone of her complaints about her mother. Although her father had subjected her to brutal beatings from the time she entered puberty at around 11 to the time he died, when she was 18, Lena rarely mentioned his faults. Instead, she enumerated her mother's failings in great detail, portraying her as frail, nervous, and remarkably ill-suited to the demands of motherhood, a woman so inordinately preoccupied with herself she had little time for a daughter. As Lena put it, "She is always on her mind."

I subsequently learned that Lena's paternal grandmother had been the principal caretaker in her early life. Lena believed her mother had always hated her mother-in-law and had deeply resented her husband's attachment to her. Nonetheless, the grandmother appears to have been tolerated as a member of the household as long as she was useful in freeing Lena's mother from the drudgery of child care. Lena described her grandmother as gentle and caring but overindulgent toward her only son. Lena recalled her deep sense of loss at the age of ten when bitter fights between her mother and grandmother led her father to establish his mother in an apartment in a distant city where one of her daughters lived.

It was only after his mother moved away that Lena's father began his vicious beatings. Lena suspects that his rage was, in part, triggered by his resentment at his wife for forcing his separation from his mother. Only his mother and Lena herself as a young child were spared from the abusiveness with which her father apparently treated everyone else in his life. Lena recalls having been well aware that he was considered a tyrant by his employees and a "willful hothead" by other family members.

Despite her avowed contempt for her mother, Lena still lived at home. She explained that she had decided not to move out on her own after her father's death: "My mother could never manage without me. She's so inept, it's a wonder she can tie her own shoes." Lena seemed to have virtually no social life of her own but spent a great deal of time chauffeuring her mother on frequent shopping excursions, accompanying her to various doctor's appointments, and going out with her for dinner and the theater.

For all her criticisms of me, Lena never once expressed any doubt about my ability to help her. However, after six months of sessions that seemed repetitive almost to the point of ritual, I worried that the treatment was stalemated. My failure to understand the strange nature of the transference troubled me. Then, one day in her eighth month of treatment Lena entered my office looking uncharacteristically depressed. She began to describe a movie she had seen the night before in which a little girl had been beaten by her drunken father. As she spoke, tears streamed down her cheeks. Without changing her expression or pausing to wipe her eyes, Lena struggled to continue her account of the movie until, at last, she broke into sobs. With her face contorted by rage and pain, she screamed, "I'm not crying for myself, I'm crying for the little girl in the movie."

"Lena," I asked quietly, "Would it be so bad to cry for yourself?"

"It would be disgusting!" she cried. "It would make me sick. I would be just like my mother. She never stops moaning and groaning. She even used to cry for herself when my father beat me."

Asked to elaborate, Lena recalled the first time her father had hit her:

> I had just tried on a new dress that I loved because it made me look so grown-up—like a real teenager. I pranced over to my father to ask if I could show my dress to a friend. Instead of beaming at me as I expected, his face got all red and angry. Suddenly, he slapped me hard and he said. "Stop showing off." Then he stormed out of the house. I was stunned and began to cry. My mother, who had been standing nearby, screamed at me and broke into tears. "Look what you've done," she said, "You drove Daddy away. Now what am I going to do?" I ended up comforting her.

In the next few sessions Lena recounted many similar incidents in which she had assumed a caretaking role vis-à-vis her mother at times when she herself was at her neediest, that is, when her connection to her beloved father was being threatened by his abusiveness. I understood Lena's experience of his violence toward her as betrayals of her trust in him as a mirroring and idealized selfobject (Brothers, 1989, 1990a, 1990b, 1992), traumas that shattered the unconscious fantasies organizing her self-experience (Ulman and Brothers, 1988).

Overwhelmed with disintegration anxiety at the rupture of these vitally needed selfobject connections to her father and grandmother, Lena had turned in desperation to her mother. It appears that her strongest hope of establishing a trustworthy bond with her mother involved repudiating her own neediness and offering herself as a caretaker. "I guess you could say that my mother and I switched roles," Lena said. "I'm a lot better at taking care of her needs than she is at taking care of mine." Consequently, Lena's self-experience became increasingly organized by selfobject fantasies in which she was the provider of selfobject functions for others (e.g., her mother and her patients), rather than the recipient, a situation common among abused children (see Brothers, 1989, 1990a, 1990b).

From a reconstruction of the trauma-filled years of Lena's childhood it became apparent that an important way in which Lena took care of her mother was by "staying a little girl for her." Lena believed that she had been conceived to keep her parents' marriage alive. "I don't think my father liked my mother very much," she confided. "He stayed home with her because he was crazy about me." After a long pause she added, "Until I started to grow up. Then he stayed out more and more. Whenever he spent time in the house, I ended up getting beaten."

I now realized that the flaws Lena decried in my personality represented aspects of herself that she had disavowed as a means of maintaining a bond with her mother. For example, what she took for my weakness, cowardice, and passivity reflected her own disavowed neediness and fearfulness. What she saw as my temerity, self-indulgence, and willingness to exploit others reflected her own sense of entitlement, her ambitions, and her wishes for gratification. Only by presenting herself as a strong, fearless, giving caretaker who would not make demands of her own could she hope to maintain a relationship with her mother. Her predominant transference fantasy apparently involved a merger with me as an alter ego selfobject in the presence of whom she was enabled to achieve a sense of connection with hidden aspects of her own self. The more she condemned me for possessing these "flaws," the more she seemed to attain an experience of herself as whole.

Although Lena often bragged about her altruistic devotion to others, she appeared to have unconsciously elaborated numerous sadistic fantasies. In many recurrent dreams and some intrusive waking fantasies she saw herself as inflicting humiliating and painful torture on those entrusted to her care. Her sadistic fantasies were often manifested in her interactions with her mother. For example, in the guise of describing her own helpfulness Lena would publicly reveal her mother's foibles; she once told a roomful of her mother's guests that she had really cooked the food her mother had taken credit for preparing.

Lena's sadistic fantasies and enactments may be understood as further efforts at self-restoration following her shattering traumas. As the abuser (like her father), instead of the abused, Lena may well have attempted to regain an experience of herself as powerful and effective and may have temporarily restored archaic selfobject fantasies of idealized merger with her father. It is likely that in addition to experiencing me as an alter ego selfobject, Lena may have used her critical attacks on me to serve similar functions.

After some months of sessions filled with Lena's detailed descriptions of traumatic scenes from her childhood, the character of the treatment slowly began to change. Increasingly, as Lena related incident after incident in which her parents had profoundly disappointed her need for them as selfobjects, she gave greater expression to her pain and anger. At times she wept unashamedly over her deep sense of loss for the father of her early childhood, the father who had seemed to cherish and enjoy her as she was. At other times she raged at his abusiveness.

Encouraged by Lena's growing freedom to express a fuller range of feelings, I responded to her with many statements I hoped would convey my empathic understanding. Whereas in sessions at the beginning of treatment similar statements of mine had elicited a barrage of criticism, Lena now seemed comforted and appreciative of them. With her growing trust that I would respond to her affective expression with affirmation and acceptance instead of the exasperation and withdrawal she had come to expect from her self-absorbed mother, Lena increasingly acknowledged her sense of deprivation and her conviction that she deserved more ("I have a right to get what I need in life"). Moreover, she spoke freely about her terror of "losing all sense of who [she was]" and admitted experiencing deeply dissociated states in which "the edges of reality get blurred." Her criticisms of me decreased as she began to integrate these heretofore disavowed aspects of herself. Her need to experience me as an alter ego selfobject was diminishing.

Nevertheless, the therapeutic relationship remained turbulent for many months. The following incident is representative of this period in treatment, which was dominated by the working through of Lena's alter ego transference. An unexpectedly lengthy phone conversation in my break between patients caused me to be a few minutes late in inviting Lena into my office for her session. Flushed and tense, Lena seemed to be fighting back tears as she entered my office. "How can your patients put up with your lack of professionalism?" she asked contemptuously. "You don't even start your sessions on time." After apologizing for starting late, I observed that Lena seemed very upset with me and asked what my failure to begin promptly had meant to her. Instead of answering, Lena berated me for being selfish and inconsiderate. She then described a recent episode that vividly illustrated her mother's selfishness and inconsiderateness. Obviously feeling miserable, Lena fell into a stony silence that lasted until the session was over. I doubted that my lateness was sufficient cause for her intense reaction and tried, without success, to reconstruct our previous session in the hope of finding the meaning of the disruption between us.

In her next session Lena reported the following dream:

> I am in a subway train on my way to see you. A man who is sitting opposite me unexpectedly stands up, walks up to me, and smacks my face. I get off the train and run to your office. When I come in, I start to cry. You greet me as usual. Suddenly you grab my shoulders and shake me. Then you say in a hard voice, "Stop being a baby!" Another patient comes in and you tell me that you have to give her my time.

Responding to my questions about the dream, Lena mentioned that she had arrived early for her previous session and had watched me say good-bye to the female patient I see before her. This stylishly dressed, middle-aged woman had struck Lena as "someone who really doesn't need therapy." Somewhat hesitantly she noted, "You seemed sad to see her go."

"And then I kept you waiting," I said. "You must have wondered if I were pleased to see you or if I wished to have another session with that woman."

"I guess so," Lena responded. "She looks so mature and self-sufficient. It's probably like a tea party in here when she comes."

I now surmised that Lena had interpreted my keeping her waiting after a session with this seemingly self-sufficient woman as confirmation of her fears about me, namely, that I, like her mother, could not be trusted to accept her needs, demands, and fears. I would be happier with her, Lena apparently concluded, if only she were more self-sufficient. Moreover, I could hardly be depended on to comfort her after a humiliating blow (my keeping her waiting). In that moment I had seemed the very personification of her mother, whose own neediness prevented her from comforting Lena following her father's brutal assaults. With all hope that I might serve her mirroring and idealizing needs dashed and faced once again with the terror of disintegration, Lena had attempted to reinstitute a much-needed selfobject connection to me as an alter ego with her barrage of criticisms.

Lena accepted my interpretation that my actions before our previous session had understandably alarmed her, that she felt I was really no more accepting of her neediness than her mother and no more capable of soothing her distress. As was true following many similar episodes during this period, Lena's criticisms of me then abated. At the present, time, in the fourth year of treatment, Lena no longer appears to experience me as an alter ego selfobject. Her predominant transference fantasies now involve her experience of me as a mirroring selfobject who admires and appreciates her with all her needs and fears and as an idealized maternal selfobject in whose presence she feels soothed and protected. She becomes critical of me mainly when she experiences me as failing to provide these essential functions. For example, on my return from a recent vacation she chided me for having neglected her. "And I had begun to think you were someone I could depend on," she huffed.

Although Lena still struggles over the prospect of leaving her mother, she has begun to spend time with people her own age. She also dresses more age-appropriately and has cut her hair in a "grown-up" style, further indications that she is integrating those aspects of herself that had been disavowed.

LENA AND MR. C

There are several points of difference between the transferences of Lena and Mr. C. First, Mr. C initially attributed to Kohut qualities in himself that hid those he had disavowed (e.g., experiencing himself and Kohut as devoid of ambition masked his untransformed grandiosity). In contrast, the qualities Lena criticized in me directly corresponded to those she disavowed in herself (e.g., her neediness, fearfulness, and sense of entitlement). Second, the working through of Mr. C's alter ego transference initially involved his locating the conflict over the integration of disavowed aspects of himself within Kohut, whereas Lena did not experience me as conflicted. In fact, it was only after finding it possible to express within the transference aspects of herself that she had previously disavowed that Lena appeared to become aware of her conflicts. And, third, unlike Mr. C, Lena did not continue to find new qualities in me to criticize after one set of her own disavowed attributes had been worked through.

Nevertheless, the function of the alter ego transferences in both cases appears to have been very similar. Both Mr. C and Lena suffered traumatic disappointments in parental selfobjects that shattered the fantasies of self in relation to selfobject organizing their self-experience. Evidence of these shattering traumas is to be found in their bizarre and sadistic fantasies, which may be understood in several ways: (1) as disintegration products of their fragmenting selves, (2) as expressions of the archaic (untransformed) nature of these fantasies, and (3) as faulty efforts at (defensive) self-restoration.

Moreover, in response to the shattering of their selfobject fantasies both Mr. C and Lena disavowed aspects of themselves. Both apparently sought the presence of the therapist as a means of experiencing, through transference fantasies of alter ego merger, a sense of being reconnected with these hidden parts of themselves. Having been split off and disavowed, these aspects of self were unable to undergo further transformation. In the context of alter ego transferences transformation is resumed.

Lena's disavowal of her sense of entitlement and her "altruistic devotion" to her mother and her patients resemble the efforts undertaken by Anna Freud's governess. In other words, like the governess who craved closeness with vain women, Lena sought to experience her mother as an alter ego selfobject in relation to whom she could obtain vicarious satisfaction of her own needs. However, this effort was doomed to failure insofar as her relationship to her mother foreclosed the possibility of reintegrating and transforming split-off realms of herself.

Like Kohut, I never directly interpreted the patient's alter ego transference; I did not tell Lena she criticized qualities in me that she disavowed in herself. Had I done so, I would have interfered with her fantasy of me as an alter ego, a fantasy she relied upon as a means of stemming the tide of self-fragmentation. Instead, I would interpret my selfobject failures as they threatened her with transference repetitions of traumatic betrayals in her early life.

SUMMARY AND CONCLUSIONS

In keeping with the definition of alter ego as "another side of oneself, a second self," I have proposed a new understanding of alter ego transferences. These transferences reflect a patient's need for the presence of another person who functions as a selfobject in whom disavowed or hidden aspects of self-experience are found. With the activation of an alter ego transference fantasy an experience of self-cohesion is attained. Kohut's case of Mr. C, Anna Freud's case of the "altruistic" governess, and my case of Lena were used as illustrations.

It is my contention that alter ego transferences are most likely to arise among trauma survivors who attempt to restore shattered selfobject fantasies by means of disavowal and dissociation. It is the therapist's trustworthy demonstration of empathic responsiveness to the affects, wishes, and needs that were disavowed, in contrast to the dreaded response typical of the traumatically disappointing selfobjects in the patient's life, that sets the stage for the establishment and working through of these transferences.

Twinship and alter ego transferences are similar in that both reflect the patient's need to experience another person as like himself or herself. However, each serves strikingly different functions. While twinship transferences provide reassuring "confirmation of the feeling that one is a human being among other human beings" (Kohut, 1984, p. 200), thereby enabling patients to *maintain* a sense of cohesive selfhood, alter ego transferences offer opportunities for patients to *restore* a sense of cohesive selfhood following shattering traumas.

REFERENCES

The American Heritage Dictionary of the English Language, 1980, New College Edition, s.v. "alter ego."

Basch, M. F. (1981), Psychoanalytic interpretation and cognitive transformation. *Internat. J. Psycho-Anal.*, 62:151–175.

_____ (1983), The perception of reality and the disavowal of meaning. *The Annual of Psychoanalysis*, 11:125–153. New York: International Universities Press.

Brothers, D. (1989), Treating trust pathology in trauma survivors: A self-psychological approach. Presented at the Twelfth Annual Conference on the Psychology of the Self, San Francisco, October 14.

_____ (1990a), The trustworthy selfobject: Psychological giving and the therapeutic relationship. Presented at the annual Conference of The Training and Research Institute for Self Psychology/The Society for the Advancement of Self Psychology, New York City, May 5.

_____ (1990b), The recollection of incest as a consequence of working through trust disturbances in the transference. Presented at the Sixth Annual Meeting of the Society for Traumatic Stress Studies, San Francisco, October 31.

_____ (1992), Trust disturbance and the sexual revictimization of incest survivors: A self-psychological perspective. In: New Therapeutic Visions: *Progress in Self Psychology, Vol. 8*, ed. A. Goldberg. Hillsdale, NJ: The Analytic Press, pp. 75–91.

Detrick, D. W. (1985), Alterego phenomena and the alterego transferences. In: *Progress in Self Psychology, Vol. 1*, ed. A. Goldberg. New York: Guilford Press, pp. 240–256.

_____ (1986), Alterego phenomena and the alterego transferences. In: *Progress in Self Psychology, Vol. 2*, ed. A. Goldberg. New York: Guilford Press, pp. 299–304.

Fraiberg, S. (1987), Self representation in language and play. In: *The Selected Writings of Selma Fraiberg*, ed. L. Fraiberg. Columbus, OH: Ohio State University Press, pp. 536–537.

Freud, A. (1966), *The Ego and the Mechanisms of Defense*. New York: International Universities Press.

Harvey, N. A. (1975). Imaginary playmates. In: *A Study of Imagination in Early Childhood*, ed. R. Griffiths. New York: Arno Press.

Kernberg, O. F. (1987), Projection and projective identification: Developmental and clinical aspects. In: *Projection, Identification, Projective Identification*, ed. J. Sandler. New York: International Universities Press, pp. 93–115.

Klein, M. (1946), Notes on some schizoid mechanisms. In: *Developments in Psycho-Analysis*, ed. P. Heimann, S. Isaacs & J. Riviere. London: Hogarth Press, 1952, pp. 292–320.

Kohut, H. (1971), *The Analysis of the Self*. New York: International Universities Press.

_____ (1977), *The Restoration of the Self*. New York: International Universities Press.

_____ (1984), *How Does Analysis Cure?* ed. A. Goldberg & P. Stepansky. Chicago: University of Chicago Press.

Manosevitz, M., Prentice, N. M. & Wilson, F. (1973), Individual and family correlates of imaginary companions in preschool children. *Develop. Psychol.*, 8:72–79.

Sandler, J. (1987), The concept of projective identification. In: *Projection, Identification, Projective Identification*, ed. J. Sandler. New York: International Universities Press, pp. 13–26.

Ulman, R. B. & Brothers, D. (1988), *The Shattered Self*. Hillsdale, NJ: The Analytic Press.

Chapter 16

To Free the Spirit from Its Cell

Bernard Brandchaft

> PASTOR MANDERS: I refuse to discuss such questions with you, Mrs. Alving—not while you're in such an unstable state of mind. But what do you mean by calling yourself a coward just because . . .
>
> MRS. ALVING: I'll tell you what I mean by it. I'm timid and frightened because I can never be free of the ghosts that haunt me.
>
> PASTOR MANDERS: What do you mean by that?
>
> MRS. ALVING: I'm haunted by ghosts. When I heard Regina and Osvald out there, it was just as if there were ghosts before my very eyes. But I'm inclined to think we're all ghosts, Pastor Manders; it's not only the things we've inherited from our fathers and mothers that live on in us, but all sorts of old dead ideas and old dead beliefs, and things of that sort. They're not actually alive in us, but they're rooted there all the same, and we can't rid ourselves of them. I've only to pick up a newspaper, and when I read it I seem to see ghosts gliding between the lines. I should think there must be ghosts all over the country—as countless as grains of sand. And we are, all of us, so pitifully afraid of the light.
>
> Henrik Ibsen, *Ghosts*, Act Two

The conference out of which this volume grew marked the tenth anniversary of the final appearance of Heinz Kohut at our deliberations. It was a time to acknowledge how sorely we missed his presence. Our memories turned to Berkeley and we were inevitably reminded of his tearful farewell, a scene of unforgettable heroism and tragic eloquence. Heinz Kohut's departure from our proceedings left a yawning space of which we were acutely aware. In the past decade self psychology, the discipline he founded, has confounded those critics who, too eagerly, wrote it off as a fad and prophesied its demise (Rangell, 1982). It has firmly established its importance in the therapeutic community. Self psychology came into existence because Kohut had come to believe that by converting hypotheses into doctrine classical analysis had brought psychoanalytic development to a cul-de-sac. He contrasted the world of dogmatic religion with that of creative science, and he recognized that to the latter, absolute truth is essentially unknowable. And so, acting in fidelity to his own observations and his own experiences, he forged a new and historic path that freed frozen potentialities of his patients and his own.

I wish here to acknowledge my personal and professional debt to Heinz Kohut. I was reminded again of this only recently, when I reread "The Two Analyses of Mr. Z" (Kohut, 1979) a dozen years after I had last read it. I was amazed to find how many of the understandings that I discuss in this chapter were anticipated in that paper.

The ten years have, however, also provided us with a wealth of clinical experience with the basic principles Kohut elaborated so brilliantly. Nothing in a creative science stays the same. "Even the most convincing conclusions, seemingly self-evident and beyond question, may ultimately come into serious question " (1984, p. 57), Kohut (1984) wrote, leaving this as an essential part of his legacy. Now we face the challenge of addressing the great tasks remaining before us. It is a time to take a fresh look at problems yet unsolved. For us, as for Kohut, what is unquestioned cannot be changed. Our theories are different, but to see only what our own theories make recognizable to us remains a continuing hazard of our occupation. These new concepts must not be allowed now to become accepted and passed on as established or revealed truths. That is the danger that Arnold Goldberg (1990) portrayed so elegantly in *The Prisonhouse of Psychoanalysis*. Every previous innovative development within our field has been overtaken and circumscribed by that somber fate. Perhaps my own personal experience over the past 40 years in psychoanalysis especially alerts me to this peril. Perhaps, equally, I choose this focus here as my way of honoring that special bond that I share with colleagues with whom I have had the privilege of collaboration in this unique enterprise over the past nearly 15 years. It is a bond best defined in the words of Albert Einstein: "The right to search for truth also implies a duty. One must also not conceal any part of what one has recognized to be true."

Over the past decade I have come to recognize certain problems that call into question important concepts and common practices within self psychology. In order the better to illustrate these problems I will present some excerpts drawn from the treatment of two patients. The first, an architect, and the second, a writer, were each painfully saddled with conceptions whose underlying assumptions they had never recognized or been able to question. These pretty much determined their perceptions and ideas about who they were, which in turn predetermined what they were doing—and were unable to do—on this planet. Both the concepts I brought to the patients and those they brought to me had to be reconsidered in order to establish the "space" in which, in one case, a new edifice might be created and, in the other, a new script written. In the depths of that dimension of experience which is my focus here there was operative a pervasive fear, one more difficult to identify and engage directly and therapeutically: *a fear not to repeat*, a terror of change.

The fear of repeating traumatic childhood experiences creates a resistance that is now readily recognizable. It takes the form of defense structure that Kohut (1984) described as involving

> activities undertaken in the service of psychological survival, that is, as the patient's attempt to save at least that sector of his nuclear self, however small and precariously established . . . , that he has been able to construct and maintain despite serious insufficiencies in the develop-ment-enhancing matrix of the selfobjects of his childhood [p. 115].

According to Ornstein (1990), these defense organizations "continue to be reactivated whenever the patient is experiencing his environment as unresponsive and unempathic" (p. 42). Their treatment constitutes a challenge "to be able to interpret habitual, deeply unconscious defensive positions from within the patient's own perspective and to recognize—and appreciate—the functions they serve in protecting the vulnerable self in less than optimal environmental circumstances" (p. 46). These defensive structures are considered to constitute "the most powerful obstacles to change" and must be subjected to the process of working through in a successful analysis (pp. 41–42).

With the patients I am describing here our focus was drawn increasingly to a defensive structure different from that described by Kohut in the passage just quoted. Rather, operating at an unconscious level, this formation acted as a stubborn resistance to change by dismantling and preventing the consolidation of new structures of experience. It was triggered in response to the patient's experiencing the analyst not as unresponsive or unempathic but as an invaluable ally in the maintenance of a therapeutic bond that was based on sustained empathic inquiry into deepening recesses of the patient's subjective experience. The fear here arose with the patient's perception of the approach of imminent and profound change. It appeared whenever the process of inquiry illuminated and thus threatened some deeply entrenched unconscious principle of organization of experience of the self, a principle in which the essence of an archaic tie to a primary caretaker continued to live on.

The direct observation of the operation of this defense organization indicates that resistance to change is stratified and multidimensional and that the working-through process must provide access to and address this layer of unconscious experience if the analysis is to have its most important mutative impact. Thus, I would take the position that analysis of the defense organizations that cluster around the need to protect vulnerable self-structures is an essential but not ultimately conclusive target of the analytic procedure. In order to become engaged in the serious task of analyzing the more deeply embedded psychological configurations, "the patient has to be certain that the current selfobject, the analyst, is not again exposing him to the pathological milieu of early life" (Kohut, 1979, p. 13). On the other hand, neglect of the more deeply embedded sources of resistance to change will lead to a result in which improvement may be limited to certain areas while the patient's essential perspective on himself and his world remains unchanged, with the possibility foreclosed for examining and transcending a relentless, unconscious contribution to the forms and quality of his life.

It was this deeper source of resistance to change that kept the patients I am describing here imprisoned in gulags of their minds. Its treatment is complicated, for it involves an investigation into and an essential realignment of the ordering principles that shape experience and determine the nature and structure of subjective realities. In order for this development to occur in a patient, the analyst is likely also to have to undergo a painful process of realignment in what he observes and in the focus of his interpretive activity. It is to the case of the architect to which I now wish to turn in order to illustrate my thesis.

Patrick, the architect, had earned an outstanding reputation for the quality of his work and for the dedication and absolute integrity he brought to it. Still youthful and athletic in appearance, he had achieved much of what he had set out to do in life. He was looked up to and regarded as an unqualified success by many who knew him. He had participated actively in his family life, raising three children who appeared successful in their own right, and he maintained a stable marital relation of many years' duration. Nevertheless, life had become not only joyless but a source of almost ceaseless torment for him. His feelings of emptiness and depression had some years ago driven him to a severe addiction. He acknowledged almost wistfully that even such costly relief had become foreclosed for him.

What was it that continued to agonize Patrick so cruelly? He was the eldest son of a father who had freed himself from his own childhood impoverishment to become a legend in the ranks of pioneer developers of housing tracts and shopping centers, a man who had amassed undreamed-of wealth. The father attempted to pass on the lessons life had taught him to his son, whom he loved, with the same tenacity that had served him so successfully in his business affairs. He espoused the virtues of hard work with a missionary ardor, and he heaped scorn and predictions of apocalypse upon anyone whose zeal in this direction was less than his own. Attention to detail he elevated to the status of *the* nuclear art form. "Make certain you do the little things," he would preach, "and the big things will follow." As a boy, Patrick had drawn the unfortunate "little thing" assignment of raking the leaves of their fine new house each afternoon after school. In the evening before the family could sit down to supper, dad would accompany the lad into the yard and inspect the results of his labors. No white-gloved marine sergeant was more dedicated to his task. His father's reproaches and his own forebodings as neglected leaves were discovered and pointed to, his indolence or fraudulence thus unmasked, remained indelibly seared in Patrick's memory.

Having set an example in his own world that his contemporaries fell over themselves trying to learn and emulate, Patrick's father could not understand why he should be having such difficulties in getting his firstborn son to follow simple instructions. Equally difficult for him to comprehend was how Patrick could find appealing any interests or entertain any ambitions other than those he had determined were in the boy's best interest. Increasingly, Patrick's father came to treat such expressions with disdain and as personal rejections of him and his values. He especially could not understand why the boy was so offended whenever they visited one of his new development projects. Instead of seeing his father's entrepreneurial wizardry, Patrick could only see mindless and garish desecration being inflicted on the environment, and having experienced it at shorter range on himself, he reacted viscerally. Although dad regularly and cordially invited Patrick to come along on his fishing trips or sailing boat excursions, he never attended a baseball game in which his son, who took pride in his feats as a second baseman, was playing.

This schism between what he saw and felt and what he was supposed to see and feel—in general, between experiences as they were and as they were supposed to be—remained for Patrick an enduring source of irreconcilable torment. Somehow out of the woof and warp of this relationship Patrick developed a firmly consolidated structure of experience. It was woven and held together by an underlying perspective toward himself and his life that created an architecture for his spirit that was almost as confining as his life with father had ever been. Patrick could never really unlearn very much of what his father had insisted on teaching him. Any spontaneous enthusiasm or fun for anything he might design for himself, including his own lifestyle, came inexorably to be erased, automatically and mysteriously, as if by some unseen master hand and as if it—and, in a profound sense, he—had never really existed.

Patrick was compelled to operate in his profession—one he had somehow had the courage to choose for himself—exactly as if it were his father's first venture in the development business. The possibility of little things turning into very big and disastrous ones had become so enshrined as a principle of not-to-be-questioned truth that Patrick could never again limit the significance to him of any imperfection. In the tight confines of his mind there was no time and no space for the enjoyment of his superbly innovative spirit. He had to concern himself with every detail of any project he undertook, as if it were the lawn that was to be inspected by his father. Patrick drew each design and bird-dogged it through the detailed drafting process. He took the plans to the building authorities himself and personally followed the interminable procedures necessary to secure the required permits. He even had to see that the garbage was taken to the street from his office himself, for he was certain that anyone to whom he delegated the responsibility would forget it sooner or later. If he departed in the slightest from this ritualized existence, he was filled with terrible foreboding. He was compelled to conclude what his father had always maintained—that his insistence on choosing his own life for himself and not accepting what his father chose for him was an unarguable demonstration of his stupidity or willfulness.

Nor could Patrick enjoy even the acclaim and rewards his talents and energies brought him. Helplessly manacled to his father's values and unable to consolidate any of his own, he continued to harbor the unyielding conviction in some corner of his mind that he was fraudulent and undeserving of those tributes. His admirers were reacting to his beautiful buildings; he, unyieldingly, to the neglected and unraked leaves they had not yet seen!

Whatever transient feeling of well-being, confidence, enthusiasm, or hope, arising from some still-active spring inside himself, Patrick experienced in his sessions would regularly disappear, relentlessly vitiated by some self-disparaging thought. Then the space that had been occupied by the feeling of aliveness would be replaced by the more familiar empty malaise and joylessness that had pervaded his childhood.

What happened in my consulting room, I was able to determine, was a faithful replication of what occurred when Patrick was by himself. Observing how his mental operations always came to ground zero in this repetitive self-negating process, I got a vivid sense of how like a cell Patrick's mind was. I could observe how each time the cell door opened with a fresh, innovative thought or exuberant feeling it soon clanged shut again. Only by immersing himself in work to the point of exhaustion had Patrick been able to find some measure of relief from this process.

I have come to recognize this constellation of shifting feeling states as an indication that there is an underlying process at work—ghosts, as it were—that discloses skeletons below. Within this skeletal framework experience is being shaped sequentially by two different and incompatible perspectives according to two different sets of organizing principles. These in turn reflect different and incompatible motivations. This process can assume many forms, frequently insidious and difficult to detect, and one of the two sets of perspectives and motivations, that which divests the self of what is exquisitely personal, is always preprogrammed to prevail. Thus, development on the basis of authenticity of experience and centrality of differentiated choice is repetitively foreclosed. These principles operate from within an area of experience that has been described as the prereflective unconscious (Atwood and Stolorow, 1984). As Basch points out, this corresponds to "the sensorimotor period delineated by Piaget, that is, those first 18 months of life where infants establish patterns of expectation that are not, and may never become, subject to symbolic manipulation" (personal communication).

Caught up in the affective content of their experience, patients are likely to be oblivious to the existence of the subterranean backdrop of other mental operations. As Freud first noted, patients tend unreflectively to believe that experience is explained by events and circumstance and are oblivious to the role played by the unconscious in how events are being processed. Analysts, especially those who lend themselves to sustained immersion in their patients' experience, also tend to become similarly trapped in its content. Such entrapment blinds the analyst to the shifting of affect states and subjective realities that is occurring beyond the focus of their eyes. In these circumstances it is easy to fail to recognize that the forms or symbols in which a particular constellation is finding expression are unimportant except as they provide access to the underlying process. It is easy also to fail to appreciate that the "reality" of the patient's affective state may need not so much to be affirmed or resonated with as opened wide to the processes of self-reflection so that its derivative and subjective origins can be grasped.

In patients like Patrick the process by which one way of organizing experience is usurped by another more forceful, is an internal and automatic replication of crucial developmental events of the child–caretaker experience. That point at which the shift in feeling state from enthusiasm to malaise occurs continues to mark exactly the great divide of developmental derailment. It reflects the fact that the child's attempts to differentiate were stifled by attitudes and actions of caretakers. The patient cannot exit what has become a closed and noxious system. He remains trapped in the structural remains of an archaic tie. The perspective and motivation that prevails is one in which the individual is compelled to submit to a definition of himself determined by forces external to his control or volition, a definition determined by the needs, wishes, and fears of caregivers or those who continue to represent them psychically. "I must believe that I am and must continue to be what you, my caretakers, see me to be" remains the operative organizing principle.

Let me now turn to my second example.

I treated Marco, a writer, striking in his tall, ascetic, and unaffected appearance, a number of years ago and he appeared in my office one Monday after spending the previous Saturday night at the opening performance of his play. He said that he felt "hung over," although he had not been drinking. The misgivings he had had about the staging and the acting proved unwarranted, and the play, he said, went very well. He noticed, however, that at the party afterward he felt sad—"melancholic" he termed it—and he could not explain this to himself. He remembered that he had stood in the rear of the theater while the performance was taking place, listening carefully to his lines being delivered. He felt flashes of pride as he found himself saying to himself "That's okay" and sometimes "That's good!" But they vanished and were replaced by the sadness that enveloped him. The actors at the party were effusive in their praise and the director told him that he thought the play was a major piece of work, but Marco had a sense of unreality about the whole thing. Feeling distant, dull, empty, out of place, and alone as he mingled with the celebrators, he felt as though they were talking about someone else. Surely the drama that he had presented on the stage was no more dramatic than the one taking place inside him. But whose drama was it and what part was he playing in it?

Some months before, Marco had begun to discuss the difficulties he was encountering in his writing. He wrote for television and had two partners who reviewed his work and then made suggestions for revision. Marco had great difficulty in being able to preserve and protect his own contribution in the face of their suggestions. It became clear that this difficulty arose because a familiar configuration was constantly being triggered. Marco was afraid of damaging the feelings of his partners, and this fear interfered with his retaining as central his own purpose of producing what he felt was the best possible script. He compromised himself repeatedly and thus interfered with the unfettered development of his own creativity. As a consequence, his efforts were robbed of the richness and enthusiasm only he could bring to them, and he worked without zest.

A second severe problem occurred when he began with an idea that excited him. Then he would regularly find himself procrastinating, and he was soon overcome with fatigue and lethargy. Only when he approached a deadline could he rouse himself, and then only because the fear of the consequences of disappointing his employers outweighed the vague, sinister, and unrelenting discomfort that brought his excitement, and with it his creativity, to a halt.

In attempting to understand this reaction, Marco recalled that his interest in storytelling was preceded by a childhood passion for reading. In his own room he found that he could enter into the magical worlds of the great storytellers. There he sought and could find refuge from the grey weariness of his home, his mother's unrelieved bitterness, his father's withdrawal and addiction, and the interminable arguments between them. When he was eight or nine, Marco remembered, his mother walked into his room and caught him reading. "Why are you always spending your time that way?" she scolded. "To avoid helping me?" He never showed her any of the stories he subsequently began to write. When he was 12 he wrote the school play and asked his mother to come to watch on the night it was being performed. He wanted so for her to be pleased and proud, but she sat there unmoved and unimpressed. When he was introduced on the stage at the end of the play and the audience applauded, Marco noticed that his mother's hands remained fixed at her sides.

How can one understand Marco's inability to sustain his prideful enthusiasm and its collapse into a state of profound sadness at the premiere of his play? Surely it is clear that Marco remained compelled to continue to experience as his very own his mother's sadness at his early interests, which took him away from her. His mother's perspective continued to replace his own, and this process resulted in Marco's lack of initiative and his absence of zest. It continued to paralyze him and prevented him from being able to negotiate differences with his writing partners that would have protected his own innovations from surrender. Marco's triumph at the opening of his play was being reflected back to him as an example of naughtiness, and he was responding as if he had no mind, no will, no credible experience of his own.

This process and its underlying principles also shaped Marco's personal relationships with women and stripped them also of the quality of volition. Every intimate relationship had inevitably become increasingly difficult for Marco. In each he felt himself under constant pressure to demonstrate that he continued to love his partner and had not grown tired of her, a requirement that in itself inevitably became tiring. Consequently, Marco felt burdened when he was with his partner and relieved when they were apart—relieved, that is, until he would begin to worry that when he next saw his loved one she would be expecting him to make love with her and would be checking to titrate the level of his passion after their separation against what it was before. Nothing could have been more lethal in its effect on his appetite for lovemaking. He knew, moreover, that his partner would be hurt and angry or cold and aloof. That reaction in her was intolerable to him because it made him feel that he was totally bad. Thus, Marco could not help sliding into an archaic definition of who he was. He was, he felt, the very one, unchanged, his mother had reflected back to him so long ago, the boy his mother was sorry she had. Thus he repeatedly surrendered any definition of himself of his own to criteria imposed from outside. Whenever he began to experience his personal self in a perspective of his own—for example, when he began to feel as he was watching the opening night performance of his play that he was for one brief, shining moment his own person, not his mother's, his audience's, his collaborators', or mine—he would soon after feel that he was really selfish, uncaring, and therefore undeserving. That was the principle that turned Marco's success into an incipient melancholia.

Who Marco was remained dependent on the reflection he got from his partner, a principle simple in its elegance. If she smiled, he felt he was good; if she was aloof and cold, he was bad! The particular partner didn't even have to be present for this circuitry to be activated. When he was alone, Marco was preoccupied with her, could not get her off his mind. The picture of her wounded expression, her angry mouth, or flaring eyes imprisoned him. He heard her crying, "Look what you've done to me!" and he could not turn away. He did not feel that he owned his own body, his own affection, person, or mind. Each relationship was a prison cell in which his spirit was trapped.

HISTORICAL NOTES

The phenomenology that I have been discussing has been the focus of much interest, perturbation, and varying interpretation throughout the course of psychoanalytic history. It was the basis of Freud's investigations in the case of the Wolf man, in which Freud came to feel that "something in these people sets itself against their recovery (so that) its approach is dreaded as though it were a danger" (Freud, 1923, p.49). It has been described exhaustively by analysts of the Kleinian school, who have noted repeatedly the resistance of patients to change and their inability to sustain feelings of well-being inside and outside the analysis. Operating on the basis of the paradigm of the mind as an energy-processing apparatus, Kleinians have attributed these repetitive reactions to the death instinct and to pathological biological forces of destructive envy (Bion, 1962; Rosenfeld, 1987; Joseph, 1989). Every major theoretical innovation in psychoanalysis has involved a search for a better understanding and solution to this underlying problem (see, for example, Fairbairn, 1954, pp. 137–146). The inability of his patients to sustain excitement and enthusiasm and to emancipate themselves from protracted states of emotional shallowness and malaise except by resorting to desperate and despairing attempts at self-stimulation was the cardinal symptom that captured Kohut's interest. It was the failure of classical concepts to solve this problem that ultimately motivated his call for a return to the methods of empathy and introspection as "defining the contents and limits of field and determining the theories" of psychoanalysis (Kohut, 1959). The earliest descriptions that emerged from Kohut's rededication to the empathic-introspective stance were of a particular sequencing of feelings. He noted that "a pervasive hypochondriacal brooding may disappear," usually as a result of external praise or interest.

> The patient suddenly feels alive and happy and, for a while at least, shows initiative and has a sense of deep and lively participation in the world. These swings are usually short-lived and they tend to become

the source of uncomfortable excitement. They arouse anxiety and are then soon followed by a chronic sense of dullness and passivity, either experienced openly or disguised by long hours of mechanically performed activities [Kohut, 1971, p. 17].

To explain the anxiety that caused his patient's "heightened pleasure in himself and his increased vitality" to be replaced by a state of depletion, Kohut fell back on the concepts of ego psychology. "These and many other similar complaints," he wrote "are indicative of the ego's depletion because it has to wall itself off against the claims of the grandiose self, or against the intense hunger for a powerful external supplier of self-esteem and other emotional sustenance in the narcissistic realm" (Kohut, 1971, p. 17). Kohut never abandoned this explanation of the anxiety his patients experienced when authentic, demarcated, and poorly consolidated structures began to emerge. It was the crucial element in the dream interpretation that distinguished the second analysis of Mr. Z from the first (Kohut, 1979).

It was inference based on the model of an inadequate mental apparatus that led Kohut to conclude, fatefully, that the anxiety behind the failure to sustain experiences of enthusiasm and joy in the self was triggered by a deficit of psychological structure, thus providing self psychology with a defining organizing principle at its outset as a psychology of deficit rather than a complex psychology of empathically accessible subjective experience. The joyless existence of "tragic man" was the outcome of massively faulty responses to his strivings in childhood for mirroring and idealizable experiences from caretakers. The transmuting internalization that would have laid down cohesive structures in the presence of adequately empathic and optimally frustrating responses had not taken place. The enthusiasm and vitality that emerged episodically with expressions of archaic self-structures (and affirming responses to these) could not be sustained, and they collapsed.

However elegant this perspective, it fails to take adequately into account the nature and extent of the structure that has evolved and become firmly consolidated, a structure I have attempted to describe in the cases of Patrick and Marco. That structure is the consequence of the attitudes reflected back to the child in his formative relationships; within it the archaic ties to parental caretakers are perpetuated. In the psychic reality of unconscious organizing principles is to be found the enduring truth of Freud's observation that the ego never willingly abandons a libidinal object choice (Freud, 1917). The structure that develops out of the matrix of emotionally enslaving early ties forestalls the emergence of new structures, based centrally on inner and distinctive feelings, because these continue to constitute a challenge to those of the parents.

In analysis, when the observational focus is placed on deficit, on what is absent, the importance of identifying and analyzing the imprisoning structure is obscured. The therapeutic endeavor shifts to ways of filling in the deficit by processes of "optimal frustration" and "transmuting internalization" and away from the task of liberating the patient from ties that continue to bind him and that continue to impair his ability to sustain experiences of "the exhilarating bliss of growing self-delimitation" (Kohut, 1979, p. 17) and the joy of recognizing and aggressively pursuing the unfolding design of a self of his own.

In these circumstances it is apparent that the urgent needs for mirroring or idealizable qualities that appear in the selfobject transferences cannot be taken as identical to or comparable with the original selfobject needs now revived in an empathic setting (Schwaber, 1983, p. 60). Only the extension of the process of empathic inquiry can reveal a context in which such selfobject needs are being derivatively activated in order to countermand automatized self-depleting operations. Specific attunement to and recognition of Patrick's and Marco's perceptions and experiential states were unquestionably necessary for the establishment of a firm therapeutic bond (Brandchaft and Stolorow, 1990). These preconditions must be fulfilled if the analytic work is to focus on the enduring and defining impact of early experience on the sense of self and to focus on its continuing contribution to the automatic, invariant, and nonreflective organization that expropriates, redefines, and redirects experience.

When Patrick experienced a reflection of himself, in or outside the analytic transference, at variance with one that his tortured state of mind allowed him to retain, he generally seemed appreciative. However, such experiences, I noted, left him without the tools he needed to be able on his own to identify and ultimately counteract the predetermined shift in perspective that continued to nullify the impact of any beginning positive experience of himself regardless of the source from which it emanated. Consequently, expressions of pride or enthusiasm could be observed regularly to be sucked back down into the more familiar organizing perspective. I believe that continued therapeutic interaction of the kind that purports to provide the "mirroring" affirmation that was denied the patient in his childhood may, in fact, superimpose a well-intended but misguided perspective of the analyst over that which is afflicting the patient. I have observed that these therapeutic interactions tend to contribute to the prolongation of the pattern that Kohut early took note of. "The analysand becomes addicted to the analyst or the analytic procedure and the transferencelike condition which establishes itself in such analyses is indeed the reinstatement of an archaic condition" (Kohut, 1971, p. 46). The uncritical and, I believe, erroneous application of the theory that the path of development of the self consists of progress from archaic to mature selfobject relations can lead to a situation in which addictive attachments can be recycled and perpetuated, relatively unchanged in their depths, through a succession of relationships, including the one between analyst and analysand.

In the patients I am describing the nuclear structures are no longer freely mobilizable. They have become inextricably enmeshed with highly organized and unyielding internal structures in precisely the way their psychological organizations became enmeshed with that of their caretakers in childhood. Whatever the specific intersubjective factors that produced this particular character structure, the mandate has been established that the person continue to define himself by how well or poorly he fulfills what the caretakers needed, expected, and required of him, in both positive and negative aspects. No situation more clearly shows the influence of the observer on the observed than the effect of caretaker on child, and in none is the consequence of that influence more enduring. The first caretakers occupy the role of reflector of an ultimate reality and the absolute definer of who the child is. Their constructs, communicated in a thousand ways—verbal, gestural, and attitudinal—impart meaning to the child's experience. Enduringly negative or positive, hopeful or despairing, nourishing or depleting, these meanings continue to shape the quality and direction his inner life takes. It is the operation of this underlying configuration that dooms people like Patrick and Marco to suffer the fate of Tragic Man, realizing in despair that they have not been living their lives, have not "been true to their inner design" (Kohut, 1977, p. 241).

If the shift in affect state that I have described can be carefully observed over a protracted period and the invariance and automaticity of that shift made evident to the patient, he can be helped to become aware of the processes within him that are codetermining the nature and quality of his life, processes that are outside his control and volition. The anxiety that underlies and motivates the shift, no longer obliterated by unrecognized surrender to an alternative perspective, will then become more accessible to analytic investigation and work.

Perhaps I can illustrate the operation of these therapeutic principles in a brief excerpt from the associations of a patient who has been described previously (Stolorow, Brandchaft, and Atwood, 1987, chap. 4). I will here omit pertinent details except to mention that the patient was getting his chaotic professional affairs in order and, in the process, had engaged a competent and professional office manager upon whom he had become very dependent for the achievement of this goal. The patient's associations were as follows:

> I was aware of being swept along, away from the centrality of my own center of initiative, and I noticed the tendency for this to occur whenever others' spheres of influence intersected with my own. For example, Katherine. She is my office manager and she has certain priorities in the organization of my time, so I found myself fitting in with her schedule for me. If she couldn't fit my appointments with you into her schedule for me, I found myself incredulously fitting in her priorities for me as if they were my own. Her perspective became dominant and obscured any of my own. I became aware of the importance to me of not interfering with her enthusiasm and a gnawing apprehension of what would happen if I did. Gradually and insidiously I became aware of a feeling of not being on top of, but one step behind, always one step behind and never able to catch up. I saw myself rationalize my behavior: "Things at the office are a mess and I have to go along with this routine until things get straightened out and then I'll be able to go back to my analysis."

> Not wanting to undermine her initiative, I found myself swept along, *becoming resentful and unhappy because my life was not my own, even though it always seemed that what was going on was for my own good!*

> I was aware that what was lacking was the quality of ownership, that it was not I who was directing my life, and therefore there was an unmistakable lack of pleasure even in those things that appeared to me to be in my own best interest. What was enormously helpful to me was to continue to be able to be reflective while all this was going on, and so to be able to stay in that space with more wholeness, not lose my self.

Stolorow and I have proposed that "developmental traumata derive their lasting significance from the establishment of invariant and relentless principles of organization that remain beyond the accommodative influence of reflective self-awareness or of subsequent experience" (Brandchaft and Stolorow, 1990, p. 108).

The most serious and lasting damage incurred by developmental traumata is that sustained by the emerging and fragile sense of self and involving the establishment of rigid criteria by which the self is defined. Thus, it becomes essential to observe how the shift in affect states I have described is rooted in automatic relentlessly recurring translocations in the sense of self. Each step toward the realization of a demarcated and authentic personality, each appearance of an emerging sense of personal agency, is initially but fleetingly accompanied by a vitalizing and transcendent sense of self. This was the case with Marco, for example, when he initially felt exultant while watching his play being performed, but such a basis for self-definition was regularly erased and replaced by a feeling of debased fraudulence and dishonor. I have described this process in detail in a previous work on a patient with a seemingly intractable depression (Brandchaft, 1988). The shift from liberating exuberance to the malaise and depletion of defeat and surrender is rooted in this underlying shift in the foundations of the sense of self. To make possible changes at this nuclear level, it is essential that the therapeutic process open these unexplored areas of self-experience to the processes of reflection and analysis in depth.

The operations of unconscious principles of organization that create and maintain an established cohesive psychological structure while continuing to disarticulate and prevent the consolidation of new psychological structure are responsible, in one form or another, for the most frequent, pervasive, and disabling of the disorders of the self. Marco's and Patrick's dullness of existence is in its essence a function of the relentless enfeeblement of a distinctive core, a core trapped and continuously drained of its own vitality, part of the gift of life.

I have referred to the myriad of forms in which this underlying psychological configuration and the unconscious organizing principles that hold it in place can find expression. Marco and Patrick, for example, have each been transfixed with tormenting doubt concerning the truth about who and what they really are, and this doubt extends to the most profound and nuclear of their feelings. In this ceaseless and paralyzing doubt are contained the roots of the obsessive dilemma and its concretizing compulsive rituals. Kohut (1979) described the appearance of this doubt in the case of Mr. Z: as the patient became aware of the extent of his enmeshment with organizing principles established in his early relationship to his mother, as a consequence

of the crucial fact that the mother's emotional gifts were bestowed upon him under the unalterable and uncompromising condition that he submit to total domination by her, that he must not allow himself any independence, particularly as it concerned significant relations with others, he retreated from the pursuit of the analytic task, voicing instead serious doubts as to whether his memories were correct, whether he was not slanting them in his presentation to me [p. 13].

Patrick's enslavement to detail, another patient's periodic torment as to whether he had left a gas jet open, compulsive hand-washing routines I have observed—all have as a central organizing principle, as did the behavior of Mr. Z, a persistent and agonizing doubt concerning the truth about the essence of their humanness. These individuals are continually asking if they are bad or good, destructive or innocent, hateful or lovable. In this torment is the echo of the central and still-unresolved dilemma of childhood: Whose versions and whose perspective is to be believed? The failure of analysis to penetrate to this area of experience, which is exquisitely available to the analytic method of empathic inquiry, has resulted in the tragedy of the virtual therapeutic abandonment of the treatment of this disorder to the neurobiologists, who operate according to impersonal and statistical criteria and neglect the personal.

In a more florid form this oscillation between enthusiasm and malaise in the experience of one's self can also be seen in the manic–depressive syndrome. Narcissistic object choice has generally been recognized as the point of loss in the melancholia that forms part of this picture whereas mania has been ascribed to the defensive denial of that loss (Klein, 1950, pp. 282–283). Without the primary focus on self-experience and the use of empathic inquiry into that experience from within, it was not possible heretofore to identify the manic phase as emerging from the experience of transient shedding of an enslaving tie to a self-annihilating selfobject or to attribute the melancholia to the reestablishment of that tie and, consequently, to the loss of a vital part of the self (as described by my patient Marco in the passage I referred to previously). And underlying an addiction to substances and sexual enactments or rituals can regularly be found the deeper imperative to countermand the tormenting effects of corrosive experience of self not only as reflected in the eyes of another but as arising from within, from an unyielding self-abusive or self-deflating structure.

In whichever of the myriad forms this underlying configuration may come to expression, it is an unerring indicator of a specific developmental derailment. The need of Patrick's and Marco's care-givers to commandeer the child's developmental processes caused a fateful and specific transition. In both cases the individual was deprived of that developmental progression by which he could come increasingly to rely on his own spontaneous, authentic, and noncom-pliant experience as central in his perception, motivation, and inter-pretation. This failure has momentous consequences. It renders the individual permanently the hostage of the responses of another for the determination and definition of who he is. He is imprisoned by a feeling of responsibility for the state of mind of another, and he is utterly unable to use his own unfettered volition in the choices he makes in the fulfillment of his attachments and in the interests he attempts to freely pursue and fully enjoy. Thus, it becomes mandatory that the analytic process reinstate the developmental process at the point at which it was interrupted. This necessarily involves the analysis providing a setting in which the patient can live through whatever anxiety lies in the path of his reclaiming the ownership of his self and determining the laws by which his sense and definition of self are governed. Only in that way will it be possible for him at last to depend upon another without placing himself at risk of surrendering the determination of who he is to that other.

The anxiety that accompanies the shift that occurs each time the person strives once more to break free from the constraints of established principles of organization and the habitual processes built up over a lifetime may be so subtle as to escape notice. In attempting to provide a therapeutic milieu the analyst must be aware of the extent to which this dreaded affect state may have been repressed developmentally because it met with an unattuned or misattuned responsiveness from caretakers. Socarides and Stolorow (1984/1985) emphasize the sensitivity of patients to any indication of such attitudes in the analyst and describe how these attitudes initiate a resistance of their own, the dread to repeat (Ornstein, 1974). There may be feelings of unreality and profound strangeness or estrangement. Frequently, the anxiety takes the form of various concrete symbols of disaster, such as earthquakes, thunder, lightning, and the like (Brandchaft, 1991), or of pervasive hypochondriacal concerns (Kohut, 1979, p. 19). These experiences all convey the sense of threat to the self if there is a shift in its familiar orientation and allegiance. The challenge to existing ways of organizing experience continues always to constitute a painful and, not infrequently, cataclysmic psychological event.

In understanding the resistance to change in the analysis of disorders of the self and the fear that underlies it, Kohut's (1979) description in the case of Mr. Z is pertinent: "As we discovered— *without which progress would surely ultimately be halted*—his fears concerned the loss of the mother as an archaic selfobject, a loss that . . . threatened him with dissolution, with the loss of a self that at these moments he considered to be his only one" (p. 13; italics added). Kohut went on to write that the deepest anxiety experienced by his patient was that in response to movements toward "independent maleness." These continued to reproduce in him the frightened reaction he had had as a child at the "icy withdrawal" of his mother in response to similar steps, a withdrawal to which he had always responded with an emotional return to her. The account of the second analysis of Mr. Z is replete with passages that describe the intense anxiety Mr. Z experienced over and over again as his movements toward autonomous and demarcated selfhood challenged the principles that had hitherto dictated his surrender of such a developmental course.

The fear of being alone and, in that state, the terror that Kohut regarded as the greatest, that of fragmentation, has been frequently isolated and identified as a primary and irreducible factor in maintaining existing and familiar organizations of experience (Adler and Buie, 1979). In treating these patients, however, I observed, as Kohut recognized in the passages cited, that this anxiety is itself an aspect of a more complex state. When he is alone the patient has no access to any information or reflection with which to counteract insistent representations arising from unchallenged archaic and authoritarian definitions of self. He is trapped in an unreflected perspective, one that he does not recognize as perspective but accepts as not-to-be-questioned reality. He is apt to be unaware of the existence of any core of self save that caught in the enmeshing perspective. There is an escalating negation and abuse of the self which suggest experiences of being browbeaten into submission. Unable to find refuge, the patient may then begin dissociating from his experiencing self because he has developed no strategies with which to defuse the bombardment of the stimuli of his internal surround. He may suddenly feel overwhelmed and increasingly frightened by the mechanical and robotic quality of existence. This cycle is especially likely to occur when the patient is alone and at night, when there are no distracting preoccupations and when it may be terminated by desperate and joyless attempts at sexual stimulation, by chemical or alcoholic means, or by sheer exhaustion.

The attempt to organize experience in a new way frequently results in a pervasive and disarticulating doubt about the truth of subjective experience. However, if the context in which this experience regularly recurs can become familiar to the patient, that is, if it regularly follows an attempt to free himself from some constricting relationship or ongoing organizing principle, he will recognize it as a sign of forward movement, even if it is subjectively frightening. When the therapeutic focus has resulted in supporting the processes of self-reflection, the patient can become familiar with the enmeshing structure and its invariant impact on the way experience automatically evolves within it. A third perspective will then have become established within which the assumptions underlying the patient's shifting sense of self become accessible and are no longer sacrosanct and immutable. Then also the experience of dissolution can come to be recognized as involving only one sector of the patient's self-experience, not its totality and not the central sector he wishes to consolidate. In each case the frightening experience and the accompanying distress need subsequently to be carefully investigated in a therapeutic environment in which a firm bond has been established. At this point in the therapeutic interaction the preconceptions of the therapist can have a determining effect upon the subsequent course and outcome. Nowhere are the words of Kohut (1984) more prophetic:

> The difficulties, at times well-nigh insurmountable, that the observer faces are not due to his influence on the field of observation, but to his own shortcomings as an observing instrument. Prejudicial tendencies deeply ingrained within us will often decisively influence what part of the potentially available data we perceive, which among the perceived items we consider important, and ultimately how we choose to explain the data that we selectively perceive [p. 38].

If in the conduct of a therapeutic analysis of a self disorder the unfolding process is not interfered with, the operations of the underlying defensive structure will inevitably emerge. This will have a decisive impact upon the subsequent course of the analysis. Such a process necessitates the formation from the beginning of a therapeutic bond with the patient based upon a commitment to the stance of empathic inquiry (Brandchaft and Stolorow, 1990). This will lead to an awareness, deepening investigation, and gradual illumination of existing unconscious organizing principles and their continuing contribution to the repetitive course that life takes. The accompanying recognition that the existing structure must be disarticulated and its power curtailed so that alternative ways of organizing experience and new implementing structure may develop has profound implications insofar as treatment modalities are concerned. Such a procedure involves a reconsideration of the role of such modalities as affective attunement, resonance, or engagement, as well as of the relative merits of optimal frustration and responsiveness. Central to such reconsideration is an assessment of the extent to which the tool facilitates or impairs the processes of empathic investigation and illumination. I trust I will not be misunderstood here as making a plea for a lesser responsiveness. It is my intent, rather, to emphasize a greater discernment on the part of the therapist, one that leads to continued curiosity and observation and that, so informed, determines the nature of the response and the area to which it is directed.

The basic tools of sustained empathic inquiry that led Kohut to his revolutionary discoveries have persuaded me that a most essential facet of the patient's developmental process is the shift from other-referenced to independent and noncompliant criteria as the central basis for the sense of self. Such a development is necessary in order for the individual to continue to operate from a self that acts as a center of authentic and voluntary initiative. I acknowledge here a similar thesis in *The Sovereign Self* by Francesca von Broemsen (1991). In the cases of Patrick and Marco I have described how their development was constantly being stripped of what was most exquisitely spontaneous and personal and how malaise and lifelessness accompanied that process. It is my impression that the truest measure of the depth of the success of an analysis lies in the extent to which it has helped the patient free himself from the organizing principles that dictate this usurpation and surrender of the self. Only by reclaiming the ownership of his own sense of self and proceeding from a center of initiative within it can the patient experience the joy and enthusiasm of a life more truly his own.

The empathic investigatory process that formed the basis of Kohut's original theories of the psychology of complex states is uniquely suited to the exploration of this area of continuing repetitive derailment and resistance to change. It is to this enduring contribution that we need to periodically return, and we continue to be inspired by Kohut's courageous example. Beyond any specific set of concepts, it continues to be the indispensable tool and compass of the creative science of psychoanalysis. It is a sobering realization, but one we cannot evade, that the future of the heritage Kohut left us is now in our charge. It can be a future of expanding scope and influence if we ourselves, inspired by his example, recognize and overcome our own resistances to change. This is our challenge if we are to illuminate and free the still-imprisoned spirits of our patients from the darkness of their cells and our spirits from the continuing fetters of our own.

REFERENCES

Adler, G. & Buie, D. (1979), Aloneness and borderline psychopathology: The possible relevance of child development. *Internat. J. Psycho-Anal.*, 60:83–97.

Atwood, G. & Stolorow, R. (1984), *Structures of Subjectivity*. Hillsdale, NJ: The Analytic Press.

Bacal, H. (1985), Optimal responsiveness and the therapeutic process. In: *Progress in Self Psychology*, Vol. 1, ed. A. Goldberg. New York: Guilford Press, pp. 202–227.

Bion, W. (1962), *Learning from Experience*. London: William Heinemann.

Brandchaft, B. (1988), A case of intractable depression. In: *Learning from Kohut: Progress in Self Psychology, Vol. 4*, ed. A. Goldberg. Hillsdale, NJ: The Analytic Press, pp. 133–154.

_____ (1991), Whose self is this anyway? Presented to a conference on self psychology, Los Angeles, March 17.

_____ & Stolorow, R. (1990), Varieties of therapeutic alliance. *The Annual of Psychoanalysis*, 18:99–114. Hillsdale, NJ: The Analytic Press.

Fairbairn, W. R. D. (1954), *An Object-Relations Theory of the Personality*. New York: Basic Books.

Freud, S. (1917), Mourning and melancholia. *Standard Edition*, 14:243–258. London: Hogarth Press, 1957.

_____ (1923), The ego and the id. *Standard Edition*, 19:12–63. London: Hogarth Press, 1962.

Goldberg, A. (1990), *The Prisonhouse of Psychoanalysis*. Hillsdale, NJ: The Analytic Press.

Joseph, B. (1989), *Psychic Equilibrium and Psychic Change: Selected Papers of Betty Joseph*, ed. E.B. Spillius and M. Feldman. London: Tavistock/Routledge.

Klein, M. (1950), A contribution to the psychogenesis of manic–depressive states. In: *Contributions to Psycho-Analysis*, London: Hogarth Press, pp. 311–338.

Kohut, H. (1959), Introspection, empathy and psychoanalysis. *J. Amer. Psychoanal. Assn.*, 7:459–483.

_____ (1971), *The Analysis of the Self*. New York: International Universities Press.

_____ (1977) *The Restoration of the Self*. New York: International Universities Press.

_____ (1979), The two analyses of Mr. Z. *Internat. J. Psycho-Anal.*, 60:3–27.

_____ (1984), *How Does Analysis Cure?* ed. A. Goldberg & P. Stepansky. University of Chicago Press.

Ornstein, A. (1974), The dread to repeat and the new beginning. *The Annual of Psychoanalysis*, 2:231–248. New York: International Universities Press.

_____ (1990), Selfobject transferences and the process of working through. In: *The Realities of Transference: Progress in Self Psychology, Vol. 6*, ed. A. Goldberg. Hillsdale, NJ: The Analytic Press, pp. 42–58.

Rangell, L. (1982), The self in psychoanalytic theory. *J. Amer. Psychoanal. Assn.*, 30:863–892.

Rosenfeld, H. (1987), *Impasse and Interpretation*. London: Routledge.

Schwaber, E. (1984), Psychoanalytic listening and psychic reality. *Internat. Rev. Psycho-Anal.*, 10:379–392.

Socarides, D. and Stolorow, R. (1984/1985), Affects and selfobjects. *The Annual of Psychoanalysis*, 12/13:105–119. Madison, CT: International Universities Press.

Stolorow, R., Brandchaft, B. & Atwood, G. (1987), *Psychoanalytic Treatment: An Intersubjective Approach*. Hillsdale, NJ: The Analytic Press.

von Broemsen, F. (1991), The sovereign self. Unpublished manuscript.

Chapter 17

Reversals: On Certain Pathologies of Identification

Russell Meares

Fluctuations in self-state are a feature of severe personality disorder. This chapter concerns a particular category of changing self-state, one that involves pathological identification and that I am calling a "reversal." This phenomenon, though not uncommon, has received relatively little attention and has generally been conceived in terms of defense. An alternative explanation, given here, depends upon a psychology of self.

In order to approach this subject I figuratively conceive the experience of self in relationship to the other, at any instant, in three dimensions. The first of these dimensions is vertical. On this axis self experiences can be placed up and down along the chronology of the individual's life. A second axis is horizontal and consists of a range of selves of the individual at a particular point in development. The third axis, also horizontal, is orthogonal to the second and reflects the process of identification. It consists of the back-and-forth oscillations between self-experience and the experience of the self as other. The subject of this chapter lies in this dimension and focuses on sudden, salient, and often perplexing "reversals" of the relation between self and other. I begin with two examples.

REVERSALS AND THE INTEGRITY OF SELF

The first case is of a woman of 19. She has a history of multiple suicide attempts. She is talking with a trainee psychiatrist who has recently

An earlier version of this chapter appeared in Meares (1993). Reprinted by permission of the publisher.

become her therapist and is asking him about the suitability of multiple sexual liaisons. The question has arisen because several men have told her they wished to live with her. Within a few sentences of listening to her inquiry, however, the therapist finds himself accused of advocating a life of sexual license. The patient reprimands him for this moral stance. The therapist is bewildered because, as far as he knows, he has done nothing of the kind. What is particularly baffling for him is that there has been a very rapid shift in roles. At one moment the woman is treating him like a parent, asking for advice about the complexities of relationships of late adolescent life. A few moments later *she* becomes the parent, lecturing him about morality.

A second and more subtle reversal comes from a patient who does not have a borderline personality, although she could be described as having a disorder of self. She is sophisticated and intelligent and is telling the therapist about a book she has been reading. The therapist's response is misinterpreted by the patient and sensed as belittling. A few sentences later, without apparent reason, the therapist finds that she is being lectured to by the patient on Freudian theory, of which the patient has a very comprehensive grasp. Once again the therapist is perplexed by a reversal of roles, which in this case finds the patient switching from something like a child/pupil role to that of parent/teacher.

What has happened in these two cases? Before we proceed to attempt an answer, consider two more illustrations of reversals. The first of these is a well-known case reported by Karl Abraham (1924). A woman was very attached to her father. In Abraham's words, she clung to him "with all an unmarried daughter's love" (p. 434). A terrible crisis occurred in her life when her father was discovered to be a thief and was arrested. As a consequence, she became psychotically depressed. The main feature of this psychosis was that she held the delusional belief that *she* was a thief. It was as if having lost her father—not only in a physical sense (since he was now in prison) but also in her idealized view of him—she now *became* him.

The second story also concerns loss. Simone de Beauvoir (1969) described her experience after visiting her mother in the hospital following an operation in which it was discovered that she was in the last stages of cancer. De Beauvoir's response was catastrophic. She went home late at night and, after an outburst of tears, talked to Sartre:

> I talked to Sartre about my mother's mouth as I had seen it that morning and about everything I had interpreted in it—greediness refused, an almost servile humility, hope, distress, loneliness—the

loneliness of her death and of her life—that did not want to admit its existence. And he told me that my own mouth was not obeying me any more: I had put Maman's mouth on my own face and in spite of myself, I copied its movements. Her whole person, her whole being, was concentrated there, and compassion wrung my heart [p. 28].

In a very subtle way, only detected by someone who knew her well, de Beauvoir also showed a reversal following catastrophic loss.

Might it be that the transient reversals shown in the first two examples had a somewhat similar basis? That is, they were responses to miniature losses that precipitated a disruption of the sense of self. This, then, is the hypothesis: *Reversals are a consequence of a severe disruption of the sense of self*. This disruption occurs when there is a disjunction or disconnection with the other who is sensed as necessary to the subject's going-on-being, that is, with the selfobject. When the other is not available as selfobject or is physically not there, the threat to self emerges. The reversal is an attempt to shore up a sense of existence by becoming the necessary other who has gone.

How does this idea help us to understand the first two vignettes? In the first case the young woman was frightened by the possibilities that confronted her. Although she seemed confident, in fact she was scared, not knowing how to cope with the men around her. The therapist, however, responded to her in a manner that he considered to be nonjudgmental. There was nothing particularly wrong with this response except that he did not pick up the patient's anxiety and so, for her, there was a feeling of being grossly misunderstood. A disconnection or disjunction occurred of which the therapist was unaware. In the second case, the therapist did not realize that the book about which the patient spoke had an intense personal significance for her. Although the therapist tried to respond in a way that was empathic, the response was not perceived in this way. Once again, the patient was not understood and a disconnection or disjunction occurred, and of a very subtle kind. In both these cases, then, I postulate that the reversal was a consequence of a break in the sense of connectedness between self and selfobject that was experienced as a threat to the patient's sense of existence, although this threat was slight and transient compared with the massive losses of Abraham's patient and Simone de Beauvoir. A reversal, then, is the consequence of a pathological situation in which anxiety of a fundamental kind is aroused, in which something akin to annihilation or disintegration is momentarily experienced.

It was perhaps Anna Freud who first drew attention to the phenomenon that I am calling a reversal. In her essay "Identification with the Aggressor" (1966) she suggests that behavior that seems to mimic the other is a form of defense against an anxiety that was precipitated not long before. At the beginning of the essay she gives an example of a boy who made faces in class. These were so gross that at times the whole class would burst out laughing. When the child was examined in the presence of the teacher, the psychologist Aichorn saw that

> the boy's grimaces were simply a caricature of the angry expression of the teacher and that, when he had to face a scolding by the latter, he tried to mask his anxiety by involuntarily imitating him. The boy identified himself with the teacher's anger and copied his expression as he spoke, though the imitation was not recognized. Through his grimaces he was assimilating himself to, or identifying himself with, the dreaded external object [p. 113].

As Anna Freud put it, "a child introjects some characteristic of an anxiety object and so assimilates an anxiety experience which he has just undergone" (p. 113). How do these ideas of defense relate to the phenomenon I have been describing?

If we consider the first example of the girl besieged by several men, we find that a reversal is indeed due to anxiety. There are, however, two levels to the anxiety. The first is the anxiety about not knowing how to manage her relationships. Underneath this anxiety is a second and more fundamental anxiety, one that arises from *the failure of the therapist* to understand her feelings. This anxiety, which arises through the disjunction and which momentarily poses, in a limited way, a threat to the sense of existence, is fundamental; this more primitive kind of anxiety seems to be the necessary trigger to a reversal. Following this postulate, one would suppose that the boy who made faces was not merely afraid of scolding. Underlying this fear, presumably, was a more basic and powerful form of terror associated with a disintegration of self.

We must next consider whether, in fact, a reversal is a defense. What I am saying is that a reversal is a consequence of a situation in which a connection with the other is felt as necessary to going on being. When the other fails as a selfobject, the child (or the patient) responds by taking on for himself or herself a salient aspect of the other in order to shore up a threatened sense of existence. Insofar as the reversal is a response to anxiety, it is a defense. It is not, however, the kind of defense proposed by Anna Freud (1966). She conceived the child's angry appearance as a defense against an "external object" (p. 110). It was meant to frighten the aggressor.

However, I would speculate that the basis of this boy's behavior was different. Most children are afraid of a scolding, but they do not make bizarre faces. It seems not unreasonable to suppose that when the reversal occurred, the little boy was so afraid of the teacher that all sense of self had been obliterated.

The story of this boy suggests the possibility that originally in the child's development *the behavior of the other at the point of the disjunction becomes the behavior of the subject during the reversal.* This idea is supported by a case report from Kohut (1984). In essence, the integrity of self of his patient was threatened by the shaming responses of the selfobject. However, "the patient was able to preserve the integrity of his self by mobilizing his aggression, that is, by turning passive into active. In this way, he became a sadistic voyeur, exposing the selfobject or its substitutes and making the selfobject ashamed and embarrassed in its exposure" (p. 144). Kohut believed that this tendency of his patient came from early life and was a well-established or "ingrained" part of his personality (p. 123).

REVERSAL AND TRANSFERENCE

Further evidence concerning reversals following disruptions of the self–selfobject bond comes from a study whose principal aim was to evaluate the outcome of cases in which patients with severe personality disorders were treated according to the principles of a psychology of self by trainee therapists working under close supervision. As far as can be judged, the report of the findings describes the first prospective follow-up, at least in the English language literature, of outpatient psychotherapy, of any kind, with borderline patients (Stevenson and Meares, 1992). All sessions were audiotaped, with the patients' written consent. These tapes show that disjunctions of the self–selfobject connectedness produced not only affect shifts but also changes in language toward more linear and outer-directed speech (Meares, 1990). They also precipitated transference phenomena (Meares, 1993), which sometimes involved the mechanism of reversal when the disjunction was severe. The following is an example:

The patient is 35. Her background includes repeated sexual abuse by her father, with which, apparently, her mother colluded. The mother was an unstable woman who was neglectful of her daughter and whose responses to her were unpredictable. The patient has been admitted to a psychiatric hospital over 30 times with manifestations of borderline personality, including quasi-psychotic phenomena, suicide attempts, and self-mutilation. She has responded to a change in session time by mutilating herself. At the beginning of the following

session the therapist notices that there is something different about
the patient and remarks on it. There is no initial response but after
about ten minutes the patient says, "The only thing I can sort of think
when I arrived, I had been pondering on what was different about
it . . . the only thing I can think of . . . you know, I felt such utter
contempt towards you." She then goes on to talk about anger and
how she wants to hurt her husband when he hurts her. This,
however, is an ordinary anger, different from the extraordinary anger
she felt for her therapist, an anger that, although this was not made
explicit, was expressed during her self-mutilation.

The therapist replies by saying, "I was wondering if it seemed I
was contemptuous of you, that I was sort of dismissing you and your
feelings."

"Yeah, well it sort of felt like I'd been given the bum's rush," says
the patient.

"I wondered if you'd had that feeling with your mum, that she was
contemptuous of you."

"Very much, hmm." Irrespective of what you thought or felt or
what you would have liked to have been, if she'd already decided on
something, it didn't matter, you didn't enter into the conversation.

Later in the session the patient describes the background to her
self-mutilation. When she was six or seven, she found that the only
time she would get a cuddle from her mother was when she would
hurt herself accidentally. She then started to cut herself to gain this
solace, but her plan soon began to fail since her mother realized what
was happening and reverted to her system of neglect. Nevertheless,
the child found that cutting herself was still soothing. There remained
something of the soothing effect of her mother's care within the act of
cutting. In the patient's words: "I remember I used to feel much better
inside. I didn't feel so empty, so lonely somehow." In this way the
self-mutilation, which involved something of a reversal, was an
integrating act.

A relationship between reversals and transference phenomena is
evident in the reverberations of contempt. We might suppose that the
child's integrity of self was originally threatened by parental contempt. In the case of the self-mutilating patient the disjunction
between self and selfobject comes about in another way. Nevertheless, there is a reversal during which the patient becomes contemptuous. Furthermore, she perceives the therapist as also contemptuous. Put another way, "a whole series of psychological experiences
are revived, not as belonging to the past but as applying to the
physician at the present moment" (Freud, 1905, p. 116). In this case,
then, the reversal is accompanied by a transference experience.

A second illustration of the relationship between reversal and transference comes from the therapy of another borderline patient, one who also suffered from severe anorexia nervosa. Her relationship with her mother was fused or symbiotic; that is, there was little sense of boundary between the child's subjective space and that of the mother. Accordingly, the mother was able to inflict severe sanctions upon the child by withdrawal. When this occurred the patient was threatened with a sense of annihilation. A therapy session that had been preceded by a severe disjunction, a vacation, opened with the patient withdrawn and practically mute. Later in the session the patient was able to say that she experienced the therapist as withdrawn and "cut off," although the tape showed that the therapist responded appropriately. In this case also a severe disjunction brings about a reversal in which the patient replicates the role of the original other in the earlier trauma. However, she also experiences the other of the present in the same way.

INTROJECTS

How do these ideas relate to previous conceptualizations? The phenomenon I have described has sometimes been seen as a manifestation of projective identification that is "called upon to externalize aggressive self and object images" (Kernberg, 1968). However, the connected mechanism of introjection (the word Anna Freud used) might be more suitably invoked since during the reversal the subject is as if inhabited by another. One of the problems with the word *introjection* is that it is used to describe not only a pathological situation based on anxiety but also a normal one. For example, Melanie Klein (1955), in her famous paper "On Identification," wrote that "identification as a sequel to introjection is part of normal development" (p. 141). This collapsing of pathology and normality into one concept seems unsuitable. Nevertheless, there is a case for retaining the use of the term *introjection*, or *introject*, but using it in a specific and confined way.

I am suggesting that an introject is the end product of a reversal that has become relatively fixed. Since it is hedged about with anxiety, it cannot be integrated within the self-representation. The introject is "undigested" (Kohut, 1971, p. 49). As Glasser (1986) suggests, introjection might be seen as an incomplete process. The object does not become part of the self but remains separate within it and is sometimes experienced as alien.

The normal process of identification is different. It is anxiety-free and is fostered by an atmosphere in which the individual feels understood. Its first phase is simple copying. For example, a little boy of two swaggers around with his hands in his pockets, looking like his father. This is different from the first stage of introjection, the reversal, which is almost echopraxic at times (as in the case of the little boy who made faces) and where there is little distinction between self and other. On the other hand, the two-year-old who is swaggering around like his father shows this distinction. He is *not* his father, he is like him. It is *as if* he were his father. His behavior has about it a duality described by Stern (1985):

> To perform delayed imitations, infants must have two versions of the same reality available: the representation of the original act, as performed by the model, and their own actual execution of the act. Furthermore, they must be able to go back and forth between these two versions of reality and make adjustments of one or the other to accomplish a good imitation [p. 164].

Identification progresses, we suppose, from a first stage in which the experiences of the other is taken in as an "aliment," as a kind of perceptual food. Gradually, through the processes of assimilation and accommodation, the object representation is taken into the self-representation completely. Or, as Sandler and Rosenblatt (1962) put it, at the completion of the taking in of the object representation the self-representation changes shape. The form of the original other can no longer be found. This is the opposite of reversal, in which the lack of integration causes the self to be experienced not as a single "shape" but as a conglomerate. The absence of duality, or poor differentiation between self and object, together with the impediment to integration imposed by anxiety, leads to a collapsing together of experiences of self and experiences of the other, without space between them. This is exemplified by the patient who was contemptuous. When she cut herself before the session, at least three experiences could be distinguished: firstly, there was the child hurting herself; secondly, the child hurting someone else; and thirdly, the mother soothing the child. Three people, as it were, on top of each other. In some cases the "undigested" nature of the introject is extreme. The individual has the experience of being occupied or inhabited by somebody else, as in the following example.

A woman, frightened about her anger toward her small son, enters therapy. There is a background of physical abuse by her father. During one session she is able to describe her strange experience when she was about to strike her son. She said, "I saw my dad and me in place of me and John [her son]. Him yelling and screaming and threatening me. Getting ready to hit me. Fear, like a knot, in that situation. I was feeling it as a little girl. It was the same feeling I'd had through my whole life, which is the trigger for a worrying situation." She went on:

> I didn't want to be like that. The awful thing, I was repeating a memory that was totally abhorrent to me and I didn't want to be like. I had no control. I always said I would never be like him and here it was happening beyond my control. It was as if subconscious, like I was being controlled by something out of my power. It was like being demonized. Like having someone in your body making you speak and making you act, even though you're fighting it the whole time. Like your body's not your own. You don't have control of your body or your speech.

This description supports the notion that a reversal first occurs in a situation of high anxiety, even terror. Accounts such as this one are helpful in trying to understand the phenomenon of the victim of abuse later becoming a perpetrator (Johnson, 1988; Deltaglia, 1990). Such behavior is not explicable in terms of, say, learning theory. The theoretical position put forward here leads to the hypothesis that reversal is produced by the more extreme form of abuse, in which little remains of the sense of self. This idea conforms with the observations of some authorities in this area. Steele (1986), for example, notes that

> although there is no absolute correlation between the type of maltreatment occurring in infancy and the type of maltreatment expressed in later life by the adult parent, there seems to be a tendency toward direct literal repetition. Victims of more severe physical punishment tend to repeat the severe spankings and whippings with belts which they have undergone [p. 285].

"Literal repetition," rather than a "digested" or transmuted form of internalization, is a principal characteristic of the phenomenon of reversal.

SOME THERAPEUTIC IMPLICATIONS

Kohut (e.g., 1984, p. 70) regarded his conceptions of "transmuting internalization" and the therapeutic error as central to his therapeutic method. The method depends on appropriate responses to disjunctions that occur in the sense of connectedness between self and selfobject. It is essential, therefore, that the disjunction be detected. It sometimes appears as a reversal, which may be brief, perhaps indicated only in a phrase or single word, as in the following example.

A patient who had spent much of his early life in an orphanage could not remember anything before the age of ten. He began a session by announcing that his girlfriend was pregnant. This, he said, was "no problem" since she would get an abortion. After a few connecting sentences, the patient, showing little affect, went on to say that he wondered if some early memories were beginning to be recovered since he had had "images" of himself as a terrified child being dragged from under a bed, presumably to be taken to the orphanage. The therapist then remarked that the forthcoming abortion seemed to have triggered feelings relating to his having been "got rid of" by his own mother. In a rather pompous voice the patient replied, "Good point." He then, without any apparent reason, recounted successive incidents in which he had been physically attacked and injured, humiliated after revealing an emotional state in which he had been feeling "paranoid" and in which he had become enraged. The disjunction was signaled by the momentary reversal indicated by the authoritarian voice. There had been a swift change from "passive to active," to use Kohut's words. The therapist's response was sensed as an intrusion threatening a precariously held inner zone, as in a paranoid system (Meares, 1988). The therapist, however, failed to notice the change of voice at "Good point," and afterward the session seemed to lose its way.

A second important reason for the need to detect a reversal is implied in the concept of "intersubjectivity" (Stolorow, Brandchaft, and Atwood, 1987). The reversal has an effect on the therapist, of which he or she may be unaware. It creates a disruption that causes the therapist's behavior to change. The language becomes grammatically less "impersonal" (Meares, 1983) and begins to focus on fact or reason rather than on the more emotional "inner" aspects of the patient's experience. A further disjunction is now inflicted upon the patient. Our tapes show that in the treatment of those with a very attenuated and precarious sense of self, a spiral of anxiety reminiscent of "the persecutory spiral" (Meares and Hobson, 1977) is now set in motion. It may culminate in a relatively fixed reversal, in which the patient seems relatively mature. The conversation that ensues may appear to be useful and adaptive but, in fact, goes nowhere.

The notion of the relatively fixed reversal leads to another of the therapeutic implications of the concept. The individual may present in this state. Since the posture is frequently difficult to recognize, there may be a long period of treatment in which nothing can happen because the wrong person, as it were, is being spoken with. Sometimes the patient is able to describe what is happening, sensing that his or her role is not quite real. In this sense, it is one of the manifestations of a "false self system." In extreme cases the individual replicates his or her experience of someone else. In other cases, in which the original anxiety was presumably less, the individual seems to take on some of the functions of the failed selfobject. A variation of this phenomenon may be the so-called "grandiose false self," in which case the individual maintains a stance of arrogance and superiority of a brittle and unstable kind. This situation was described by Kohut (1971): "If the child suffers severe narcissistic traumas, then the grandiose self does not merge into the relevant ego content, but is retained in its unaltered form and strives for the fulfillment of its archaic aims" (p. 28).

A final therapeutic implication concerns the possibility that reversals may sometimes be iatrogenic. There is a style of therapy in which interpretations are based on the idea that the patient's reality is disturbed by fantasy. When the therapist's remarks are directed unremittingly at the unconscious, there is a danger that those with a fragile sense of self will have this precarious personal reality overthrown. Each interpretation has a strong potential to create a sense of disjunction. In cases where the patient's response unsettles the therapist, a "persecutory spiral" may develop. In the ensuing state of high anxiety very little of the patient's self remains. The patient now takes in, in undigested form, a reality which is not his or her own. He or she becomes the other, even copying the therapist's mannerisms of speech and gesture. This dispiriting picture is the end point of a therapy in which neither partner detects the falseness.

SUMMARY

Reversal is the term applied to a fleeting change of self-state in which the individual *becomes* the other. It is induced, in the first place, by intense anxiety that obliterates inner reality. In the therapeutic situation it is particularly likely to come about through a break in the connectedness between self and selfobject. This break, however, is experienced as massive, as compared to the break produced by an "optimal frustration," in which the individual's sense of personal existence remains. When the break is optimal there emerges a duality, a double awareness made up on one hand of an inner life, and on the other of a response to it that does not fit and that is experienced as external. The reversal, on the other hand, is adualistic. In the therapeutic situation a reversal is most likely to occur in those individuals whose sense of self is somewhat precarious, that is, in borderline personalities. An attenuated sense of self produces a vulnerability that may lead to a series of rapidly changing, and often perplexing, reversals during a single session.

When the personality structure is more stable than that of the borderline, the reversal may become relatively fixed. In this case, it might be called an introject. Since it is surrounded by anxiety, it cannot be integrated into the self-representation and remains relatively sequestered. Its adualistic basis fosters its permanence. Without reflection upon it, the system cannot change. The concept of reversal may be useful in the understanding of perpetrators of abuse who have themselves been victims.

These pathological identifications are contrasted with those that are normal and anxiety-free and that arise in a state of connectedness with another who is experienced as a selfobject. The way toward healthy identification begins with the individual having within him or her the *dual* experience of both self and other. It is supposed that something like an oscillation goes on between these two poles, leading to an eventual integration of the experience of the other into the self-representation so that the original form of the experience of the other is no longer apparent.

REFERENCES

Abraham, K. (1924), A short study of the development of the libido, viewed in the light of mental disorders. In: *Selected Papers of Karl Abraham*. London: Hogarth Press, 1949, pp. 418–476.
de Beauvoir, S. (1969), *A Very Easy Death*, trans. P. O'Brian. London: Penguin.
Deltaglia, L. (1990), Victims and perpetrators of sexual abuse: A psychosocial study from France. *Child Abuse & Neglect*, 14:445–447.
Freud, A. (1966), *The Ego and the Mechanisms of Defense*, rev. ed. New York: International Universities Press.
Freud, S. (1905), Fragment of an analysis of a case of hysteria. *Standard Edition*, 7:7–122. London: Hogarth Press, 1953.
Glasser, M. (1986), Identification and its vicissitudes as observed in the perversions. *Internat. J. Psycho-Anal.*, 67:9–17.
Johnson, T. (1988), Child perpetrators: Children who molest other children: Preliminary findings. *Child Abuse & Neglect*, 12:219–229.
Kernberg, O. (1968), The treatment of patients with borderline personality organization. *Internat. J. Psycho-Anal.*, 49:600–619.
Klein, M. (1955), On identification. In: *Envy and Gratitude and Other Words: 1946–1963*, ed. R. Money-Kyrle, B. Joseph, E. O'Shaughnessy & H. Segal. London: Hogarth Press, 1975, pp. 141–175.
Kohut, H. (1971), *The Analysis of the Self*. New York: International Universities Press.
_____ (1984), *How Does Analysis Cure?* ed. A. Goldberg & P. Stepansky. Chicago: University of Chicago Press.
Meares, R. (1983), Keats and the "impersonal" therapist: Notes on empathy and the therapeutic screen. *Psychiatry*, 46:73–82.

_____ (1988), The secret, lies and the paranoid process. *Contemp. Psychoanal.*, 24:650–666.

_____ (1990), The fragile Spielraum: An approach to transmuting internalization. In: *The Realities of Transference: Progress in Self Psychology, Vol. 6*, ed. A. Goldberg. Hillsdale, NJ: The Analytic Press.

_____ (1992) Transference and the playspace. *Contemp. Psychoanal.*, 28(1):32–49.

_____ (1993), *The Metaphor of Play: On Disruption and Restoration in the Borderline Experience*. Northvale, NJ: Aronson.

_____ Hobson, R. (1977), The persecutory therapist. *Br. J. Med. Psychol.*, 50:349–359.

Sandler, J. & Rosenblatt, B. (1962), The concept of the representational world. *The Psychoanalytic Study of the Child*, 17:128–148. New York: International Universities Press.

Steele, B. (1986), Notes on the lasting effects of early child abuse throughout the life cycle. *Child Abuse & Neglect*, 10:283–291.

Stern, D. (1985), *The Interpersonal World of the Infant*. New York: Basic Books.

Stevenson, J. & Meares, R. (1992), An outcome study of psychotherapy in borderline personality disorder. *Amer. J. Psychiat.*, 149 (3):358–362.

Stolorow, R., Brandchaft, B. & Atwood, G. (1987), *Psychoanalytic Treatment: An Intersubjective Approach*. Hillsdale, NJ: The Analytic Press.

Applied

Chapter 18

Countertransference, Empathy, and the Hermeneutical Circle

Donna M. Orange

If Thou is said, the I of the combination I-Thou is said along with it.
Buber, I and Thou

. . . a human being who actually exists *must be somewhere*.
Schreber, Memoirs of My Nervous Illness

Countertransference, a favorite topic in many psychoanalytic circles since the 1950s, has been until recently less than prominent in the literature, and particularly in the case studies, of self psychology. Two questions thus emerge: (1) Has the study of countertransference become peripheral in self psychology, and if so, why? (2) Is the conception useful or necessary in self psychology, and if so, how? A consideration of this second question will involve some discussion of recent developments in philosophical hermeneutics. This discussion will clarify the central claim of this chapter, namely, that a self-psychological understanding of the psychoanalytic process requires some notion like countertransference. It will also become clear that we need to distinguish the narrower from the more inclusive meaning of the term.

In part two of this chapter I use a broad conception of counter-transference as the whole of the analyst's experience of the analytic relationship. For the sake of clarity I suggest renaming this inclusive notion. In this first section, however, the word *countertransference* will mean whatever the theorist under discussion apparently intends, whether or not that theorist defines it.

THE APPARENT NEGLECT OF COUNTERTRANSFERENCE IN SELF PSYCHOLOGY

Kohut (1971) began his revolutionary *The Analysis of the Self* as follows: "The subject matter of this monograph is the study of certain transference or transferencelike phenomena in the psychoanalysis of narcissistic personalities, and of the analyst's reaction to them, including his countertransferences" (p. 1). By countertransference Kohut meant those remnants of the analyst's own narcissistic disturbances that interfered with the development and analysis of the selfobject transferences. He cited, for example, "the tendency of some analysts . . . to respond with erroneous or premature or otherwise faulty interpretations when they are idealized by their patients" (p. 138). If such countertransferences are stable, according to Kohut, they often consist of "quasi-theoretical convictions or of specific character defenses, or (as is frequently the case) of both" (p. 263). In the final chapters of *The Analysis of the Self* Kohut devoted considerable attention to countertransferential responses of analysts to the various narcissistic transferences.

He returned to countertransference briefly in his posthumous *How Does Analysis Cure?* where he continued to regard it as harmful by definition. "If we want to see clearly," Kohut (1984) wrote, "we must keep the lenses of our magnifying glasses clean; we must, in particular, recognize our countertransferences and thus minimize the influence of factors that distort our perception of the analysand's communications of his personality" (p. 37). He went on to deny the applicability of the influence-of-the-observer-on-the-observed principle in psychoanalysis and to attribute difficulties in analytic understanding to the analyst's "shortcomings as an observing instrument" (p. 38).

Since Kohut saw countertransference as interference, it has perhaps been difficult for self psychologists to view it as an essential part of the theory and process of psychoanalytic cure. In addition, Kohut (1971) thought that a good psychoanalytic theory, like a good analytic treatment, should have little or nothing to do with the analyst's personality (pp. 222–223n), that analysis should be a nonidiosyncratic science that can be taught to noncharismatic practitioners. The practitioners were not, however, to be traditionally neutral; sustained listening to understand and to explain, he thought, is not a neutral activity. To summarize, Kohut was torn between a desire, even in his last years, to emphasize the human determinants in psychoanalysis and his adherence to his classical training, which made him want to sift the personal elements out. This ambivalence may have prevented him from conceiving of countertransference as his survivors have done.

Wolf (1988), for example, adopts Gill's (1982) usage and sees countertransference as the analyst's experience of the relationship (p. 137). He distinguishes among countertransferences, identifying (1) the analyst's pleasure in effectiveness; (2) the "countertransferences proper," which are "based on the analyst's residual archaic selfobject needs" (p. 144); and (3) reactive countertransferences, that is, the tendencies, identified by Kohut, to defensively unmask the idealizing, mirroring, and merger transferences. Wolf does not claim that his classification is exhaustive, nor does he explain how analysts might use their experience of the analytic relationship.

Intersubjectivity theory, articulated by Stolorow, Brandchaft, and Atwood (1987), goes even further toward making countertransference self-psychologically respectable. For these authors the psychoanalytic process emerges from the intersection and interplay of two differently organized subjectivities. "Patient and analyst together form an indissoluble psychological system," they claim (p. 1). Their vision of psychoanalysis is reminiscent of philosopher Hans-Georg Gadamer's (1976) account of play, games, and language usage:

> Now I contend that the basic constitution of the game, to be filled with its spirit—the spirit of buoyancy, freedom, and the joy of success—and to fulfil him who is playing, is structurally related to the constitution of the dialogue in which language is a reality. When one enters into dialogue with another person and then is carried along further by the dialogue, it is no longer the will of the individual person, holding itself back or exposing itself, that is determinative. Rather, the law of the subject matter [die Sache] is at issue in the dialogue and elicits statement and counterstatement and in the end plays them into each other [p. 66].

Within such a dialogue Stolorow, Brandchaft, and Atwood (1987) understand countertransference as "a manifestation of the analyst's psychological structures and organizing activity" (p. 42, chap. 3, written with F. Lachmann) and hold that "transference and countertransference together form an intersubjective system of reciprocal mutual influence" (p. 42). We shall explore further some theoretical justifications for this view as well as some of its further ramifications.

Self psychology has thus shifted significantly from Kohut's negative view of countertransference toward a broader definition of the word. In addition, we find a greater appreciation, at least in theory, of the importance of recognizing the influence of the analyst/observer (whose experience of the analytic relationship is countertransference in the inclusive sense) on the observed. Where, then, are the discussions of the analyst's organizing activity, history, and personality in our case reports? Why are many of us still writing as if the analytic patient were the only one organizing or reorganizing experience?

With a few notable exceptions (e.g., Goldberg, 1988; Thomson, 1991), we self psychologists are, I think, so involved in and devoted to our efforts to get and stay close to the patient's experience that we often forget that we are there too. Thus, our cherished effort to understand patients from their own vantage point may prevent us from recognizing our contribution to shaping the patient's experience (the influence of the observer on the observed). It may also interfere with our recognizing that we can understand another's experience only through our own equally subjective experience. In the words of Lomas (1987):

> By the very nature of things people cannot attain perfect openness to each other. Our perceptions are based on past experience. Nothing is entirely new to us, otherwise we would completely fail to appreciate it. However much we strive towards an unencumbered, receptive state of mind, we bring to each exchange the sum total of our history, an interpretation that is unique to us, the most coherent, manageable and least anguished *Gestalt* that we have been able to attain [pp. 39–40].

The apparently spreading opposition to regarding transference as distortion, which should expand to eliminate the distortion idea from countertransference, is consistent with the acknowledgment that two subjectivities are always at work.

In addition, I think the word *countertransference* sometimes puts off clinicians who do not subscribe to theories of innate aggression. Instead, we view anger and hostility as understandable responses to deprivation, to abuse, and to the frustration of crucial emotional needs for appreciation, affirmation, validation, and consistent support. *Counter* means, among other things, "against" or "opposing," and we self psychologists usually view ourselves as allied with the patient. Perhaps *cotransference* would better acknowledge our participation *with* the patient in the intersubjective field or play space of the psychoanalytic dialogue. This inclusive term would remove the assumption that the analytic relation is automatically or in most respects adversarial.

The notion of *cotransference*, like the related ideas of intersubjectivity and mutual influence, does not imply that there are no differences between the participation of analysts and that of patients in the analysis. It does imply and acknowledge that two differently organized subjectivities are always involved in the dialogue. Nevertheless, the analyst or therapist is always there primarily for the sake of the other. To acknowledge, as the cotransference notion does, that two subjectivities are fully involved does not preclude important differences between them.

COUNTERTRANSFERENCE AND SELF-PSYCHOLOGICAL THEORY

Self psychology requires an inclusive notion of countertransference (or cotransference) as a necessary, though not sufficient, condition for the possibility of empathy. Empathy has occupied a pivotal place in the theory of self psychology because Kohut (1959) insisted that the psychoanalytic realm was by definition coextensive with whatever introspection and empathy (or vicarious introspection) could reveal. By empathy Kohut did not mean warmth or responsiveness—though he did regard these as necessary conditions for analysis, he referred, instead, to the focused attempt to enter another's subjective reality. Stolorow, Brandchaft, and Atwood (1987) call this process "decentering" to understand the patient's subjectivity. Dialogic or perspectival realism (Orange, 1992) requires such vicarious introspection for the communication and sharing of perspectives in dialogue. Such empathic dialogue may result in both the understanding of previous perspectives and the creation of new ones. Relying on one of the old hermeneutic rules to achieve empathic understanding, I widen my perspective (I do not abandon it) by asking myself how the other person's point of view, feelings, convictions, and responses could make sense, could be reasonable.

Philosophical hermeneutics may help us further here. Hermeneutics was originally a set of rules or methods for interpreting biblical texts. More recently, Schleiermacher and Dilthey saw hermeneutic inquiry as an attempt to read the meaning of a text by reference to the author's intentions (*mens auctoris*). How to gain access to the author's intentions was a further practical problem. With the growth of historical consciousness in the past century, hermeneutics has come to include history—we might say development—as vital to understanding anything. Modern hermeneutics has come to view a text or a painting or a dream as a *"Sache selbst"* (a thing itself), partly understandable from the perspective of an interpreter. The interpreter participates in a dialogue with the text. From this dialogue new meanings are always emerging. We can know nothing of the text without knowing the interpreter, including the interpreter's theories, personal history, and organizing principles. There is no single completed truth about the text, person, or dream. Rather, there is an indefinite number of possible interpreters and perspectives whose communication may make possible more inclusive and coherent—and thus truer—views, perspectives, understandings, and theories.

Gadamer, quoted earlier, is now the most prominent proponent of this view. Several of his favorite themes are pertinent to the more inclusive psychoanalytic notion of countertransference. Gadamer claims, first, that prejudice is inevitable. By prejudice he means the inevitability of being somewhere vis-à-vis whatever we seek to know or understand. He thus intends to strip the word *prejudice* of its negative connotations, as difficult a task as making *countertransference* a neutral or positively valenced term. Here is Gadamer's (1976) attempt:

> It is not so much our judgment [about truth or value] as our prejudices that constitute our being. This is a provocative formulation, for I am using it to restore to its rightful place a positive concept of prejudice that was driven out of linguistic usage by the French and the English Enlightenment. It can be shown that the concept of prejudice did not originally have the meaning we have attached to it. Prejudices are not necessarily unjustified and erroneous, so that they inevitably distort the truth. In fact, the historicity of our own existence entails that prejudices, in the literal sense of the word, constitute the initial directedness of our whole ability to experience. Prejudices are biases of our openness to the world. They are simply conditions whereby we experience something—whereby what we encounter says something to us. This formulation certainly does not mean that we are enclosed within a wall of prejudices and only let through the narrow portals those things that can produce a pass saying, "Nothing new will be said here." Instead we welcome just that guest who promises something new to our curiosity [p. 9].

Similarly, American philosopher C. S. Pierce (1931–1935) explained:

> We cannot begin with complete doubt [in the style of Descartes]. We must begin with all the prejudices which we actually have when we enter upon the study of philosophy. The prejudices are not to be dispelled by a maxim, for they are things which it does not occur to us *can* be questioned [Hartshorne and Weiss, 1931–1935, v. 5, p. 156].

Another way to speak of the necessity of prejudice (or of cotransference) is to consider the historicity, or personal/relational history, of the interpreter. For Gadamer, interpretation is not an attempt to read an author's mind, as Schleiermacher and Dilthey believed. Instead, the dialogic process, the interplay of interpreter and text (or patient), creates something new: the interpretation. Interpreter and text are equally important, and the historicity, including the prejudices (organizing principles), of the interpreter takes on an organizing role. Gadamer regards the attribution of subjectivity to the text and objectivity to the interpreter as a dangerous denial of the interpreter's contribution to the making of meaning.

It is not that we should simply accept our prejudices or organizing principles; rather, we must continually test them. We test them not by empiricist criteria to check for distortion but in dialogue. Continental philosophers often use the notion of horizon to mean the field of vision, or whatever perspective is available from where one stands. We test our prejudices by attempting to see whether they fit with broadening horizons. Similarly, we revise organizing principles to take new experience into account (as in Piagetian accommodation). Colloquially, we sometimes speak of education or travel as "broadening our horizons," enlarging our perspective on the world. Rightly or wrongly, people commonly make the assumption that a broader perspective is likely to be truer, that narrowness is somehow wrongheaded. The psychoanalytic version of the assumption is that deeper is better. (To the objection that delusional people claim to see broadly and deeply into meanings, a response might be that we are speaking of the elaboration of complexity whereas delusions usually oversimplify.) In the hermeneutical view we attain a broader or deeper experience of anything by knowing and acknowledging who we are— our historicity and our prejudices. Only thus can we enter the playful dialogue that broadens and deepens our understanding.

In psychoanalytic language, we must know and acknowledge our countertransferences, our cotransference, our point of view or perspective, if we are to become capable of empathy or vicarious introspection. We must acknowledge the lenses through which we are reading the text in order to do authentic psychoanalytic work, or to speak authentically of our work.

This is, by the way, not a discussion of the advisability or inadvisability of countertransference disclosures. This question belongs under the principle of optimal responsiveness (Bacal, 1985). Normally, I decide such matters on pragmatic grounds. The central pragmatic maxim can be expressed as follows: "By their fruits shall ye know them." Thus, if an intervention or response usually yields understanding and self-consolidation, then it deserves serious consideration (and vice versa).

Under discussion here, instead, is the nature of understanding itself. At issue is the thesis that cotransference (or countertransference in the inclusive sense) is a necessary though not sufficient condition for the possibility of empathy. Countertransference here includes both historicity and the prejudices/horizons of philosophical hermeneutics, which are roughly equivalent to personal history and organizing principles. To understand psychoanalytically, and to understand psychoanalytic understanding, we must acknowledge our historicity and examine our prejudices. To work psychoanalytically we must have access to our historicity and prepare ourselves to criticize our horizons and to revise those prejudices that limit our capacity to understand another's experience.

Finally, to reexamine the whole question of the place of countertransference in self-psychological theory, let us turn to the old question of the hermeneutical circle. The paradox that understanding is inevitably circular has been expressed in many ways. Palmer (1969) summarizes the view of the early Romantic philologist Friedrich Ast: "Because *Geist* is the source of all development and all becoming, the imprint of the spirit of the whole (*Geist des Ganzen*) is found in the individual part; the part is understood from the whole and the whole from the inner harmony of its parts" (p. 77). Similarly, for Schleiermacher, the whole of the text and the parts of the text explain one another. Dilthey provides the example of a sentence whose meaning can be grasped only via the inevitable interaction of whole and parts. In Palmer's words:

> Dilthey cites this example and then asserts that the same relationship exists between the parts and whole of one's life. The meaning of the whole is a "sense" derived from the meaning of individual parts. An event or experience can so alter our lives that what was formerly meaningful becomes meaningless and an apparently unimportant past experience may take on meaning in retrospect. The sense of the whole determines the function and the meaning of the parts. And meaning is something historical; it is a relationship of whole to parts seen by us from a given standpoint, at a given time, for a given combination of parts. It is not something above or outside history but a part of a hermeneutical circle always historically defined [p. 118].

Dilthey's view of understanding has implications for the debate between those who favor here-and-now focus and those who emphasize history and development in clinical work. Neglect of either, in his view, would hinder understanding. For our purposes here, however, Dilthey illuminates the necessity of the dialectic of whole and part, past and present, for understanding. It has remained for Gadamer to include the future in the dialectic and to show that the hermeneutic circle is not a vicious circle once the historicity and horizons of the interpreter take their rightful place.

Gadamer sees clearly that the risking and testing of prejudices in "dialogical encounter" is the path to understanding through the hermeneutical circle. The nature of understanding is that we can come to understand only what we already understand. Risking testing our organizing principles in dialogue with a text or a person makes possible a new meaning, a newly complexified organizing principle, a future form of experience that could emerge only through the dialogue. This fully relational and intersubjective account of the process of psychoanalytic understanding is completely incompatible with objectivist and empiricist theories of truth or with an exclusive focus on the subjectivity of the patient.

Gadamer's solution to the feared subjectivism and solipsism of the hermeneutical circle is to say that the path to understanding in the hermeneutical circle is via the self-knowledge of the interpreter. If for his "understanding" we read "empathic understanding" and for "text" we read "patient," the implications for psychoanalytic self psychology become clear:

> In reading a text, in wishing to understand it, what we always expect is that it will *inform* us of something. A consciousness formed by the authentic hermeneutical attitude will be receptive to the origins and entirely foreign features of that which comes to it from outside its own horizons. Yet this receptivity is not acquired with an objectivist "neutrality": it is neither possible, necessary, nor desirable that we put ourselves within brackets. The hermeneutical attitude supposes only that we self-consciously designate our opinions and prejudices and qualify them as such, and in so doing strip them of their extreme character. In keeping to this attitude we grant the text the opportunity to appear as an authentically different being and to manifest its own truth, over and against our own preconceived notions [1979, pp. 151–152].

To summarize, I use a perspective derived from philosophical hermeneutics to elucidate my claim that countertransference in the inclusive sense is indispensable to empathy, is a necessary condition for empathy, and thus will find a prominent place in a self psychology aware of its own nature and nuclear program. I further suggest that this inclusive sense be renamed *cotransference* and that we reserve the term *countertransference* for the analyst's emotional memories that interfere with empathic understanding and optimal responsiveness.

REFERENCES

Bacal, H. (1985), Optimal responsiveness and the therapeutic process. In: *Progress in Self Psychology, Vol. 1*, ed. A. Goldberg. New York: Guilford Press, pp. 202–227.

Gadamer, H. (1976), *Philosophical Hermeneutics*, trans. D. E. Linge. Berkeley: University of California Press.

_____ (1979), The problem of historical consciousness. In: *Interpretive Social Science*, ed. P. Rabinow & W. Sullivan. Berkeley: University of California Press, pp. 103–160.

Gill, M. (1982), *Analysis of Transference, Vol. 1*. New York: International Universities Press.

Goldberg, A. (1988), *A Fresh Look at Psychoanalysis*. Hillsdale, NJ: The Analytic Press.

Hartshorne, C. & Weiss, P., ed. (1931–1935), *Collected Papers of Charles Sanders Pierce*. Cambridge, MA: Harvard University Press.

Kohut, H. (1959), Introspection, empathy, and psychoanalysis. *J. Amer. Psychoanal. Assn.*, 7:459–483.

_____ (1971), *The Analysis of the Self*. New York: International Universities Press.

_____ (1984), *How Does Analysis Cure?* ed. A. Goldberg & P. Stepansky. Chicago: University of Chicago Press.

Lomas, P. (1987), *The Limits of Interpretation*. Northvale, NJ: Jason Aronson.

Orange, D. (1992), Subjectivism, relativism, and realism in psychoanalysis. In: *Progress in Self Psychology, Vol. 8*, ed. A. Goldberg. Hillsdale, NJ: The Analytic Press, pp. 189–197.

Palmer, R. (1969), *Hermeneutics: Interpretation Theory in Schleiermacher, Dilthey, Heidegger, and Gadamer*. Evanston, IL: Northwestern University Press.

Stolorow, R., Brandchaft, B. & Atwood, G. (1987), *Psychoanalytic Treatment: An Intersubjective Approach*. Hillsdale, NJ: The Analytic Press.

Thomson, P. (1991), Countertransference in an intersubjective perspective: An experiment. In: *Progress in Self Psychology, Vol. 7*, ed. A. Goldberg. Hillsdale, NJ: The Analytic Press.

Wolf, E. (1988), *Treating the Self*. New York: Guilford Press.

Chapter 19

The Child-Pet Bond

Lindsey Stroben Alper

It is the thesis of this chapter that pets can play a critical role in providing selfobject functions to the young and developing child, particularly in an otherwise impoverished or exploitive selfobject environment. I will explore some initial ideas on this topic, drawing from my clinical experience, case material of other therapists, and empirical studies on the human–animal bond. Together, I hope that these ideas will illuminate the variety of ways in which pets may amend or enhance the fulfillment of the particular developmental needs of a child whose available selfobjects are unable to do so.

THE CHILD-PET BOND: RESEARCH

A number of studies have illustrated the positive role that pets can play with special populations. Programs have been developed that place pets with the elderly (Garrity et al., 1989), the handicapped (Frith, 1982; Ross, 1983), psychiatric inpatients (Holcomb and Meacham, 1989), prison inmates (Katcher, Beck, and Levine, 1989), and children with special needs (Gonski, 1985; Redefer and Goodman, 1989). Absent, however, is a theoretical explication of why human–pet relationships consistently have been found to have positive psychological effects; in particular, "there is very little analysis of the role of pets in child development" (Robin & ten Bensel, 1985, p. 63).

Despite the lack of a theoretical conceptualization, several studies have directly explored the child–pet bond. Levinson's early studies

(1961, 1972) suggest that in their roles as companions, confidants, playmates, and admirers pets can provide rich learning experiences, expedite adaptation to emotional trauma, regulate emotional problems, and enhance psychosocial development. Condoret (1973) posits that pets are important in regulating affective functioning, particularly in psychotic and mentally retarded children.

Other research has confirmed the hypothesis that interactions with pets can play a role in the emotional world of the child. In an exploration of children's feelings about their pets, Kidd and Kidd (1985) found that 32 percent of the children they interviewed confirmed statements indicating the emotional soothing they received from their pets (e.g., "comforts me when I'm sad" and "keeps me from being lonely"). Twenty-eight percent of the children confirmed that their pets provided a source of learning, teaching them about responsibility and relationships. Twenty percent viewed their pets as playmates, and 15 percent said that they received love from their pets. In a study of adolescents, Wolfe (1977) suggested that pets can function as "transitional objects" by providing consolation, reducing stress, and mitigating maladaptive responses to traumatic events. Further support for the salutary impact of pets includes Sherick's (1981) description of the role of pets in a young girl's expression of unconscious conflicts and as a symbolic substitution for her ideal self and Melson's (1990) work suggesting the positive role of pets in the development of nurturance.

While the benefits of pets for children have been demonstrated, a theoretical conceptualization of why child–pet relationships are beneficial is lacking. An analysis of the child–pet bond from a self psychology perspective provides a framework for a deepened understanding of this bond and and of the past and current significance of adult patients' relationships with their animals.

A SELF PSYCHOLOGY FRAMEWORK

Clinicians and theoreticians of personality development have long contended that social stimulation and affective connection with others form the bedrock upon which healthy growth proceeds (Spitz, 1965; Mahler, Pine, and Bergman, 1975; Bowlby, 1982). Self psychology has elaborated on these themes and has contributed to an understanding of the process of self development by elucidating the crucial importance of empathic responsiveness from the child's self-object environment (Kohut, 1971, 1977). According to self psychology, the ideal developmental scenario is one in which the child's caretakers provide consistent recognition, appreciation, and reflection of the child's actions and accompanying affect states. Such an optimum environment enables children to form a sense of themselves that is cohesive and resilient. The resultant self-structure has the capacity to regulate affect and to withstand blows to self-esteem. Healthy narcissism, ambitious strivings, and the capacity for empathy develop and mature.

Research with infants suggests that structuralization and the unfolding of inherent capabilities are potentiated through interaction with other people (Stern, 1983). However, even in families where caretakers have some capacity for emotional attunement, certain important selfobject functions are not met or are met incompletely, ambivalently, or erratically, impairing the growth and development of the child. The unfolding process stagnates, and vital psychological structures do not develop. Stolorow, Brandchaft, and Atwood (1987) define these "developmental derailments" as the swerving off course of normal developmental lines owing to the failure of caretakers to provide age-appropriate selfobject responsiveness. Another way to view this process is in terms of the *degree* of derailment: The less significant the deficits in the selfobject environment, the more cohesive and unified is the self and the less significant the derailment. Minor detours are not believed to preclude a later rekindling and integration of developmental processes. The defensive structures protecting the nuclear self are less firmly ensconced, and the archaic, nascent self is less ossified.

THE INTEGRATION OF AFFECT

Stolorow et al. (1987, p. 20) contend that "selfobject functions pertain fundamentally to the integration of affect into the organization of self-experience, and that the need for selfobject ties pertains most centrally to the need for attuned responsiveness to affect states in all stages of the life cycle." In families where the range of allowable affect expression is constricted, children may find it safer to explore the vicissitudes of emotionality and affect with their pets because animals do not judge, criticize, or humiliate the child's embryonic rehearsal of new behaviors and emotions. They do not retaliate, feel overwhelmed, or reject the child who is expansive in displaying her or his grandiose self. They can, however, provide approximations of mirroring, idealization, and twinship selfobject functions.

In "dysfunctional" families, where there is a paucity of emotional attunement and a limited capacity for sustained intimacy, there are multiple unmet needs and a greater likelihood that the child will be unable to experience one or both parents as idealizable figures.

Furthermore, when clear mirroring or the capacity to maintain a consistent relationship of attuned responsiveness with the child are compromised, the child forms an inaccurate, negative, empty, or fluctuating sense of self, one that is susceptible to disintegration and fragmentation.

Children, however, are often adept at seeking out and utilizing whatever objects are available in order to supplement—or to provide altogether—the functions that are necessary for the development of a cohesive self. In some instances, members of the extended family provide crucial selfobject ties. Neighbors, teachers, and peers can also assist in facilitating the growth of a stable and coherent self through the selfobject functions they provide. The term *object* has traditionally referred to a person, and the term *selfobject* has to some extent absorbed and been limited by this connotation. My clinical experience, however, has led me to understand that for many patients animals have provided a primary attachment in which they feel comforted, esteemed, and unabashedly loved. It is a relationship in which they receive the longed-for gleam of love and delight that the dull eyes of their primary caretakers do not reflect. I hope that through descriptions of experiences in which a child's pet provided rough functional equivalents of important selfobject responses the concept of selfobject can be expanded to the nonhuman domain. The consequences of pets, rather than humans, providing these needs will also be discussed.

CLINICAL EXAMPLE: HILARY

The following is a case study of a young woman whose relationship with her dogs provided her with experiences of attuned responsiveness. According to Stolorow, Brandchaft, and Atwood (1987), the overarching selfobject need is for affect attunement, which when consistently available forms the foundation for the integration of the child's affective states.

Hilary entered therapy at 28 years of age with vague complaints of unhappiness, lack of self-esteem, and drug dependency. She described her family of origin as close-knit, a family whose members enjoyed being together and "had a lot of fun." Hilary, her younger sister, older brother, and her parents lived in the same town and spent most weekends together.

After several months of discussing her family, Hilary began to see that the facade of a fun-loving family belied a pervasive sense of depression and anxious interpersonal interactions. As therapy progressed, Hilary began to reconnect to memories of her attempts to gain the interest and attention of her parents and to express her emotional world through the writing of stories and poems. Her father, a busy sales executive, was frequently away on business trips. Hilary saw her mother as an emotionally reticent and inhibited woman who had never fully recovered from the death of her twin sister, who had died while she was pregnant with Hilary. The mother could not allow herself to be emotionally spontaneous and responded with palpable discomfort to her daughter's unbridled emotionality. She was also unable to mirror aspects of the daughter's emotional experience that were expressed through Hilary's writing; when Hilary excitedly showed her mother her stories and poems, her mother appeared bored and unimpressed. Repeated experiences of a flattened response from her mother eventually resulted in a dampening of Hilary's exuberance and creativity. She turned away from seeking out her mother for this need in order to avoid the painful invalidation that came with exposure to her mother's "excitement boundaries" (Benjamin, 1988). Other family members were not available to provide the needed mirroring either. Hilary's sister was withdrawn, and the unspoken but insidiously competitive relationship between them prevented a close attachment.

About a year after therapy began, Hilary brought into a session several scrapbooks that she had assembled as a young girl. These scrapbooks, which resembled "baby books," chronicled the life of each of her dogs in exquisite detail. In the scrapbooks, which included snapshots of the dogs in hundreds of poses, Hilary had described their personalities, favorite foods, dog friends, relationships with each family member, and favorite activities. Although she had spoken in therapy about her pets, it was through the books' careful accounting of her dogs' lives that I began to think about the importance of these pets in keeping alive and expanding Hilary's emotional and affective capacities.

Idealizing

As we began to explore more deeply her relationship with her dogs, Hilary revealed that she had spent a great deal of time training them in obedience classes and entering them in professionally judged competitions. This aspect of her relationship, with one dog in particular, was, I believe, central in providing an idealizing selfobject function. Idealizing refers to the child's need to merge with the perceived omnipotence and greatness of an admired other, and it requires a selfobject who exhibits positive qualities and who can tolerate the child's need to idealize. When idealizing needs are thwarted, as when idealized figures are noxious or even when, more benignly, the object cannot tolerate the idealization, children are deprived of a template and cannot identify with an idealized other. In the best of circumstances, such an identification allows the child to absorb and internalize a sense of self-worth that evolves into healthy narcissism. In Hilary's family, the prototype for the development of healthy narcissism was minimal. Her mother's frequent self-disparaging remarks communicated to Hilary that she was not worthy of idealization, thus preventing Hilary from internalizing and establishing an ideal self. On the other hand, Hilary's dog embodied many positive qualities and was "willing to tolerate" her idealization. This was particularly important for Hilary because of her gradual disillusionment in her mother.[1] Showing her dog, an extension of herself, provided Hilary with an avenue for the development of her thwarted narcissism, channeling it into a form that was given public and familial approval; The dogs provided her with an opportunity to feel proud and worthwhile.

Mirroring

According to Kohut (1971, 1977), mirroring refers to children's need for positive recognition and confirmation of their uniqueness and greatness. In the privacy of her room, Hilary conducted poetry readings in which her dog was the enthusiastic audience. The dog sat attentively through the readings, and when Hilary enthusiastically asked, "Did you like it?" the dog would wag her tail, lick her mistress, and jump up and down. She responded with enthusiasm and activity, a rough functional equivalent of the attuned responsiveness Hilary's parents were unable to provide. The dog provided Hilary with a positive image of herself, reflected back her own natural joy in her creative productions. Her internal experience of excitement was validated, allowing her to develop an awareness and appreciation of her own creativity. Through her dog Hilary saw mirrored a worth-while, interesting, and expressive self, and it was this mirroring response that made her feelings and actions meaningful.

I believe that repeated interactions of this nature greatly contrib-uted to the integration of Hilary's emotional experience into a more cohesive self. Although Hilary entered into therapy with a certain fragility of self, I would suggest that repeated interactions in which

---

[1]It is important to note that a confluence of societal factors also contribute to the phenomenon of maternal disillusionment (Lang, 1990; Wolfe, 1990). Sands (1989) argues that cultural devaluation of mothers results in a premature deflation of little girls' grandiose exhibitionistic self.

she experienced mirroring from her dog contributed to a more resilient self-structure and mitigated against other selfobject failures that rendered her susceptible to fragmentation.

Hilary attributed to her dog a capacity to understand her and to respond to her feelings in a comforting way. Her dog's responses were validating and affirming. She found in her dog a much needed recognizing other. In this relationship was the self–other matrix where empathic resonance and affective interchange were available. Although this may appear to be no more than projection, Hilary's experience, like that of many pet owners, was that her pet "knew" what she was feeling and responded to it. Like other children with cold, withdrawn, or overwhelmed parents, whose lack of responsiveness can leave them feeling impotent and dead, Hilary needed a responsive other whom she could affect and allow herself to be affected by. Recent research has confirmed that there exists a reciprocal relationship between children and their dogs in which each acts upon and reacts to the other (Filiatre, Millot, and Montagner, 1986). This mutual recognition is crucial in the formation of the self. The lack of reciprocal recognition is frequently a hallmark of dysfunctional families.

Hilary's experience is echoed in the work of Gonski (1985), who studied the interactions between dogs and children in foster care who had been abandoned, neglected, or abused. She found that these children were significantly affected as a result of contact with a dog. Specifically, "the mere presence of the dogs was often sufficient to elicit laughter, lively conversation, and excitement among even the most hostile and withdrawn of the children" (p.97).

Pets' behaviors are frequently perceived as straightforward (i.e., unconflicted and unambivalent). This may help a child to begin to differentiate between different affect states. Tail wagging, growling, hissing, and purring (some dogs even "smile") are relatively easy to differentiate and correspond with other overt behaviors of the animal. This function of assisting the child to distinguish and differentiate between different affect states is particularly useful in homes where affect is repressed, ambiguous, dulled, or unacceptable.

This is not to say that pets can completely compensate for absent or distorted mirroring. It is likely that children who rely on pets as mirroring objects may, later on, be unable to make subtle discriminations between affective states because no pet can provide more than a rather gross approximation of a child's state. Children may feel confirmed and their affects may not be completely split off, but they may later lack the ability to make subtle discriminations between their own (and others') affective states. This was certainly true for Hilary, who in stressful situations frequently could make only gross differentiations between her own affective states. For example, she would frequently make statements like "I'm not sure if I'm sad or just bored."

Hilary began to do more creative writing and to bring in her work soon after we looked at her dog books together. Discussion of the dogs' importance seemed to unleash a flurry of creativity in the therapy. Because I was able to value and appreciate the importance of Hilary's dogs, and in a manner paralleling the dogs' function, an intersubjective field was created that provided an opportunity for the disavowed and undeveloped aspects of the self to reemerge. I believe that this repository of creative energy was accessible because it had been kept alive by Hilary's interactions with her dog. Prior to our exploration, this patient had demonstrated a visible yet inhibited remnant of this creative potential. It is possible that repeated experiences of responsiveness from her dog prevented the total derailment and splitting off of this capacity for affectively charged creative expression.

CLINICAL EXAMPLE: TERRY

Terry entered therapy at the age of 50, complaining of a repetitive pattern of emotionally abusive relationships. She had been a diabetic for 42 years, and her family's concern for her health had created an environment of overprotection, particularly in the area of emotional expression: her mother believed that if Terry became too excited, an insulin reaction would be precipitated, resulting in convulsions, coma, or death. Because Terry was a brittle diabetic, these fears were reinforced by frequent medical complications, including severe insulin reactions, and periodic convulsive episodes.

Terry's diabetic condition and her parents' subsequent overprotective behaviors isolated her from her playmates. Her cat Samuel was her primary companion; he was constant, loyal, and devoted, remaining attentive regardless of her emotional state. He provided a twinship selfobject function. Terry could cry, feel upset, and be crabby, sullen, or hyperactive without fear of criticism. In therapy Terry described many instances of confiding her innermost feelings to Samuel. He provided the unconditional acceptance that her parents, because of their own fears, and her siblings and peers, because of Terry's "differentness and limitations," could not consistently provide. With Samuel, Terry had an opportunity to practice the vicissitudes of her emotional world. Her affects could not be integrated in the context of her family because family members were unable to provide the requisite responsiveness.

In therapy sessions Terry spoke about her childhood and her current relationship in a flat and matter-of-fact way. It was not until she began discussing her relationship with her cat—fortunately, the therapist was able to recognize its importance—that Terry began to show and experience emotion in the therapy. During one session Terry described an incident that occurred when she was eight: She and her sister had been playing a "camping game" indoors when the makeshift tent they had built collapsed and fell on her new kitten. The kitten's back was broken and he died. While she was unable to grieve for her own disability, Terry was able to deeply grieve over the death of her kitten. As she related this trauma in therapy, she sobbed and finally said, "The only time I remember ever feeling anything was when it had to do with one of my cats." In discussions concerning her cat, affects that were once available to her (and partially integrated) vis-à-vis her cat were revivified and emerged in the therapeutic milieu. Although these experiences were infrequent, they did give Terry some opportunity to experience feelings, to label them, and to develop a vocabulary for describing them, and, over time, to experience a sense of validity in her own unique subjective inner experience.

Terry's bond with her cat also helped her to reexperience herself in a new way. Because of the diabetes, others were always caring for her. Her caretaking of her cat allowed Terry the opportunity to see herself as nurturant and allowed her to incorporate an image of herself as caring, kind, and giving, as opposed to needy, bad, and taking. This redefinition is particularly important if it is in contradistinction to previously introjected negative attitudes of the self, such as "bad," selfish, mean, and so on. It seems likely that Terry's prolonged attachment to Samuel and her experience in caring for him assisted her in elaborating a narrow view of herself into a fuller, richer sense of self that incorporated positive qualities.

In therapy Terry frequently described the sensual pleasure of stroking and petting her cat. Research has shown that pets provide opportunities for soothing tactile stimulation, and touching a pet has been shown to affect the cardiovascular system by reducing blood pressure (Friedmann, 1979; Friedmann et al., 1983). Stroking her cat enabled Terry, who felt isolated and rejected, to feel soothed and connected with another sentient being. From Terry's descriptions, it appeared that she actively sought out her cat to hold and stroke when she experienced states of internal disorganization. She described, for example, a frustrating experience with her father: He had walked into

the kitchen while she was eating a candy bar. He began to criticize
and lecture her and then told her not to get too excited when she
became agitated and angry. She tried to explain that she was aware
that she needed glucose and that she had been attempting to regulate
her blood sugar. This experience was pivotal for Terry as it represented both her repeated attempts to take responsibility for and
respond to her own internal states and her father's implicit injunc-
tions against her doing so. On that day, as on many others, Terry
sought out her cat to hold and to talk to. Her cat was particularly
reinforcing, settling into her lap and soothing her with reassuring
purrs.

In families where the boundaries for appropriate sexual expression
are blurry or nonexistent, this tactile connection with animals can
provide a safe outlet for affectional contact and sensual relating. On
the other hand, if this contact is the primary physical outlet, it may
interfere with the development of an expressive and comfortable
sexual self. The primacy of Terry's physical relationship with her cat
may have contributed to the many ambivalent feelings she had
regarding her own sexuality.

WHAT ABOUT TURTLES? A NOTE ON PETS WHO DO NOT RESPOND

Pets differ in the extent to which they are perceived to respond to
one's actions and affective states. The higher the animal on the
phylogenetic scale, the more likely it is that it will be perceived as
differentially responding to or mirroring the child. A goldfish, gerbil,
snake, or hermit crab, while not responsive in the traditional sense,
can nevertheless function as a stable or soothing selfobject that can
mitigate the liability and instability of a child's affect states and may
thereby play a role in the integration of affect. To learn to self-soothe,
one first needs a soothing other, and pets may become that soothing
other. Evidence supporting the calming effect of nonresponsive pets
is seen in a recent study which found that coronary patients were
significantly less anxious and recovered faster than control subjects
when a well-stocked aquarium was placed in their hospital room
(King, 1989).

Clearly, the characteristics of the pet will affect the nature of the
attachment experienced by the child (this is true within as well as
between species), but any pet provides the child with an opportunity
to caretake, to own, to name, and to feed it and offers the child an
outlet for expressive affectional needs as well as an emotional/
affective connection. Owning and caring for a pet may facilitate the

capacity to put oneself in another's position, the keystone of empathy; in fact, there is evidence of a positive relationship between pet ownership and empathy (Hyde, Kurdek, and Larson, 1983; Melson, Sparks, and Peet, 1989; Michaels, 1989).

Secondarily, nonresponsive pets may function as a medium through which selfobject functions are provided by others, that is, as a social catalyst. For example, a recent program at the University of California, Davis Veterinary School paired handicapped children with animals and found that the children were approached more frequently by their peers, indicating that owning a pet can help to mitigate a child's sense of social isolation and can provide the child with opportunities for the development of social competencies.

CLINICAL IMPLICATIONS

In addition to understanding and appreciating the client's relationship with a pet, the particular meanings attached to that relationship, and the selfobject functions provided by the pet, it is also important for the therapist to keep in mind the fact that children who establish an intense or exclusive relationship with a pet may suffer in the development of sophisticated and meaningful relationships with people. If a child's primary affective tie is with a pet (especially when it is developmentally appropriate to be making attachments to peers), he or she may be at risk for problems in subsequent psychosocial development.

An examination of the patient's bond with a pet can be a valuable avenue for garnering information about the selfobject deficits of the family as experienced by the child. Therapeutic efforts can be directed toward (1) generalizing the positive aspects of the patient's relatedness from pets to humans and (2) using the safety of the empathic therapeutic relationship to establish the subtler and more differentiated human–human contact.

Although I have focused in this chapter on the child–pet bond, the variables of age and gender need to be addressed in additional work. Adults do not outgrow their need for selfobjects, and the refueling of selfobject ties is crucial to the maintenance of cohesiveness, vigor, and self-esteem. The bond with animals can be a vitalizing and beneficial attachment throughout the human lifespan. As particular needs become ascendant, a person's attachment to a pet may take on new shape and form.

A thorough discussion of the impact of gender is beyond the scope of this chapter, but it is clear that gender is an important variable in how children use their pets to provide particular selfobject needs. The affective outpouring boys give to and receive from their pets may be particularly crucial because of societal sanctions against emotional expression in boys. Several interesting studies bear upon this issue. Guttman, Predovic, and Zemanek (1985) found that 11-to-16-year-old boys with pets were better at decoding facial expressions than were boys without pets, whereas girls, who were generally superior on this task to boys, were unaffected by pet ownership. G. F. Melson (personal communication, January 3, 1992) found that while by age five boys and girls see mothering a child as a female activity, nurturing and caring for a family pet was not seen as an exclusively male or female activity, suggesting that a boy's relationship with his pet may provide a socially acceptable context for the development of nurturance.

SUMMARY

I have attempted in this chapter to explore the implications of self-psychological theory for an understanding of the child–pet bond. I have found from my work with patients and in my discussions with colleagues that pets can play an essential role in preserving potentialities of the nuclear self. As Atwood and Stolorow (1984) point out, "when the psychological organization of the parent cannot accommodate to the changing phase-specific needs of the developing child, then the more malleable and vulnerable psychological structure of the child will accommodate to what is available" (p. 69). Fortunately for many children who are at risk, a pet is an integral part of the family and is available to play a vital role in remediating derailments, remobilizing development, or redressing affective imbalances. Aspects of the child's self that may otherwise have been thwarted or defensively sequestered may be affirmed and kept alive vis-à-vis this essential self–selfobject bond.

REFERENCES

Atwood, G. & Stolorow, R. (1984), *Structures of Subjectivity*. Hillsdale, NJ: The Analytic Press.
Benjamin, J. (1988), *The Bonds of Love*. New York: Pantheon Books.
Bowlby, J. (1982), *Attachment*. New York: Basic Books.
Condoret, A. (1973), *L'Animal Compagnon de l'Enfant*. Springfield, IL: Charles Thomas.
Filiatre, J., Millot, J. & Montagner, H. (1986), New data on communication behaviour between the young child and his pet dog. *Behavioural Processes*, 12:33–44.
Friedmann, E. (1979), Pet ownership and survival after coronary heart disease. In: *Proceedings of the Canadian Symposium on Pets and Society*. Vancouver, B.C., Canada: Standard Brands Food Company, pp. 26–34.
_____ Katcher, A. H., Thomas, S. A., Lynch, J. J. & Messent, P. R. (1983), Social interactions and blood pressure: Influence of animal companions. *J. Nerv. Ment. Dis.*, 171(8):461–465.

Frith, G. (1982), Pets for handicapped children: A source of pleasure, responsibility and learning. *Pointer*, 27(1):24–27.

Garrity, T. F., Stallones, L., Marx, M. B. & Johnson, T. P. (1989), Pet ownership and attachment as supportive factors in the health of the elderly. *Anthrozoos*, 3:35–44.

Gonski, Y. A. (1985), The therapeutic utilization of canines in a child welfare setting. *Child and Adolescent Social Work Journal*, 2:93–105.

Guttman, G., Predovic, M. & Zemanek, M. (1985), The influence of pet ownership on nonverbal communication and social competence in children. In: *The Human–Pet Relationship*, ed. Institute for Interdisciplinary Research on the Human–Pet Relationship. Vienna: Institut für Interdisziplinäre Ersogschung der Mench-tierbeziehung, pp. 58–63.

Holcomb, R. & Meacham, M. (1989), Effectiveness of an animal-assisted therapy program in an inpatient psychiatric unit. *Anthrozoos*, 2(4):259–264.

Hyde, K., Kurdek, L. & Larson, P. (1983), Relationships between pet ownership and self-esteem, social sensitivity, and interpersonal trust. *Psychol. Rep.*, 52(1):110.

Katcher, A., Beck, A. M. & Levine, D. (1989), Evaluation of a pet program in prison: The PAL Project at Lorton. *Anthrozoos*, 2(3):175–180.

Kidd, A. H. & Kidd, R. M. (1985), Children's attitudes toward their pets. *Psychol. Rep.*, 57:15–31.

King, K. M. (1989), Facilitating hospital patient recovery rates by aquarium viewing. Unpublished master of social work thesis, California State University, Sacramento.

Kohut, H. (1971), *The Analysis of the Self*. New York: International Universities Press.

——— (1977), *The Restoration of the Self*. New York: International Universities Press.

Lang, J. (1990), Self psychology and the understanding and treatment of women. *Rev. Psychiat.*, 9:391–408.

Levinson, B. (1961), The dog as co-therapist. *Mental Hygiene*, 46:59–65.

——— (1972), *Pets and Human Development*. Springfield, IL: Charles Thomas.

Mahler, M., Pine, F. & Bergman, A. (1975), *The Psychological Birth of the Human Infant*. New York: Basic Books.

Melson, G. F. (1990), Fostering inter-connectedness with animals and nature: The developmental benefits for children. *People, Animals, Environment*. Fall.

——— Sparks, C. & Peet, S. (1989), Children's ideas about pets and their care. Paper presented at the annual meeting of the Delta Society, Parsippany, New Jersey, November 10–12.

Michaels, Y. (1989), The relationship between pet attachment and self-esteem in latency age children [Abstract]. *People, Animals, and the Environment: Living Together in Cities*. Renton, Washington: Delta Society, p. 8.

Redefer, L. A. & Goodman, J. F. (1989), Pet-facilitated therapy with autistic children. *J. Autism Develop. Disorders*, 19(3):461–467.

Robin, M. & ten Bensel, R. (1985), Pets and the socialization of children. *Marriage & Family Review*, 8:63–78.

Ross, S. (1983), The therapeutic use of animals with the handicapped. *Internat. Child Welfare Rev.*, 56:26–39.

Sands, S. (1989), Eating disorders and female development: A self psychological perspective. In: *Dimensions of Self Experience*, ed. A. Goldberg. Hillsdale, NJ: The Analytic Press, pp. 75–103.

Sherick, I. (1981), The significance of pets for children: Illustrated by a latency-age girl's use of pets in her analysis. *The Psychoanalytic Study of the Child*, 36:193–215. New Haven, CT: Yale University Press.

Spitz, R. A. (1965), *The First Year of Life*. New York: International Universities Press.

Stern, D. (1983), The early development of schemas of self, of other, and of various experiences of "self with other." In: *Reflections on Self Psychology*, ed. J. Lichtenberg

& S. Kaplan. Hillsdale, NJ: The Analytic Press, pp. 49–84.

Stolorow, R., Brandchaft, B. & Atwood, G. (1987), *Psychoanalytic Treatment: An Intersubjective Approach*. Hillsdale, NJ: The Analytic Press.

Wolfe, B. (1990), Female development: Perspectives from self psychology. Paper presented to Self Psychology Study Group, La Jolla, California, November 3.

Wolfe, J. (1977), The use of pets as transitional objects in adolescent interpersonal functioning. Unpublished doctoral dissertation, Columbia University (DAI, 38(5-b), 2391).

Chapter 20

Review of *The Prisonhouse of Psychoanalysis** by Arnold Goldberg

Estelle Shane

To put Goldberg's third book, *The Prisonhouse of Psychoanalysis,* in perspective, I should remind you that the author not only occupies a central role in self psychology but was also the president and director of the Institute for Psychoanalysis in Chicago and, as such, sat on the Board on Professional Standards of the American Psychoanalytic Association. If ever there was a member in good standing of a community of scholars that represents American psychoanalysis, it is Arnold Goldberg. Yet he writes a book that challenges the central position of organized psychoanalysis, questioning the authenticity and validity of its training procedures, its scientific publications, and its clinical theory and practice. He sees established psychoanalysis as, if not already dead and confined to a mausoleum of its own making, at least showing a senescent "creaking stiffness" (p. 147) of its joints. And he views the individual practitioner in the field as hamstrung and made excessively uncomfortable by the technical restraints required of him if he wishes to be recognized by others and to consider himself (as Goldberg ironically puts it) as an authentic member of the profession, one who upholds the standards and ideals of Freudian analysis.

"Shall we pity the poor psychoanalyst?" Goldberg is led to inquire in the first chapter of the book (p. 16). His answer is that we shall indeed, and he makes his points unrelentingly, convincingly, and with biting sarcasm and humor. Now while it is always good to ask an author, in this case an exceedingly well-established member of the

---

community of psychoanalysts, just who the audience he has in mind for his book is, in this case it becomes an unusually relevant question. Whom does he think he will convince of the rightness of his position? It seems clear to me—although it is not always easy to separate out his irony from his straightforward efforts to persuade—that Goldberg wants desperately to influence, so as to *remain* a respected member of it, the community of psychoanalytic scholars, a community he cannot help but respect, one he feels he cannot totally ignore, one he feels no science can totally do without. Therefore, he wishes to enlighten at least some of this community as to the error of their ways and to persuade them to join with him in the direction he is suggesting that psychoanalysis must go if it is to do more than merely survive, if it is to live well and prosper.

And yet I know Goldberg to be too much of a realist, too much of an ironist, to be too hopeful about the numbers of authentic analysts he can influence with this publication. At the same time I was rereading and thinking about Goldberg's book for this discussion I happened to be reading a new novel by Milan Kundera called *Immortality*. Given the context, it will not be hard for you to understand why I was struck by a particular passage in Kundera's book, a passage in which a leading scholar, not unlike Goldberg, who is both intelligent and iconoclastic, given to irony, humor, and direct action, wishes passionately to persuade his own community of scholars, in this case a community of ecologists, of the importance of eradicating the automobile so as to preserve the planet, just as Goldberg would like to eliminate the polluting and choking constraints in the *trade* of psychoanalysis in order to preserve the *science* of psychoanalysis. In this passage the author, Kundera, is speaking in his own voice to this leading scholar, so like Goldberg, who is named Professor Avenarius. The author says to the professor, "I can never quite understand to what extent one should take your projects seriously." And Avenarius responds, "Everything I do should be taken absolutely seriously." Kundera continues: "For example, I try to imagine you as you were, actually lecturing the ecologists about your plan to destroy cars. Surely you didn't expect them to approve it!" After a pause, during which Avenarius too keeps silent, the author goes on: "Or did you by any chance think they would burst into applause?" Avenarius replies, "No, I didn't." The author returns, "Then why did you make the proposal? In order to unmask them? To prove to them that in spite of all their nonconformist gesticulations they are in reality a part of what you call 'Diabolum' [a reference to the devil and to the enemy]?" Avenarius responds, "There is nothing more useless than trying to prove something to idiots." "Then," says the author, "there is only one explanation: you wanted to have some fun. But even in that case your behavior seems illogical to me. Surely you didn't expect that any of them would understand you and laugh?" Avenarius shakes his head and says rather sadly, "No, I didn't expect that. Diabolum is characterized by the total lack of a sense of humor. Joking no longer makes sense." Finally, Kundera is driven to ask, "Well if it wasn't for the sake of fun, why *did* you submit that plan? Why?" Avenarius is interrupted before he can answer—and he never does.

We could pose this same question to Goldberg, along with a number of others, but perhaps a review of some of the highlights of this truly challenging, very funny, and deeply serious book will lead us to some answers.

Prisonhouse is a book about the constraints that have arisen in the practice of psychoanalysis and about the need to rethink and restructure these constraints if we are to free ourselves from them and advance the field. Goldberg's plan for the book, as well as the field, can be clearly discerned merely by examining the table of contents. It is both liberating and frightening to consider seriously what Goldberg is proposing here; it may be, in fact, all too easy to dismiss all of it with cowardly relief because of the very boldness of his design. He begins, after an introduction, with a chapter on the prisonhouse within which we practice our field. He goes on to propose a series of striking sacrifices as a way out of this prison. We are to do without our heroes, including Freud, Klein, Hartmann, and Kohut; we are to do without any foundations, including those traditionally held givens that we have considered, perhaps naively, to constitute the bedrock on which we stand; we are to do without mental representations, including self and object representation; and we are even to do without the usual concept of a subject, a self separate from others. With all of this, we must then, perforce, give up the idea that an authentic analysis can be easily distinguished from an inauthentic one. Finally, Goldberg requires us to give up our addictions to the kind of theory and the kind of practice that have kept us going, however inadequately, these many years. What Goldberg proposes to offer us in exchange for all of these sacrifices is an unmitigated freedom to teach, learn, practice, publish, advance the field and, finally, redefine ourselves and resume our own development as analysts, which development has been sadly neglected, arrested, stagnated, and skewed.

Of course, Goldberg offers us more: he offers us new ways of conceptualizing these crucial topics in psychoanalysis and new possibilities for a more active participation in the world. These ideas are based on a self-psychological model that Goldberg supports with his understanding of philosophy and neurophysiology.

Goldberg recognizes that psychoanalysis is peculiarly attached to its heroes, those men and women who have provided its most fruitful ideas and who seem to evoke a continued fealty far beyond what is necessary and useful, and far beyond what characterizes the practice in most other sciences. He asks, Is there something about our field that requires us to cling to our heroes? Does it have something to do with the inherent lack of certainty in what we know and practice? In other words, is there some unexamined defect or deficit that leads us in this unusual direction, creating an inhibiting and restraining force within us that restricts our critical examination of the ideas as separate from the person who promulgated them? Consider, for example, the obsessive study of Freud as a man, the unmitigated hero worship that surrounds him, and, above all, the loyalty to his authority as a godlike or fatherlike figure of supreme knowledge. We need only remember Young-Breul's biography of Anna Freud, who could not free herself from her father sufficiently to assess his ideas independently and use her own powerful intellect and position to move psychoanalysis beyond him and his thinking. This limitation is understandable in Anna Freud. What Goldberg communicates is that the whole field remains in this same archaic trap, and he uses his knowledge of self psychology to tell us why, that is, why we need our heroes, why we remain addicted to them, and how we can free ourselves from this limiting position.

Kohut delineated the line of development of idealization from archaic to mature forms. He suggested that on the one end of the continuum there exists the Tausk-influencing-machine-like merger with the untrusted and diabolical other, leading to a frightened avoidance of any connection to such a needed, powerful object. This category does not apply to analysts but, rather, to a certain type of enemy of analysis, a person too fearful of the powerful nature of psychoanalytic ideas to make any connection with them. As a way station to the more mature form of idealization, there is a phase of normal development characterized by an addictive thralldom to the powerful and revered hero, the idealized other who completes the undeveloped, immature self.

Goldberg suggests that our addiction to heroes in psychoanalysis is based upon just such a deficit, just such a failure to fully mature to the point where we can sustain ourselves with more personal values and ideals. What keeps a whole group of analysts in this immature state is the particular situation of our field, which provides no secure foundations, no steady resting places, and which inevitably provokes insecurity and anxiety in its practitioners. Finally, the mature form of idealization in the analyst is characterized by a skepticism that allows for questioning, that alternates with an achieved and more comfortable certainty, and that returns once again. Goldberg notes that we as analysts are unable to remain alone with our ideas for too long and that we must inevitably gravitate to points of certainty. He asks us to periodically devalue our convictions and to worry when we become too sure or too certain about ourselves, our clinical technique, and our theoretical beliefs. Perhaps this seems foolhardy, he says, but it is necessary in order to regain our freedom; we have to walk through life uncertain, unsure, and a little frightened in order to redefine and transform ourselves and to advance our field. The alternative is insulated psychoanalytic groups isolated from one another and from the world, and an inevitable stagnation.

Goldberg next demonstrates, through the example of a clinical conference, the shakiness of the ground on which we stand. When a case is presented at a conference, the presenter has a certain understanding of the patient. The listeners have more or less different understandings, and each feels that his interpretation of the material is more authentic than the others. Goldberg notes that the goal of all such conferences is to find consensus and then adds that perhaps that goal is wrong. Psychoanalysis may not be able to enjoy such resolution, he says. The goal should be for each of us to understand and remake ourselves as individuals.

Goldberg distinguishes among the kinds of discussions analysts engage in: There are those discussions that psychoanalysis as a discipline carries on with related scientific disciplines, wherein, perhaps, the status of the field is under consideration; there are those discussions wherein analysts talk with one another, the debate being about what is significant in the field, as in the case conference where different psychoanalytic points of view are considered; and there are, finally, the discussions between patient and analyst, where, indeed, an exchange of meanings and an agreement about meanings can and should be achieved. Goldberg asserts that it may be a mistake to lump these three types of analytic discussion together, as if they were the same. In terms of the first, the discussion about the position of psychoanalysis as a scientific discipline, Goldberg questions our need for support from infant observation, neurology, or biology to validate what goes on inside our field and questions whether any more certainty is provided us by concurrence stemming from such sources. At best, he says, limits are placed by these disciplines on analytic speculations and reconstructions.

At this point in my reading of his book, the following questions arose: How does Goldberg reconcile his devaluation of the data gleaned from the aforementioned sources to confirm or invalidate psychoanalytic theories with his own heavy reliance on the outside fields of philosophy and neurophysiology? And which proponents of gathering such data from extreme sources, such as infant observation, would expect to establish any more than limitations on analytic speculation and reconstruction? Is not the establishment of such limitations sufficient to justify turning to outside related disciplines, as Goldberg himself does?

In terms of the discussion regarding theoretical differences among analysts themselves, Goldberg asserts, as the heart of his thesis, that there are no common places in the field, that there is no agreement about the nature of the unconscious, the value of the concepts of resistance and defense, the importance of infantile sexuality and the Oedipus complex, or the nature of transference. Rather than search for concepts upon which all analysts agree, he says, we must rely on a hermeneutic approach to achieve, via a Socratic dialogue, the synthesis of understanding that can only exist between a given patient–therapist pair. It is only on this level, with this third type of discussion, that there is any consistency or consensus or any sense of certainty for the individual practitioner. And even here, the truth is never final or complete; meanings can always change.

Having removed from us any general psychoanalytic concepts that can be agreed upon and upon which we can hope to build permanent foundations, Goldberg goes on to explain why the construct of representation, as understood in classical analysis and object relations theory, is neither a useful nor an accurate depiction of how experience is preserved in the mind. Traditionally, self and object representations are conceptualized as contents of the mind that, once laid down, are simply retrievable as such, as fixed entities, like recorded pictures. Once having been laid down, these representations, whether they approximate reality or are altered by defensive operations, remain solipsistically contained within the individual mind or brain. This view of representation influences the theory of technique and of cure, so that the goal of classical analysis is to unearth the hidden representations defensively buried within the mind.

Goldberg offers a reassessment of representation, borrowing generously from neurophysiology's new concept of connectionism. In this view, memory is not passive and representations are not laid down as complete, to be recoverable as such; rather, memory is an active creation that requires the external participation of a stimulating current object to complete the pattern, without any intermediary mental representations being reached for or discovered. This necessity for external input to complete a pattern fits well with the concept that a selfobject serves to complete an incomplete self.

This new view, then, also influences the theory of technique and of cure, so that self psychology is not concerned, or not as much concerned, with the hidden representation of the object buried in the psyche but with the representation of the deficient self, which is to be completed by experience with the selfobject analyst. That is, the analyst in the transference is most concerned with the immediacy of the connection to the analyst and most involved with the completion of the distorted and deficient self within the transference.

Goldberg concludes this chapter by saying that the nature of patients' improvement in therapy seems to depend so much on the immediate participation of the analyst that a new way of explaining cure is called for. He compares storehouse theories of representation with connectionism theories, suggesting that the latter are more accurate and provide a more useful way of understanding the person's connection with the world. Connectionism serves to justify the self psychologist's focus and reliance on the selfobject concept. However, I don't believe that Goldberg means to eliminate storehouse views of representation entirely. There are representational patterns sequestered for defensive purposes, incomplete though they may be; these are object patterns rather than selfobject patterns. There would seem to be room, therefore, for the enactment in the transference of hidden and forbidden object retrieval within the current relationship with the analyst. Perhaps Goldberg would agree but would consider this a secondary matter.

Goldberg, in an important chapter dedicated to the self in psychoanalytic theory, attacks the assumption made in almost all of psychoanalysis that there is a separate and distinct subject, or self, that either begins as an autistic being, as in classical theory, or emerges out of a merger state with the mother, as in most object relations theories. The self in these theories is viewed as coming into its own, then, by gaining distance from the object, as well as by retaining contents derived from the object, and then existing in a state of isolation only relieved by communication. Even in interpersonal theory, the subject is seen as separate and distinct from the object.

Rather than trace this theory of self and object separateness, only to then refute it, as Goldberg does so masterfully, I will instead cut right to the chase and bring in Goldberg's own favorite philosopher, Heidegger. Heidegger is the one who revolutionized the common

notion of subject as distinct from object, positing instead a fundamental position for man of being in the world and being of the world.
In effect, man is composed of relationships with others, is completed
by relationships with others, and does not exist exclusive of others at
all. There is no subject/object dichotomy, unless something goes
wrong and man is thrown out of this normative world-connected
relationship, under which circumstance the object as such is then
discoverable.

The connection to the selfobject concept is obvious. As Goldberg
suggests, if persons are composed of these relations with others, then
we embrace the self-psychological concept of the self as related to
others and thereby made up of others. Selfobjects are not experiences; they are not distinct and separate beings. Selfobjects are the
"others," the entities that allow one to achieve and maintain an
individual integrity; they are what make us what we are, our very
composition. But the individual is not merely reduced to these
selfobjects. There is a self ownership (an ownness) inherent in the
individual that goes beyond and is logically distinct from these
relationships. And, as with Heidegger's conception, it is only when
selfobjects fail, when there are breaks in empathy, that one becomes
aware of the separateness of the self, of its isolation, and of its
fragility. Goldberg specifically distinguishes this position from the
intersubjective view of Stolorow, Atwood and Brandchaft. These
theorists presuppose two separate and distinct self entities that
interact in an intersubjective field. Goldberg does not specify his
distinctions from other self-psychologically informed analysts, such
as Basch—though Basch certainly has a different conception of the
selfobject, defining it as a relationship that comes into being only
when the self is threatened and in need of selfobject sustenance and
support.

Goldberg ends the chapter on the selfobject by stating that these
ideas do not mean the abandonment of more familiar psychoanalytic
concepts, but, he says, psychoanalysis must catch up with other ways
of looking at the world; in so doing, it will be more of this world and
less autistically isolated from the larger world of ideas that surrounds
it.

We come now to the final section in Goldberg's book, where he
questions most specifically the concepts of authentic analysis and the
authentic analyst. He criticizes the training model, which is, he says,
more concerned with tests of allegiance and fidelity to established
ideas than with creating analysts who are capable of thinking for
themselves and of challenging accepted dogma. He views the litera-

ture as not helping much with this condition, with the journal "referees" being more concerned with finding agreement with their own ideas than with looking for what is new and innovative. Goldberg notes, as well, the political use made of psychoanalytic journals, namely, to keep in power those who concur with establishment ideas.

In the final chapter Goldberg reminds us that the future of analysis is unpredictable, as is any evolutionary process. His own personal prescription has to do with a change in values and a change in the hierarchy of values that has to date informed the field. Freud's principal concern, as Kohut emphasized, was the search for truth, with other values only secondary. Goldberg turns to the philosopher Rorty for a more solid debunking of truth values. Rorty asserts that it is misguided and fruitless to seek foundations, to search for the truth, to feel the world can ever be accurately represented. Goldberg assures us that he himself is not diminishing the significance of truth and knowledge, or even the value of accurately reconstructing the patient's childhood; rather, he joins Kohut in the view that these truth conditions must be secondary to other values, naming among these alternative higher goals the empathic effort to understand our patients and noting that it is really more important to understand what the patient experienced than it is to know what really happened, with the effort to discover the latter being considered less significant.

In the final chapter Goldberg also puts forward other values to be ranked within a hierarchy of importance in determining the goals of psychoanalysis, values such as aesthetic coherence (that is, how things fit together); therapeutic ambition (the wish to actually help our patients being elevated rather than shunned as a goal); and creativity, which deserves affirmation from our mentors and peers since it fosters an atmosphere in our training of intellectual stimulation, as opposed to an atmosphere of rules, regulations, and certitude, and which is currently equated with deviance, an unhealthy state for the individual and for the field.

With this I complete my review of Goldberg's book, but I am afraid I have not done it justice. There is no way to communicate what makes the book special by just revealing, however accurately, its contents. Goldberg has presented very complicated ideas, which I have only hinted at, with great humor, much lucidity, and admirable intensity. Moreover, he has illustrated what is complex with clear, cogent, and entertaining case examples. Finally, I am afraid I have conveyed the idea that the philosophical and neurophysiological underpinnings of his ideas are limited to the few points I have made, and this is far from the case. Obviously, one must read this book to appreciate it and the man who has written it.

Moreover, I believe that Goldberg's view of the future of analysis is prescient. While his fellow analysts may not all hear or regard what he has to say, there are nevertheless a growing number of them who are currently moving in the precise direction Goldberg points to.

Author Index

Subject Index

B

Bonding, 29, 34–35
  after successful mourning, 171
  analyst–patient, 29, 34–35, 56–57, 212,
    221, 222
  child–pet, 257–268

C

Child development
  interpersonal factors in, 108
Child–pet bond
  age and gender regarding, 267–268
  case illustrations, 260–266
    idealization, 261–262
    mirroring, 262–264
  impact on relationships with people,
    267
  integration of affect, 259–260
  and nonresponsive pets, 266–267
  research on, 257–258
  self-psychological framework for,
    258–259
Childhood
  experiences in, 28–29
  trauma, 32
Consciousness vs. unconsciousness, 22,
  28
Core self agency, 1
Countertransference-cotransference,
  247, see also Transference
  in analytic process, 32–34
  hermeneutical view on, 251–255
  intersubjective perspective on, 249
  and self psychology, 251–255
    neglect of in, 248–251
  types of, 249

D

Defense structures, 211–212
  case illustrations, 212–219
  reversals as, 234–235
Disruption, 29, 39, 160
  interpretation of, 25–26
  reversals and, 233
Disjunction, 239–240, 241
Dissociation, 205–206
  trauma and alter ego regarding, 196–198
Drives, 8
  and aggression, 130

from fragmentation products, 133–134
innate sexual aggression, 121–122
and mourning process, 172
state changes and satisfying, 48
Drive theory, 8, 120–121
  homosexual, mourning and, 173
Dysfunctional families, 259–260

E

Ego
  alter, 173, 191–206
  and mourning, 171
Empathic immersion, 110
  prolonged, 33–34
Empathic inquiry, 32–34, 212, 221
  definition of, 33
  sustained, 33–34
Empathy, 4–5
  countertransference and, 251, 254
  child–pet bond and, 267
  definition of, 31–32
  interpretation of analyst's lapse in,
    26–28
  and mourning, 179–180
  and psychoanalytic interpretations,
    31–36, 54–55
  and treating narcissistic rage, 133–134,
    160, 162–163

F

Families, dysfunctional, 259–260
Fears, 28–29
  of therapeutic situation, 23–25
Ferenczi, Sándor, 19
Fragmentation, 205
  drives from products of, 133–134
  and narcissistic rage, 132–135
Freud, Sigmund, 10, 117
  drive theory, 120–121
  views of, 16–17
    on ambivalence of investigating phy-
      sicians, 18–22

G

Gender
  of analyst and transference, 105–106
  case illustration of sex, sexualization,
    and, 61–74, 75–85

introjects and, 237–239
pathologies of identification regarding,
    231–242
therapeutic implications concerning,
    239–241
and transference, 235–237

S

Self, 7
    disorder, 226, 228
Self-assertiveness
    distinguished from narcissistic rage,
        147
Self, sense of, 223–224, 227, 229
Self-esteem, 174
Selfobject, 159–160, 162, 235, 277–278
    bonding 162
        with therapist, 29, 56–57
    concept of, 7–10
    disruption, 50
    experiences, 89–90
        providing patient with, 32, 36, 41
        twinship, 103, 105–106, 192
        two types of, 192
    failures, 39–41, 205
        during oedipal phase, 88, 104
        two phases of, 39
    function and child–pet bonds, 259–267
    mourning process, role of in, 174–175,
        177–180, 183–184
    transferences, 7, 39–41, 70, 112–113,
        148, 211, 221, 248
        mirroring, 68, 81, 195, 197–198
        and oedipal phase, 88–89, 103,
            116–121
    twinship, 259
        role of, in female oedipal develop-
            ment, 87–107
Self psychology
    and countertransference, 247, 251–255
        neglect of, 248–251
    framework for child–pet bonds,
        258–259
    future of, 5–6
    genesis of, 3–6
    increased interest in various countries,
        2–3
    interpretation and resistance, 23–25
    intrapsychic view of, 8
    intrinsic and external elements of, 1–3

mourning theory and, 174–177
narcissistic rage and, 130–132
open clinical-theoretical system of, 6–11
and self-object transferences, concept
    of, 6–10
as a structural theory, 27–29
therapy, relationship between, 57
Self-regulating other, 47, 50, 51–52
    definition of, 47
Self representations
    object and, 171–172, 178, 238, 276–278
Self-selfobject, 132, 161
Self-selfobject bond
    disruption of, 235–237
Self-state, 47–52
    definition of, 47
Self-state transformations, 47–52
Self structure, 259
Self system, 259
    false, 241
Seronegative survivor, 170, 180
    case illustration, 181–184
Seropositive survivor, 170, 180
    case illustration, 184–189
Sexuality, *see also* Homosexuals
    and aggression in pathogenesis and
        clinical situations, 109–124
    case illustration, 110–112, 113–114
    child–pet bond and, 266
    drives and, 121–122
    normal, 109–110
    oedipal selfobject transferences and,
        116–121
Sexualization, 118–119, 121
    case illustration of sex, gender, and,
        61–74, 75–85
    definition of, 63
Structuralization, 259
Subjectivity, 17, 34, 251

T

Therapist. *See* Analyst
Therapist–patient interaction. *See*
    Analyst–patient interaction
Therapy. *See* Analysis
Transference, 161, 164, 188, 204–205, *see
    also* Countertransference
    alter ego, 191–206
    gender of analyst and, 105–106
    interpretation, 35, 36, 38, 40